WINDSWEPT & INTERESTING

MY AUTOBIOGRAPHY

Also by Billy Connolly

Tall Tales and Wee Stories

BILLY
CONNOLLY
WINDSWEPT &
INTERESTING
MY AUTOBIOGRAPHY

TWO
ROADS

First published in Great Britain in 2021 by Two Roads
An Imprint of John Murray Press
An Hachette UK company

This paperback edition published in 2022

1

A CIP catalogue record for this title is available from the British Library

Paperback ISBN 978 1 529 31827 2
eBook ISBN 978 1 529 31828 9

Typeset in Celeste by Palimpsest Book Production Ltd, Falkirk, Stirlingshire

Printed and bound in Great Britain by Clays Ltd, Elcograf S.p.A.

John Murray policy is to use papers that are natural, renewable and
recyclable products and made from wood grown in sustainable
forests. The logging and manufacturing processes are expected
to conform to the environmental regulations of the country of origin.

Two Roads
Carmelite House
50 Victoria Embankment
London EC4Y 0DZ

www.tworoadsbooks.com

CONTENTS

WINDSWEPT & INTERESTING

MY AUTOBIOGRAPHY

INTRODUCTION

I DIDN'T KNOW I was Windswept and Interesting until somebody told me. It was a friend of mine – the folk singer Archie Fisher – who was startlingly exotic himself in the sixties. He'd just come back from Kashmir and was all billowy shirt and Indian beads. I had long hair and a beard and was swishing around in electric-blue velvet flares. He said, 'Look at you – all *windswept and interesting!*' I just said, 'Exactly!' After that, I simply had to maintain my reputation.

———

It's not difficult to become Windswept and Interesting – you just have to *BE* it. Then people will notice that you are. And once they've accepted it – and pronounced that you are – you're all set.

Windswept and Interesting people recognise each other. I was in Boston once, appearing on the *Good Morning Massachusetts* TV show. There was a drag queen on air before me, singing 'I Am Who I Am'. It was nine o'clock in the morning, but she was covered in sequins and jewels. Huge hair, startling make-up. As she came offstage, her gaze met mine. I was wearing oxblood corduroy trousers, reindeer boots with curled-up pointed toes, a frilly polka-dotted satin shirt and a big gold hoop earring in one ear. As she brushed past me, she whispered in my ear: 'Savage gypsy lover!!'

See? She knew, and I knew.

Being Windswept and Interesting is not just about what you wear. It's also your behaviour, speech, your environment, and an attitude of mind. It's perpetually classy – but it's not of a particular class. It transcends class.

It's not about money either. For example, Windswept and Interesting people don't wear new clothes. Quite the opposite. They select unusual pieces – maybe a thrift shop item like a junior musician's coat from a long-forgotten Scottish regiment or Mexican charro trousers as worn by mariachi bands. Not everyone appreciates our garb. When I was on location in New Zealand during the filming of *The Last Samurai*, I was sitting outside a cafe on one of my days off and Ed Zwick, the director, came walking along the road. I was wearing red suede Mary Jane shoes with long turquoise socks, knee-length breeches and my orange 'Jesus Is My Homeboy' T-shirt. Ed stared at me with a twisted smile. 'Billy,' he said, 'who gets you ready in the morning?'

We W & I's love style . . . but we abhor fashion. We decorate our homes any way we damn well please. If you came into this room I'm in now, you'd see that it's the abode of a Windswept and Interesting man. It's eclectic and a wee bit disorganised. I'm surrounded by things I like – musical instruments with battered cases, lots of books, banjo magazines going back many years, and a rattan writing desk on which sit sketchbooks and drawing instruments. On my wooden bedposts sit several panama hats decorated with flowers, assorted scarves, beads, bandanas and a Bob Marley shoulder bag. I sit in a leather chair that can wheech me upside down (to relieve my back). On the walls are a Celtic banner, a Mexican Day of the Dead mask, a large Tibetan mirror, a Japanese kimono and French mirror sconces with flameless candles. There are two wooden ceiling fans, Indian cushions and curtains, a gentleman's wooden valet, boxes of fishing flies, a piece of sculpture by a New Zealand artist, a pair of red boxing gloves, a wooden Inuit box, a collection of fountain pens, dogs' water bowls, TV, broken DVD player, Academy DVDs I have yet to watch, and a remote control I can't fucking operate.

'Sounds a right mess, Billy . . .' I hear you say, 'and a tad pretentious.' Pretentious? MOI?!! I say it's a stylish mix of objects – some practical, some useless – curated by a man of taste and fuck-you-ness. And yes, indeed it is messy . . . because I like it that way. That's just how we W & I's roll. You don't like it? Fuck off.

Once I'd realised that I was Windswept and Interesting it became my new religion. It was such a delightful contrast to the dour and disapproving attitudes I'd grown up with. Instead of cowering under the yoke of 'Thou shalt NOT!', I found a new mantra: 'Fuck the begrudgers!' It felt brilliant. I was no longer obliged to behave with even a smidge of decorum. Over the years I've discovered the Secret Truths of W & I, such as: 'Hell is not for sinners; it's for beige-wearers', and 'Blessed are those who yodel – for they shall never be troubled by offers of work'. I even found the Key to W & I Enlightenment: 'You can misbehave all you like – provided you leave them wanting more.'

Sometimes people ask me: 'Billy . . . I, too, would like to become Windswept and Interesting! How can I achieve it?' And I reply: 'I'm afraid you've blown it by *wanting* to be it.' You have to be *accepted* as Windswept and Interesting by *other* Windswept and Interesting people – once it *arrives* in you. And when that happens you get to write your own rules.

Here are a few of mine:

> YOU HAVE TO GENUINELY NOT GIVE A FUCK
> FOR WHAT ANY OTHER LIVING HUMAN
> BEING THINKS OF YOU.

> SAY THE FIRST THING THAT COMES INTO YOUR MIND
> AND DON'T WORRY ABOUT WHAT MIGHT HAPPEN
> TO YOU AS A RESULT.

> SEEK THE COMPANY OF PEOPLE WHO, WHEN
> LEFT ALONE IN A ROOM WITH A TEA COSY,
> WILL ALWAYS TRY IT ON.

> NEVER TURN DOWN THE OPPORTUNITY
> TO SHOUT 'FUCK THE BEGRUDGERS!'
> AT THE TOP OF YOUR VOICE.

> AND TELL YOUR STORY YOUR OWN DAMN WAY . . .

1

DO WHAT MAKES YOU HAPPY

BE WHAT MAKES YOU HAPPY

IF OTHERS DISAPPROVE TELL THEM
TO REARRANGE THESE WORDS
TO MAKE A POPULAR PHRASE:
YOURSELF, FUCK, GO

———

I LIKE BEING naked in public. I discovered this made me happy when I was only four years old. It wasn't so much the willy-pointing – more a lovely sense of naked freedom. A woman who used to babysit me from time to time told me I was a real handful – wild and funny – and that I used to take my clothes off as often as possible. I remember that feeling of nakedness; the joy of it has never left me. As an adult I've danced naked all over the world – even in the Arctic Circle. Over a hundred million viewers have seen my willy. Not many people can say that.

It's peculiar being me. Few things make me as happy as being naked. I'm not sure what my definition of happiness is. I used to think it was a daddy with a beach ball playing with his kids. But in recent years I've mainly come to think of it as what it's not. Things that please other people don't entertain me. I fucking hate talent shows, most reality shows, and those popular movies full of explosions, with unlikely heroes saving the world. On the other hand, I love watching TV evangelists. They're such grandiose con artists, urging people to send money they can't afford. 'Pop an envelope in the mail and you're bound to have a windfall!' Pricks. Capitalising on loneliness. Makes me angry, but I can't tear myself away.

My wife Pamela says I'm angry about so many things I don't leave much room to be happy. She put a board with the words *'Today I will be as happy as a bird with a French fry'* on the wall opposite my toilet so I am reminded every time I take a piss. But that just makes me angrier.

I feel happy just as I'm about to go to sleep, when I'm comfortable in my bed. Just at that final point before sleep I feel great. I've always imagined that would be the feeling you get before you die. And it makes me happy being around my children and my grandchildren. Yeah. Because I can see they're not like me. They're more complete in themselves. I like that in them and I'm a wee bit jealous.

Football makes me happy. When my football team Celtic wins I do a wee dance in my heart. As you've no doubt heard, in Glasgow we have two very famous football teams: Rangers and Celtic. And never the twain shall meet. When they're playing each other, the supporters of Celtic go to one end, and the supporters of Rangers go to the other end. They shout at each other for ninety minutes, and then they all go home. It can get quite heavy: 'Ah, ya Orange bastard!'

'Aaaagh!'

'Have some o' that, ya Fenian bastard!'

'Ooooph!'

I like to hear the crowd singing. Have you heard Welsh people singing their anthem before a rugby match starts? It's so moving. All those voices together, singing that lovely melody. That makes me happy.

You might think that being a Windswept and Interesting

showbiz personality I would love myself a lot. I suspect happiness is having a liking for yourself and having a joy in being with yourself, and I'm not sure I have it.

———

I think I might have been happy before my mother left. Until I was four, I had this feeling – and I'm sure she got the same feeling – of two creatures joined by the same material. Before she left, I was like a naked animal. Crawling around with sticky things in my hands. Sweets and buns. I was happy before I was four.

I can still smell the inside of my pram . . . plasticky, like hot rubber. And I remember the taste of the sweets. I don't remember eating anything else except the boiled sweets – those liquorice ones – in gaudy colours. Black and purple and pink. And a kind of buttery one. My stage clothes ended up looking the same – stripy, loud.

I remember being in other people's houses as a wee boy. There was a man called Cumberland who lived across from us in Dover Street. He had a big family – eight girls, and the youngest was a boy. We used to spend a lot of time in his place with all his children. I loved it. They had an easy chair that was covered in corduroy and I used to sit in it the wrong way round – I would have my back where your bum should be and my legs where your back should be, so I was kind of upside down. Mr Cumberland would take a penny and run it across the corduroy sideways, making a noise like a motorbike. I thought that was brilliant and I asked him to do it again and again. I remember being delightfully happy there, in my own wee world.

I get that same feeling now when I'm fishing. And when I

eat a biscuit. There's something wonderful about a biscuit. It lifts you off the floor. My favourite is the digestive. It's the king of biscuits. It's not filled with cream or jam or dripping with stuff. In the biscuit world it's kind of plain, but it really suits being beside a cup of tea. I like the jammie dodger too, a round biscuit, sandwiched with jam, and the Abernethy – a big, ugly biscuit that was flaky and dry and great for dipping in tea.

Biscuits make most people happy, don't they? It's amazing the number of big, muscly men who work in hard, heavy industries who will fall to their knees at the offer of a cup of tea and a biscuit. And I'm sure the Queen likes to have a digestive and a cup of tea the same as a coal miner does. When you get that into your head then you get Britain. After you've had a hard day working as a housekeeper, in the factory or the library or civil service, to settle down with a cup of tea and a digestive – the whole country is thankful for that. And it stays with you for your whole life. You never lose your love for the digestive. You never hear anybody saying: 'I used to love the digestive but now I can't be bothered.'

After I became a comedian, I met people who knew the Cumberlands and said they were pissed off at my talking about them onstage. I liked to tell the story about the time my sister Florence and I were playing in the street on a Friday night.

Mr Cumberland came home from his work, had his tea, then told his wife: 'I'm away for a pint.' But his wife said, 'You get those children off the street and into bed first before you go for any bloody pint!'

'Okay, okay, give me peace!'

And he staggered out of the house. 'Right, how many weans have I got? . . . Nine!' So, he goes into the street looking for kids. 'Right, you, you, you, you, and you . . .'

He rounded up the first nine children he came across, two of whom were me and my sister! We were washed and put to bed. I was there, tucked in with all the others, looking around, going: '*Waaaah!*' My sister's trying to calm me: 'We're all right. I've been in here before!' '*Waaaah!*' Meanwhile, my mother's going berserk! She came back late, and we weren't there – so she's out looking for us with a policeman because she thinks we're off in a kitbag with some pervert! The only reason they found us is that they spied two wee Cumberlands crying in the street. '*Waaaah!* We can't get in the house! The bed's full!' So they took them in, and we were kicked out: '*Waaaah!*'

People loved that story when I told it onstage – but I really wouldn't want to upset the Cumberland family, because I'm very grateful for the strong parental presence I sensed in that house. It felt safe.

———

I was born in a flat in a tenement building at 65 Dover Street in Anderston, near the centre of Glasgow. Tenement blocks were all over the city then; they had become the most popular kind of housing since the nineteenth century. They were solid sandstone apartment buildings with four storeys and a staircase in the middle. They had a narrow close – entrance hall – leading to a small back courtyard where people did their washing. Some Glasgow tenements were considered posh, but in my street they were overcrowded and deteriorating to the point of becoming slums.

Dover Street was noisy. Coalmen would rumble past with their horses and carts, while rag and bone men would get your attention with military bugle calls: '*doo di doo, doo di doo diddly umpum . . .*' Chimney sweeps wheeled their hand-barrows inside the close and yelled '*sweeeeeeeep*' so it echoed upstairs. Children would play football on the street, using a lamp post as the goal-post. Upstairs, women would sit on the windowsill or hang out of the windows, chatting to each other or shouting at children in the street: 'What've I told you about throwing stones . . . ?' Drunks would stumble into our back courtyard and give impromptu singing concerts. If these had merit, residents would throw down pennies. But if the singer was giving everyone a headache someone would first heat the pennies over the stove using a pair of pliers. 'There ya go, ya winey bastard!!! Take yer wailing elsewhere . . .!!!' '*Ach Oucha OUCHHHH!!!*'

We lived on the third floor of our tenement, and there was a smelly communal toilet on the landing. Our little two-roomed flat was a bit gloomy. I just remember an alcove bed, a kitchen table, and a sideboard with a drawer that was my crib when I was a baby. There was no bathroom, and no hot water; Florence washed both of us standing up in the kitchen. All this may sound a bit awful, but it wasn't. There was a warmth about tenements, because of the people who lived in them. They were colourful, vertical villages. Sure, they were considered slums. People say, 'Oh, the *deprivation*! Oh my . . .' Nonsense! When you're a wee boy it's not like that. It felt great to have all these nice neighbours. And we had a big wooden toilet seat . . . luxury! You didn't lose the use of your legs reading the Sunday paper.

Maybe it's my age, but it seems I can't walk when I've been on the lavvy. '*Heeelp!*' The only other time I've felt like that was after I'd had a drink in America, called a 'Zombie'. Have you ever had a Zombie? You get drunk from the bottom up. You're perfectly lucid, talking away – until you need to go to the toilet. But then you find out your legs are pissed! 'Excuse me, I'll just go to the toilet . . .' *Crash!* You're on the floor, and you can't get up.

I was born on the kitchen floor on the twenty-fourth of November 1942, during World War Two. That's the only date you're getting in this book, because my birthday's the only one I can remember. A few years ago, I forgot Pamela's birthday and had to get it tattooed on my arm, but I still missed it the next year because I forgot to look. Anyway, when I was born my dad was away fighting in the air force in Burma and India. I don't remember my mother being there much. Maybe she worked – I don't know. She was an attractive teenager – like a British film starlet – with wavy dark hair and a smiley face. Everybody I met later who knew her said she was funny, and so volatile she could start a fire in an empty room.

I don't remember her hugging me, although I remember her smell. It was Florence who looked after me. She bathed me, fed me, dressed me. Tried to keep me out of trouble. Florence was only eighteen months older than I was. It never occurred to us that she was far too young to be in that position, with no adult around for hours on end. Our mother would leave us alone with an open, blazing fire. One night Florence fell into burning ashes and permanently damaged one eye.

I was sickly – always sniffling. I had pneumonia three times before I turned four. But I felt jolly when Florence was next to me. We slept together in the alcove bed in the kitchen, and she used to teach me songs:

I see the moon, the moon sees me.
Under the shade of the old oak tree.
Please let the light that shines on me
Shine on the one I love.

It was a wartime song she heard on the radio. There were Scottish songs too:

Come o'er the stream Charlie
Stream Charlie Stream Charlie
Come o'er the stream Charlie
And dine wi' MacLean
And tho your heart's weary
We'll make your heart cheery
And . . .

da di di diddy de diddy dee dee . . . I forgot the rest . . .

———

At night, Florence used to shine a hand mirror on the wall, making a circle of light. She chased me with it 'til I screeched like a parrot.

The most profound memory I have from 65 Dover Street was the time when I woke early and went to look for my mother. I opened the door to her bedroom and saw a stranger – a shirtless man, sitting in a chair, putting on his socks. I realised my mother was in bed, but I couldn't see her because she was behind the door. This guy just put his foot on my forehead and gently pushed me out the door, then closed it. I found out later his name was Willie Adams, my mother's lover. Shortly afterwards, she left us.

———

I think I'll have a pizza tonight. Pizza makes me happy. Food of the gods. I don't live in New York any more but I was there last year and had a slice of pizza every single night. I like my pizza the way I like my biscuits – kinda plain. My favourite is margherita – the plainest of the plain. It makes you fat. I can't control my weight and eat the things I like, so I eat the things I like. It's a W & I thing.

2

IF NO ONE GIVES YOU A MEDAL, DESIGN YOUR OWN

———

HAVE YOU EVER wondered if you're brave? Men especially worry if they're brave or not. We're brought up with all those 'manly men' books about Biggles and Tarzan and *The Last of the Mohicans* – so you always wonder if you're a brave guy like them. I often watch that TV programme *Forged in Fire* where the guys are all shirtless giants with leather waistcoats, hand-wrestling metal into lethally sharp weapons. But then I'm equally drawn to *Say Yes to the Dress* and am frequently caught sniffling as the bride makes her choice. 'Mum! Get the tissues! Dad's crying front of the telly again!' That pretty much kills my Tarzan act.

I'd really like to be thought of as the hero type. I hope that if I ever saw a child running in front of a bus I'd dive across and shove him to safety: 'Get out the road of the bus, son! Live a full and happy life! I've had *my* life, mine is over – or it will be as soon as this fucking thing runs over me . . .' I'm about to have the word LEYLAND stamped backwards on my forehead. '*You'll* be fine, but it'll be over for me. Live a *good* life, son. All the best, cheerio!'

Yes, I hope I'd be the type of guy who'd do that kind of thing, but I probably won't. I'll more likely go: 'My God! *Look*!' It's a wee *boy*! In front of a *bus*!' And somebody else will say: 'For fuck's sake, are you just gonna *stand* there?? The bus will run him over! Flatten him like a fucking pancake!!' I'll say: 'Has nobody got a phone?' And they'll say: 'Yeah, let's phone a *brave* guy!'

———

My mother's mother Flora MacLean – my granny – she *was* brave. In the fifties, she was walking along Argyll Street in Glasgow, carrying her shopping bag and minding her own business. There was traffic everywhere – tram cars, buses, police cars, motorcycles – and she saw a child running onto the road. 'My God!' She puts down her bag – not a care for herself – and rushes into the road – *Beep! Beep!* – grabs the child under one arm and scolds him: 'Stupid little bugger!' He goes: 'Aw, leave me alone!' She yells: 'Don't you dare struggle with me!' and carries him back and puts him down on the pavement. 'Now *behave* yourself!!' But it was a wee man. With a wee moustache. 'Fuck off, leave me alone!'

After our mother left with Willie Adams, my granny offered to take me and my sister in to live with her. Looking back, I wish she had. I'd seen her occasionally before my mother left. She was a warm-hearted, hard-working woman who cleaned offices for a living and was one of the lights of my life. My granny always seemed really glad to see me. She liked boxers and gave me pictures of her favourite – the famous American Joe Louis. There's a photo of me in her house at three or four years old, hanging out of the window, and I look really happy. She used to turn up at our house in a fur coat and fancy earrings, bearing a bar of Fry's 5 Boys chocolate. The wrapper had five pictures of a boy with five different expressions: Desperation, Pacification, Expectation, Acclamation and Realisation . . . the five emotions of chocolate-eating, in order. I don't think they make Fry's 5 Boys any more, but I still seem to pass through those stages while eating a Fry's Turkish Delight, or an Aero, or a bag of Liquorice Allsorts. Nowadays I get an extra emotion at the end, especially during an acute dose of heartburn: Mortification.

I can't remember who found us alone in the house after my mother left. Maybe a neighbour. Anyhow, someone took us to a children's home. I remember sitting with Florence in the foyer. It was all wooden panels and echoes, and I didn't like it much. I was glad when my father's sisters Mona and Margaret showed up and took us out of there.

———

My father wanted us to be brought up as Catholics. Flora had grown up in a Catholic family, but she married Neil MacLean (from clan MacLean of Duart) who was a Protestant from the Isle of Mull off the west coast of Scotland. When they had children, it became a tug o' war. Flora even tried to have them baptised as Catholics behind her husband's back, but her scheme failed.

Sectarianism was much more alive then. People nowadays don't care all that much but, back then, if Catholic people married Protestants their family would never speak to them again. And if a Protestant got married in a Catholic church their parents wouldn't come to the wedding. It was a tribal war. And it was a shame, because sooner or later the young married couple would

have a child and the grandparents would be desperate to see it
– but because of the upset over the wedding, the rift could never
be mended.

The Irish . . . from whence I sprang – were very much under
the thumb of the Catholic Church. They were all 'God bless you'
and had come to Scotland as very poor, potato famine immi-
grants. They were frowned upon. Glasgow was a very successful
city. It looked upon itself as the second city of the British Empire.
It was a great merchant city for tobacco, whisky and exports,
and there were shipyards and steelworks. So, the people – while
still working class – were comparatively well off. They looked
upon themselves as successful, and the Irish as losers. To marry
one of them was considered to be marrying below your station.

———

Maybe everyone would have been better off if we'd gone to live
with my Granny Flora. But who knows? You can't know. I once
said on TV that I would have preferred going to a children's
home, where I'd be with other kids who all felt the same. A bit
later on, when I was in Australia, I was walking along the street
and a man came up to me. He was an older guy with tattoos, a
hard man – looked like a builder, or maybe a merchant seaman.
This man had been raised in children's homes. He hugged me
and said, 'You're wrong. You wouldn't have liked it.' And he was
crying.

When my aunts arrived at the children's home, they were all
dressed up in fancy coats and hats and I was in awe of them.
Aunt Margaret was my godmother. I was christened in St Patrick's
Church, which is next to the Hilton in Glasgow. When I was
told I was going to live with my aunts and my Uncle James, I

was delighted. The children's home scared me. Everything scared me after my mother left. And I've gone on being scared my whole life.

What scares me now might surprise you. Games for one thing. When people announce they're going to play games – especially 'thinking' games – I run away. I'm frightened of being found to be stupid. I avoid board games like Monopoly, or the games families play at Christmas. You won't catch me playing fucking guessing games where you have to stick something on your forehead or find your way out of a room with clues – that kind of thing is purgatory for me. Physical games are okay, though. I have fun when there's a ball and a crowd of dafties.

After my aunts took Florence and me to their small flat on Stewartville Street in Partick, they immediately held a party to launch their new life of having two children. I remember various friends and relatives being led in one at a time to see me lying there in my cot. It seemed to be a jolly affair. I was quite happy being inspected – as long as Florence was handy. Everybody seemed to like me. I had a sonsy face, as they say in Scotland: 'a face that would get you a scone at any door'. Florence and I were put in two different rooms. I shared one with Mona and Margaret, and Florence was in the kitchen. I must have sorely missed my mother, but I don't really remember that feeling. I do remember peeing the bed and being harshly scolded. And I remember there was a mouse in my room . . .

I'm not afraid of mice. I used to be afraid of sharks, although I've got used to them. I'm very scared of spiders. I saw a gigantic one in Nepal. It was so huge I thought it was a rabbit – brown and furry, moving along in the long grass. When I learned it was a spider, my heart stopped. It was the same day I saw a baby rhinoceros – and I've never seen anything quite so nice.

The mother was running in front with her baby behind her – and I was behind them both on an elephant. The baby kept looking back, scared that we were catching up.

At that early point Mona and Margaret must have thought that having two children in the house was a good idea, but I doubt they really knew what they were getting themselves into. They both had full-time jobs; Mona was a nurse and worked in the hospital at night as well as tending to a few private patients. Margaret, her younger sister, was a Wren during the war but eventually became a civil servant. Presumably they took us in out of a sense of martyrdom based on the religious necessity of saving our souls. But whatever it was, it soon wore off. I don't think they'd considered that they might want to get married one day, and that having us would be an anchor on that. Sometimes, when I'm thinking about it all, I try to pull myself up and I think, 'Maybe I'm just ungrateful'. It was really quite a sacrifice, because they were giving up their chance to be carefree young adults.

Margaret had natural wavy red hair like an American pin-up girl and modelled for a local hairdresser called Eddy Graham. Mona was thirteen years older than her. She dyed her hair blonde; it became my job to trot down to Boots the Chemist for her peroxide: 'Twenty volumes, please.' Like many people at that time, Mona had acquired National Health false teeth, but they must have been uncomfortable because she never put them in unless she went out. The two of them would get all dolled up and go out dancing to the 'F and F' (Fife and Fife) dance hall. They would bring men back home and sit around the fire, laughing and talking.

My Uncle James lived with us in Stewartville Street for a while. Since my dad was in India, James took it upon himself to show me how to brush my teeth. We had tins of Gibbs tooth-paste. He took the lid off and showed me how to rub my toothbrush on the solid toothpaste and how to clean my teeth up and down, not side to side. Uncle James had lost three fingers in an explosion during the war, but he managed well with the fingers he had. He was a nice man. Funny. I loved having him in the house. But after a while, he married an Irish lass called Peggy and went to live in Whiteinch.

Another thing that scares me is public speaking. You might find that hard to believe, but I'm not talking about being onstage – although that's terrifying too. I'm talking about making a speech at weddings and so on. The very thought makes me want to vomit. I had to give a best man's speech once and made a total arse of it. Just after the vows, while they were solemnly singing: '*Mine eyes have seen the glory* . . .' an inescapable image entered my head: I saw a line of old cowboys singing it with their hats off: '*Glory glory hallelujah*'. I burst out laughing and couldn't stop.

When I turned five, I started to attend the school across the road. It was a massive pink sandstone building – I thought it was like a castle. It had two playgrounds – one for older boys and one for girls and younger boys. I'd been observing the school since I was four. I could lean out the window and see right inside the gates. It looked like a good place to be. I could hear it too. I could hear boys singing, and adults teaching. I could see the kids coming out to play in the morning and afternoon. They seemed really delighted to be there – playing games and running about.

The pipe band practised in the school dining room on Friday nights. I loved listening to them. I waited eagerly for the lunch-time noises – all the cutlery being crashed around in the dining room, and boys being ordered about: 'Sit over here!' 'Less nonsense over there!' I could even smell the food. It was cooked somewhere else and delivered to the street outside the school in big metal cases, and it sat there, wafting, until they carried it in. Sometimes wild boys from other streets or towns would sneak along and open it, especially when the pudding was cake and custard. They would each grab a big handful of sponge cake, pry open the custard bin and dip it in, then run away before they could be caught.

The school was divided into two sides. If you were a five-year-old boy you went to St Peter's Girls' School and Infants' School until you were six, and after that you went next door to St Peter's Boys' school. Everybody went in the main entrance – a big double door in the centre of the facade. After I turned five, the big day came when I was to start at the infants' school. I was excited. I had been imagining a bright and happy place with lots of fun and kindly teachers. But once I got inside, I found out just how wrong I was . . .

The first thing that greeted me in the entrance hall was a massive crucifix on which was mounted an eight-foot bleeding Christ. Bright red blood dripped down the face, from the evil-looking crown of thorns to the near-naked body. This monstrosity hung threateningly above the stairwell and was impossible to miss. I'd been attending Mass since I was two, but I still didn't completely understand the significance of that statue. This much I did pick up: it was a dire warning. Apparently, it was all MY fault that Jesus was tortured and killed, and I'd be paying for it throughout eternity.

At first, I didn't mind the school lessons. I felt confident because I'd already learned to write letters. Florence had taught me. And I liked my teacher, Miss O'Halloran. She even paraded me around the whole school to show how clever I was. I remember writing the letter 'J' on the blackboard with a piece of chalk, to the great admiration of the merry throng.

But pretty soon, a shadow fell. The headmistress, Sister Philomena, was a humourless inquisitor who had pictures of hell on her walls – half-naked, chained people being ripped apart on torture beds or eaten by giant serpents. I already had my own, nightmarish visions of what hell was like – dark purple caves invaded by raging fires, with people moaning and shrieking, and nowhere to go. It was dawning on me that we were placed here on Earth with all that exciting stuff that constituted sin and temptation – but if we used it, we'd be punished mercilessly. I still think it's a rotten deal.

Sister Philomena was the big boss, and a huge threat because I knew she could decide my fate. On my first day at St Peter's, I wisely thought: 'These nuns and teachers are my superiors. I'm very small and they're very big. This could go badly for me.' I was right. The nuns were very violent. Their punishment tool was a twelve-inch ruler they'd crash down on our knuckles, even in the infants' school. They'd cruise by your desk and check your work, and if it wasn't up to par they'd make you put your hands on your notebook and *thwackkk!!* I never even knew exactly why I was being punished, and I never dared ask.

At least life at home in Stewartville Street was fine at first. We were not neglected. There was always someone home to watch us. There were fewer sticky sweeties, though, mainly because it was wartime. Instead – much to my horror – Aunt Mona cooked us vegetables. I liked potatoes, but I hated the carrots and onions. The absolute worst were Brussels sprouts. We always had them on a Saturday. Fucked up the whole day. To help get them down my throat, Mona would offer encouragements like a smack in the head or a bloody nose. There was no such thing as leaving them on my plate. I'd have to sit there for hours and hours, staring at the nightmarish, overcooked, wee greenish-grey things. I would miss the movie matinee I'd been looking forward to all week, but still I just couldn't put one in my mouth. Even now I have an utter disgust for Brussels sprouts; just being in the same room as one makes me want to vomit.

But as a boy, there was something wonderful about refusing to eat them. So what if the matinee was over? I was starring in my own Western movie. To me it was a life-or-death stance just like the shoot-out at the O.K. Corral. Would Flash Gordon cave in and eat the sprouts? No, he fucking wouldn't. It was a rebellious act that I believed elevated me to the realm of the heroes. This was my chance to prove to myself and others that, at five years old, I could be counted among the brave.

3

**AVOID PEOPLE WHO SAY
THEY KNOW THE ANSWER**

**KEEP THE COMPANY OF PEOPLE
WHO ARE TRYING TO UNDERSTAND
THE QUESTION**

THERE HAS BEEN no shortage of questions in my life. For example: what does snot accomplish? I used to think your nose would be much better designed to hold in snot if it was the other way up. But then, if you had a cold and you sneezed, your eyes would be full of snot. And you'd always have two partings in your hair.

Another thing: why do men have nipples? I've never been given a decent answer to that one. Perhaps that's why I had mine pierced – to provide a reason. It wasn't so much the actual piercing, it was the pride of it. I used to like showing my pierced nipples to people, hoping they'd be suitably shocked. They usually were.

It was a good day when I got those nipple rings. The piercer said, 'Why do you want this?' I said, 'I've become so ordinary. I used to be a hippy, with long hair, and dressing wild. I feel like I've joined the beige ranks.' He got his needle and pierced my left nipple.

After I'd stopped screaming, he said, 'There you go. One more of us – and one less of them.' *Oooohhhh.* It hurt like fuck. It was like being struck by lightning. There was a high from it that I'll never forget. Lasted for hours. Having my feet tattooed was painful too. Torture. The worst was going back the second time to have all the flowery patterns coloured in, knowing what the pain was like from having the outline drawn. Holy Mother.

I wish I still had my nipple rings. I had to take them out when I was in *Mrs Brown* – a movie I did with Dame Judi Dench. I had to be filmed swimming naked in the English Channel, and the director asked me to remove them. That's how I lost them. Well, I actually didn't lose them – I just didn't put them back in for a while, so when I finally tried, the holes had healed up. And that was that.

———

Once I turned six and was moved up to St Peter's Boys' School, there were no shortage of mysteries. For example, I always wondered why we weren't Jews, since Jesus was one. I got hounded for asking, and I never got an answer. I learned early on that I would be ridiculed if I dared ask my burning questions about things like: 'Did Jesus have any brothers and sisters?'

The teachers at St Peter's Boys' School used a different instrument of torture from the nuns at the infants' school. The 'tawse' was two or three feet long, with a turn at one end. At the other end it was split into two or three tails. The punisher would put it over his shoulder and brace himself, ready to take aim. You had to stand like you were holding a bowl out in front of you and they would come down hard. *Ssschwckkk!!! Ssschwckkk!!! Ssschwckkk!!!* On a winter's morning it had to be felt to be believed.

If you cried, you got mocked – especially by Rosie MacDonald. She was a psychopath. 'Big Rosie' they called her, as if she deserved affection. Her speciality was placing pencils under your knuckles to induce extra pain when she whacked you. She would thrash me for nothing – for showing interest in pigeons outside the window or glancing away when she was talking. She was a sadistic bastard. There was a guy with glasses in my class whom she called 'four-eyes'. She was supposed to be a teacher! That kind of thing leaves an indelible scar on you. One day I was late, so she got two boys in my class to grab my arms and run me up and down the classroom aisles to 'wake me up'. My little play-piece (sandwich) fell out of my jersey and was trampled to mush on the floor.

After a while I just decided to stop doing my homework. I reasoned, 'She's going to beat me anyway'. And she did. Almost every day. Hurt me beyond words. I don't really want to talk about her any more, it puts me in an awful mood.

In any case, at six years old I learned that a thwack on the hand – or even a smack in the mouth – is overrated as a pain-creator. It's not the worst thing you're ever going to feel. My aunties could fucking inflict twice that pain without lifting their hands – by humiliation. My strategy for dealing with physical hurt has always been to dream. I would just choose to think about other things.

And apart from being battered mercilessly, I rather liked St Peter's, especially the infants' school. I enjoyed the atmosphere of all the boys and girls together learning and singing songs. We learned about the Catholic vestments: the alb (robe), the amice (top garment), the girdle (belt), the maniple (ornamental armpiece) and the stole (long scarf).

That was just the beginning of our Catholic education. Between the infants' school and the primary school there were all sorts of sneaky ways they tried to nudge us towards the priesthood.

The real showdown was when the priest came to recruit us. He swished into the classroom in his long black outfit, and posed the ultimate trick question: 'Are there any boys here who DON'T want to be priests?' Nobody dared put up his hand.

———

One question my five-year-old self had was: 'Where is my father and is he ever coming back?' I had no memories of his being there when I was a baby, and my aunts never talked about him to me. But he eventually showed up just after my fifth birthday – an enormous guy dragging a huge metal trunk. When I heard him approaching, I dived for cover right away. He peered at me, under the table, then pulled me out and gave me a wonderful toy yacht. It was green and red with canvas sails, and it really sailed. I was dead pleased. My father and I sailed it together in Victoria Park near Whiteinch in Glasgow. There was a splendid pond, and a club for wealthy people who had handsome miniature racing yachts. They were really accurate sailors and brilliant to watch. My wee boat wasn't as showy as the others, but it did well. You'd put it in the water, then run like hell around the pond to catch it on the other side.

My father's name was William Connolly. People had called me 'Billy' until he came home, but then I became 'Wee Billy' because he was 'Big Billy'. He really was big – and broad – with a neck and head like a bull. His collar size was $18\frac{1}{2}$ inches. So, I was forced to be 'Wee Billy' my whole life until I became a comedian and Scottish people started calling me 'The Big Yin'. Some people in England thought that was to do with 'yin and yang', but it just means 'the big one' and it's common in Scotland. If you're tall and they don't know your name you're 'The Big

Yin', and if you're not tall you're the 'Wee Yin'. Being 'The Big Yin' was a nice change from 'Wee Billy', but there could be a lot of confusion. For example, in the pub some local guy might say to another: 'Billy Connolly was in earlier.' His pal would ask for clarification: 'You mean Big Billy or Wee Billy?' He'd reply: 'The Big Yin.' 'Ah . . .' His pal would nod, 'Wee Billy!' Anyone standing nearby would wonder: 'What the fuck are they talking about?'

I never met my dad's parents, but I knew his father was an Irish immigrant from Connemara in the west of Ireland. I went once to visit Connemara with my daughter Cara when I was performing in Dublin. I had a couple of nights off, so we drove up to see it. Local people knew the place was special to me because I had said on a talk show that my ancestors were from there, and they greeted me warmly. My grandfather came from a village in West Connemara called Ballyconneely – which is very like 'Billy Connolly'! When I was there a woman came up to me and said, 'Billy Connolly! You're the spitting image of yourself!' The place was lovely. Rural. White walls and black roofs. A beautiful place on the edge of the ocean. They get rain there that would take the skin off you.

I love Ireland. There's something very alive about the people there, something lovely and crazy and intelligent and strange about the whole culture. We're the same race, the Scots and the Irish. We're all Celtic people. The Scots came from Ireland – for reasons best known to themselves. 'Come on – I know an even *colder* place! It rains *all the time*! It's amazing! Head for the black cloud!' The Scots have done that all over the world. During the Highland Clearances in the eighteenth century, we went to Virginia. It was paradise – the Blue Ridge Mountains and all of that. 'Too hot! Further north, lads!' So, they went up to Hudson's Bay – where it was cold enough to freeze your bollocks off! If you had a piss you had to snap it off. If you farted in bed you woke up with an ice cube up your arse.

My ancestors left Ireland in the time of the potato famine, but not because of the weather. They were starving. But they arrived in Scotland barefoot with nothing and had nowhere to go and were treated appallingly. Protestants didn't want them. There used to be signs outside businesses saying: *'Worker wanted. Irish need not apply.'* My grandfather came to Glasgow when he was ten years old. It must have been very hard for him. Even my father – when he was old enough to apply for jobs – was greeted by *'Apprentices wanted. Boys' Brigade welcome.'* That was a Protestant organisation.

My father was a bright guy. He'd come top of his school, and became an engineer, making machine parts in companies like Singer. When war broke out, he went off to attend to aeroplanes in the Royal Air Force. He contracted malaria while he was in India and was sent up to the hill country to recuperate. The air force trunk he brought back home after the war was full of exciting stuff that gave me a little window into his life abroad. I loved seeing all the photos of India, mostly of white men in shorts. There were also official papers, bits of uniform, badges and eyeglasses. I used to play with his metal-framed military glasses – the type John Lennon wore. I would put them on and pose about. He even had an Australian military hat – the kind that goes up at the side – I never knew why.

My father loved India, and so do I. I love the landscape, the music, the paintings, the poetry and art, and I love Indian streets. I'm always amazed to see people riding side-saddle on motorbikes – women with saris flapping in the air, sometimes holding a baby in their arms. Such sights put my heart in my mouth. Much of the colour of India comes from the women. Their clothes are extraordinary. You'll turn a corner in your car on the way to a remote village, then suddenly three women will cross the road – one in emerald-green, one in bright yellow and the other in scorching red. Ridiculously bright and beautiful colours. *BaBoooom!!* And there'll be stalls on the side of the road selling kitchen things and bowls and cloth for saris, and they'll be blazing bright as well. And the men in white . . . it's all just stunning. Everybody walks nicely, and they swish along so gracefully.

———

I learned recently that I have Indian heritage, on my mother's side. It took me by surprise. I was doing a BBC TV show called *Who Do You Think You Are?* First, they took me to Darjeeling in the hill country, where my dad was sent to recover from malaria. It was a very pure place. Lovely air. I liked hearing the Islamic prayers in the morning. They seemed different from those I've heard elsewhere – and sung in a lovely pitch.

The TV researchers found that, at twenty-five years old, my great-great-great-grandfather John O'Brien was with the British Army at Bangalore. I went with the TV crew to the barracks where he was stationed and the soldiers who are there now performed a display march for us. Afterwards, one of the officers came up to us. 'Who is the parachutist?' They pointed to me. 'You've done your course?'

'Yes.'

'And you've got your wings?'

'Yes.'

He dived on me and gave me a hug.

I learned that John O'Brien had married a twelve-year-old

Indian girl. Apparently, that was pretty common behaviour for the time – although not in Ireland. I visited the simple Catholic church where they were married. There was a lot of intermarriage back then, but they tried to pretend it didn't exist. As far as the British were concerned, John's bride didn't have any Indian names – they wiped them from the records completely and called her Matilda.

My great-great-great-grandfather was no sooner married than he was called to Lucknow, where there was a long siege of the garrison by Indian rebel forces who no longer want to be ruled by the British Raj. During the fighting, he was badly wounded – shot in the shoulder. Some of their wives were also attacked. I went to a hostel for British army wives and learned that rebels had turned up there when the men were away fighting the Siege of Lucknow and had thrown their womenfolk down a well. Both John and Matilda were lucky to survive the uprising. After it was all over, they settled in Bangalore and had four children. Bangalore must have been very different then . . . now it's the computer capital of India. I like the name Bangalore. Wonder if that's where the word 'galore' comes from? John and Matilda's story hardly had a happy ending. John became ill with syphilis and turned haywire with the drink. He returned to Scotland with his family, whom he could no longer support, and Matilda was forced to beg on the street. But it was her line that led to my Indian ancestry, for which I am very grateful.

———

I first tasted a curry when I was twenty-something. I was with a singer called Jimmy Sneddon and some other folkies in Glasgow. They said, 'Wanna come? We're going for an Indian.' I said, 'I don't know anything about that kind of food, and I don't want to get tortured.' 'It's good,' said Jimmy. 'You'll like it.' He suggested I try dhal and I did like it – very much. This was at the Koh I Noor restaurant in Gibson Street. I went there for many years. Until they closed their doors in 2020, they still had photos of me on the wall that they took in the seventies. I was fond of Rasul, the owner. I remember when he did the hajj to Mecca. He came up and told me he was going, and I gave him a hug.

The second time I went to the Koh I Noor I tried a chicken dish, then over the years I slowly delved deeper into the cuisine. In Scotland the Indian restaurants are mainly Bangladeshi. First, I liked biryani, and then I liked madras curries. Now and again, I like tandoori, but I prefer the others. My favourite Indian meal is spinach and potatoes – saag aloo – with dhal on the side. And I love that fruity bread – peshwari naan. Delightful. I did a British tour of seventy nights and had a curry every single night. There are great curries in Manchester, Birmingham, Sheffield, Watford and Bradford. Fantastic! And delightful sweets like gulab jamun.

I found that madras was as hot as I liked to go. I didn't like vindaloo, or faal, which is even hotter and jam-packed with chillies. You can spell faal 'phall', but it's just as fucking hot with a 'ph'. I tried to like them, but they burned my arse. I started making curries myself when I was first living in England with Pamela. I became quite proficient at it, mainly using the Madhur Jaffrey cookbooks. By the time we lived in a house with a decent-size kitchen I could do an Indian dinner for twelve, with soup, main course and dessert. First, I'd serve green soup made with spinach, then my favourite main dish, which was baked cod in a yoghurt sauce with rice, and Gujarati carrot salad with black mustard seeds. The dessert would be apple pie and ice cream. I loved cooking for my pals. Very jolly occasions. That's where I discovered that if you have to make a huge salad you can toss it in a bin liner. I came up with that idea myself.

———

Here's another of my boyhood mysteries: 'Why can't I be king?' The British class structure is still baffling to me. And people kept telling me Scotland was a Protestant country, but they never explained it. I wondered: 'What do I not get? Do I have fewer civil rights than you?' At least now I've been awarded my own Vegemite jar with my name on it. THAT's royalty.

I fucking love Vegemite. I have it on my toast in the morning. You know Marmite's that wee bit runny? Vegemite is a stage denser, and not so shiny. Killer diller. Australians grow up with it, but it's an acquired taste for everybody else. My pal Whoopi Goldberg *hates* it. We were talking about Australia and she said, 'Have you tasted Vegemite?' And I said, 'Yeah, I love it.' She said, 'Ugh, how can you say that? It's like licking a cat's ass!' I said, 'Who did your research?'

When I was a boy I wondered: 'How can 25,000 tons of steel float on water?' I did an engineering course in my fourth year of school and found the answer to that one. But early on at St Peter's, most of my mysteries were about Catholicism. I could never understand the miracle of the loaves and fishes. The Bible said they turned up with a table full of loaves and fishes, but hundreds of people arrived, and they fed them all. That's the only information you get. How did they do it? Nobody could explain it, so I just assumed each fish was twelve feet long. I could never understand the 'Holy Trinity' – Father, Son and Holy Ghost. As far as I knew, the Holy Ghost just drifts around – it doesn't take part in much. But how could God give you his only begotten son when it's actually him? I didn't dare ask the nuns, but once I got to secondary school, I tried to ask teachers there. They just put me off by being absurd. I don't think they knew either. And they didn't like upstarts. 'Connolly! Pay attention! If you paid as much attention to maths as you do to these questions, you'd do far better!'

They were wrong. Maths was useless to me. Have you ever used the word 'hypotenuse' since you left school? I rest my case. Those bastards crammed it into your skull – it's of fuck all use to anybody. Why do we learn algebra when we've no intention of ever going there? Can you imagine actually using algebra in your life? You're lost in London, and you ask someone, 'Excuse me, could you please direct me to Harrods?' 'Certainly. Let's see now – let X equal Harrods . . .' 'Fuck off. I'll ask somebody else.'

From the moment I set foot in St Peter's primary school I knew that, despite all the mysteries, I should just act like I believed everything. No questions. Never question a priest. You'd go roaring straight to hell.

4

NEVER RUN IN LOOSE UNDERWEAR

——

I WISH I knew where my snow globes are. I collect snow globes. I loved them the first time I set eyes on them when I was a boy. At the beginning they were superior – glass, not plastic. Still, many people thought they were shoddy. I didn't mind that, and as I got older, I came to appreciate kitsch – lava lamps for example – and loved my snow globes more and more. Anyway, being lined up in a collection gives them a certain air.

Some of my snow globes have a wonderful surreal quality. I have a great one from Hawaii: it has a man standing on a seesaw, fishing in the snow. I also have some beauties made by artists. There's a lovely one I got in Australia – a little garden seat on a garden mound just sitting on its own. I even have one with me in it, standing in the snow with my arms outstretched. Yeah, I have loads of snow globes, but I don't know where they are. We used to have them in a display case, but I think Pamela got fed up dusting them and hid them somewhere.

——

When I was a young boy, I became a Wolf Cub. It was one of the most pleasant things about my boyhood. Every so often the Wolf Cubs held a 'bob-a-job' week. A 'bob' was a shilling – five pence. You could go to the door of nice houses in the West End of Glasgow and say, 'Anything for bob-a-job week?' And they would give you a job to do, like raking the lawn or fetching coal, and pay you a shilling.

My favourite bob-a-job location was Highburgh Road, where there were very nice Georgian tenement houses. I knew the area well because in autumn when all the leaves were piled up on the ground, I used to get up to a little prank there: I would completely cover myself with leaves and sit quietly at the park gate. When grown-ups would pass, I'd stick my head out and say, 'Hello!' It was then that I learned that the noises made by startled adults can be very weird: *'Oooooiiiwwwwhhhh!'*, *'AaaaggghheeeEEE!'*, *'Wwhhhhooiiiiuuuu!!!'*

In one of those Highburgh Road houses there lived an elderly man – I used to see him every time bob-a-job came round. He wore a cardigan and corduroys and looked like he'd been a schoolteacher or a doctor. I loved going to his place because he treated me very nicely. We would sit beside his fire and I'd polish his shoes. He had lovely brogues. It was a peaceful thing and it gave me a love of shoe polishing that has never left me. While I was polishing, he would talk to me about Trinidad and Tobago, where he'd spent many years.

My own shoes were bought by my aunties. They were so rigid they felt like they were made of steel. The soles didn't bend until I was in the third year. But I've made up for that now; I have more shoes than anyone has a right to. Some of them are brogues. I've got green and white ones for Celtic. I once wore a pair of black patent brogues with furry black and white spotted panels on a plane. A flight attendant said, 'I like your shoes.' I said, 'Thanks – I had them made abroad. The shoemaker had a big box of Dalmatian puppies, and you could pick your own . . .' It was the only time in my life I was smacked by a flight crew member.

I tend to hang on to my shoes for decades – I've had some of my cowboy boots since the seventies. But cowboy boots just keep on getting better . . . as long as you have a good cobbler. I had a great one in New York – he had a shop downtown on Bleecker Street, and repaired cowboy boots exceptionally well. I love people who are good at their craft. I can watch them for ages.

As a child I used to love looking in the cobbler's window. He always had his lasts up at the window so he could work on them with the daylight shining in. Jack O'Brian was his name. He was a friend of my father. 'Oh hello, Billy!' Nails in his mouth. 'Hello, Mr O'Brian.' My friends and I used to challenge each other to run through the cobbler's dunny – the back entrance to his close. It was the darkest of all dunnies, and lower than the front entrance. You sneaked in from the back court and immediately turned a corner into pitch darkness. Then you'd blindly edge your way up the stairs to the front close and escape out onto the street – if you made it unscathed. Everybody was scared of the cobbler's dunny. There were ghosts in it. I got caught one day when I was running through. A giant, cold hand grabbed my neck, and I got such a fright I shat myself.

———

There was a gang of about five of us – Gerald McGee, Frankie McBride, Peter Loftus and others – who became the scourge of the neighbourhood. We created an obstacle course called 'Bite an Apple, Slap a Fish and Spit on a Remnant'. There were three shops involved in this game – a fruit stall on Dumbarton Road, a fish shop round the corner on Hyndland Street with the fish all displayed just inside an open window, and a remnant shop further along in the same street with cloth hanging outside. The trick was to run in a line and perform three daring-dos in sequence: take a bite out of an apple from the fruit stall, run round the corner to slap a fish at the fish shop, then sprint to the fabric shop and spit on the remnants. It was a dangerous race, and you had to be fast. The further back in the line you were, the more likely you were to be caught. There'd be shop-keepers after us, people running onto the road, and cars going, '*Beeeeep! Watch it, ya stupid weans!!*'

When I managed to sprint the whole gauntlet without being caught, I felt like a champ. But my athletic endeavours were hampered by my clothing, especially my underpants that were huge, loose and drooped down to my knees. Fold upon fold of wobbly Airtex material. When I took my trousers off at night, I looked like a Greek folk dancer. And there was no fly – there was just a slit. Your willy just fell out – *flop, flip, flippity-flop*.

Almost everything my aunts got me was awful. They sent me to school wearing gloves joined by a piece of string. This was a custom job, designed by my aunts to prevent me from losing them. They attached each end of the string to one glove, then threaded the whole contraption through the sleeves of my jacket. The only problem was the string was a tad short, so one of my arms was perpetually bent. And pretty soon the other boys at school twigged to the fact that if they yanked on one gloved hand my other one would likely punch my nose.

My winter hat was a balaclava, kindly knitted by Auntie

Margaret. But the eyeholes were off centre, so in order to see where I was going, I had to turn my head sideways and peer out with a distorted view. It was itchy too. My skin has always been tender. I can't stand the feel of wool on my skin. When I was in the Territorial Army I had to shave the inside of my shirt with a razor.

Wellies were worn the year round. Enjoyed and loved by all. You could jump in puddles and remain dry. I wore them to school on rainy days – most days. When it was fine, we'd wear sandshoes – they were the precursors of the sneaker. But I had trouble tying my shoelaces. It was a mystery to me. I still get a little tremor when I double the knot on my shoelaces – if I did that when I was a boy, I couldn't loosen it again to remove my shoes. Even today, when flight attendants are giving passengers the life jacket instructions – 'Tie it in a double bow on the side . . .' something in me goes '*Shhhiii!!!*' If we plunged into the sea, I'd be the only guy in the ocean with a single bow in his life jacket. And we all know sharks can loosen a single bow.

Polo necks were purgatory. Drove me insane with their itchiness. But the single most uncomfortable garment was a pair of tweeds. Those trousers thought I was edible. I think they'd been knitted from barbed wire and camels' pubic hair by some fucking pervert in the Highlands. It was terrible. My willy would rub up and down my tweeds. 'Oh, fucking hell!' The thing was red raw. Glowing in the dark: *beep-beep-beep!* The teacher would ask, 'Connolly, is that a *torch* in your pocket?'

The old man in the Highburgh Road didn't just inspire my obsession with shoes. The best thing was knowing an adult who took the time to talk kindly to me. At home no one could ever do that – let alone listen. I'd say: 'Dad?' He'd say, '*WHAT?!!?*' It was the same for all my friends. Older people couldn't communicate properly with any of us. They didn't talk about generation gaps, then, because they didn't see it as a problem – they just battered the children. 'You – *slap!* – stupid – *slap!* – boy!!!' And then they'd say, 'Have you had enough?' What a *stupid* question! 'Would you like some more of the same?' Another stupid question! I think you were supposed to say, 'Would a kick in the testicles be out of the question?'

Once my father hit me and I flew backwards over the settee in a sitting position. I used to tell my audiences, 'It was just like real flying except you didn't get a cup of tea or a safety belt.' And if you asked an adult a question they'd use it against you, by turning it into a threat. For example, you'd say, 'Can I go out on my bike?' My dad would say, 'Bike?' I'll give you *bike*!!!' 'Can I go to the pictures?' 'Pictures is it??? I'll *pictures* you, my lad!' It was so confusing. 'I'll make you smile on the other side of your face!' I'd think, 'What are you gonna do, *slash* me???'

When I was a child, it was considered very healthy to beat the shit out of your children on a regular basis, so my father's treatment of me was pretty much the same as most children got at that time. But Mona was a whole different story. As a comedian, I could always turn my father's beatings into funny stuff, but never Mona's. That was deadly serious. By the time I was seven she had taken to hitting and humiliating me whenever she could. To this day I don't know why she took such a dislike to me.

The worst thing was that she instilled in me a belief that I was useless. In my adult life it has been an enormous pleasure – and my greatest ambition – to prove her wrong. Her three favourite lines were: '*It was a sad day when I met you!*' (TRUE); '*You'll never amount to anything!*' (FALSE) and '*Your powers of observation are nil.*' (FALSE, FALSE, FALSE). My school report card got it right, though: *'Billy has a fertile imagination!'* (CORRECT).

By contrast, the old man in Highburgh Road talked to me respectfully. And he gave me stamps. Stamp collecting was my first hobby. There was nothing of any value in my collection, but I had favourites. I especially liked the triangular Vatican stamps with buildings and saints on them. I liked Russian stamps as well, with industrial scenes. Much later in my life Jimmy Reid, the socialist union man, used to kill himself laughing when I would pose as an engineer on a Russian stamp with eyes on the horizon and a spanner in one hand.

I was always confused as to why we don't call countries the names they call themselves. Why is Sweden called 'Sverige' on a stamp and Switzerland 'Helvetia'? I've been brutal about Switzerland onstage: 'Nothing good comes from Switzerland. Cuckoo clocks and fucking Toblerones. It's impossible to eat a Toblerone without *hurting* yourself. They should come with a wee toolkit. It's a stupid shape – pointy, sharp and offensive. What kind of sick mind thought that one up? An aggressive sweetie! A bar of chocolate that *hurts* you . . . Switzerland!'

By the time I was twelve I had several stamp albums. I bought them with pocket money our dad gave us every Saturday. He'd get paid on a Friday and come home with comics – *Eagle* for me and *Girl* for Florence – and our pocket money would be doled out in the morning. I'd run out and buy a bag of assorted stamps – a real lucky dip! Other people specialised in stamps of certain countries, or those depicting aeroplanes, tractors or flowers; I just merrily collected my little Vatican section.

———

When I was around eight, reading became my main hobby. Florence, who was already an avid reader, introduced me to the Partick Library. She helped me join and showed me how it worked. There were sections, divided into ages. From age four to age six you'd read the baby books. From six to eight it would be *Just William*, Enid Blyton, and a series of books called 'Cowboys Cowboys Cowboys', 'Pirates Pirates Pirates', 'Sailors Sailors Sailors' and so on. I found them really interesting, and they didn't namby-pamby you either. From eight to ten you'd get *Biggles* and a few easy novels. Then from ten to twelve things would get really interesting; that's when I read all sorts of fantastic adventure books, such as Robert Louis Stevenson's *Treasure Island*. By the time I was in the twelve-to-fourteen section I was loving Dickens. You just had to rifle through the books in your age group, see what you fancied, and take one home. After a few years – I think it was when you were twelve – you were entitled to take out two books. But the ultimate was to become a fourteen-year-old, *three-book* guy. Walking up the road with your three books had a certain cachet. It was a lovely system. Everything I've achieved in my life has been because of the library.

At least I know where my pens are. I have a wee collection of fountain pens. Writing with a good pen has been a joy since I was nine. My first writing instrument was a pencil but, at around eight years old, we began to attempt cursive using wooden pens with metal nibs. Those contraptions made the task near impossible. Every Sunday we got an 'ink exercise' for homework. There was always some bum in the class who managed to make it look great but, all in all, those first pens were pretty primitive writing instruments. There was a hole in our desks where a little porcelain inkwell sat. I still love ink.

My current favourite is brown, but back then our ink was a murky, blue-grey colour. I drank it once. It tasted okay but it made my tongue blue. I wonder what happened to all those wee inkwells?

Once you had mastered cursive, you could bring a fountain pen to school. From that point on my father would give me a fountain pen every Christmas – usually a Conway Stewart tortoiseshell pen-and-pencil set. I would have it until about mid-January and then it would disappear. Some bastard at school probably nicked it. As the year rolled on, I would have to pretend it was still in my school bag, to avoid a belting.

———

Over the years my various wee collections have meant a lot to me – my stamps, my snow globes, my pens. They were . . . mine. It's like my penchant for trying to see faces and other forms in clouds. Nobody else cares, but it means a lot to me – a little art form of my own. People have always laughed at me about it. I should move to New Zealand. They've got the best clouds on earth.

I sometimes see people in rock faces as well. There's a great rock face I always pass when I'm fishing the Green River in Utah. I often spot Johnny Cash among those rocks. Fishing's another big hobby of mine. It's my absolute favourite thing to do. I've been enjoying it for many years now – fly fishing mainly. I first fished in Cardross in Scotland and on the River Clyde for cod. Then I fished in the Scottish Highlands for salmon and trout with a wonderful guide called Ian Murray. Later, with my son Jamie, I fished for bonefish, tarpon and permit in Mexico and brown trout in Utah. I can't tie my own flies, though. I wanted to, but I never learned how. That would have been a great hobby.

I learned to tie all kinds of knots when I was in the Wolf Cubs. We had meetings every Tuesday at 5 p.m. in the church hall. One evening we were practising our knots when a priest came in and asked for volunteers to be altar boys at benediction. There was a shortage of altar boys. For Mass you only need two altar boys, but for the midweek benediction you need quite a few to make up a procession. I put up my hand. Then the priest announced that each volunteer first had to be vetted. So, eight of us went to the sacristy – that's the room where the priest gets ready for Mass – and formed a queue to be interviewed. I became bored waiting. My eye wandered around the room, and I noticed that the metal container in which they placed hot charcoal for incense – the thurible – was hanging on the wall. Now, I fancied being that front altar boy – the thurifer, or thurible-swinger. I was keen to be the one waving a smelly, clanging thing with smoke belching out all over the place. The other boys in the procession only got to carry candles, but I was desperate for that special, front-man job.

Unfortunately, both I and Matt McGinley spied the thurible at the same time, and we both had the same idea. We rushed over, yanked it down and started fighting over it. *Boof!* 'Gimme it!'

'It's MINE! Get *aarrf*!' By then everyone else wanted it too, and there was a furious rumble – all eight of us fighting savagely over it. This ended when the priest rushed in and smacked each of us in the ear. 'GET OUT!' That was my interview – and thurifer career – well and truly over.

The priests weren't beyond getting physical with you in more ways than one. There was one priest who used to go after your bum. If he met you in the street he'd find a way to touch it.

We didn't think that was especially weird – just priesty kind of behaviour. We talked about it to each other: 'Keep your eye out for Balducci! He'll feel your bum.' I suppose even priests need a hobby.

5

INTERFERE WITH YOURSELF
ON A REGULAR BASIS

———

IN THE CATHOLIC Church, you start the ritual of confession when you 'come of age' at seven – the Age of Reason. At that point you are educated about confession and Communion, and how they are linked. You're warned that you must confess before you go to Communion so that you're 'clean of sin' when you receive the sacrament. My first confession took place in a school-room. I remember thinking I was made of glass; you could see right through me. The priest sat behind a little banister, and there was a kneeler beyond that. I entered and said, 'Bless me, Father, for I have sinned. This is my first confession.' I'd been racking my brain to think of something I'd done wrong. I just blurted out, 'I've told lies' – which was the only sin I could think of. He blessed me, and off I went happily to my first Communion.

Going to confession as an older boy was different. You knelt by a window covered in a kind of black gauze. There was a little rectangular hole at the bottom where the priest could pass you something – or you could pass something to him. I never knew what could be passed, but I could always see inside to where he was. You could spot the sports newspaper on his knee. On Saturdays, the *Evening Times* was pink, and the *Evening Citizen* was green. So, you'd be telling him about your lies, and he'd be reading about Motherwell versus Partick Thistle.

After confessing your sins, the priest would murmur, 'Thanks for your confession. Say three Hail Marys.' Then you left, and the next person went in. The sins I confessed as a teenager were mainly 'thinking bad thoughts'. I'd always hope to leave it there, but the priest would ask for details. You'd tell him you'd seen women's breasts in a magazine, and you'd thought it would be nice to touch them. The newspaper would be put down quick smart. Sometimes I would confess masturbation. It's not a mortal sin, it's a venial sin, so you can be forgiven for it after you've said quite a few 'Hail Mary' prayers – a good ten of them. The punishment was chosen to fit the sin, so anybody sitting outside could more or less guess what you'd been up to by how long it took you to do your penance.

———

Whenever I talked about masturbation onstage, I could see men in the audience going, 'Aw, *no*! Please change the subject! Oh, Billy, I'm with a girlfriend here, give us a break! If I laugh, she'll know I've done it!' But I felt that my stage piece about 'what to do if you get caught masturbating' was a public service. Thinks not you? Because it's exceptionally difficult to find an excuse. My advice is this: Be quick with the excuse. You're in mid-masturb, and the door suddenly bursts open. It's your nosy brother: '*Oouuhhhhh!!!!* What the FUCK are you doing . . . ?' Don't let him complete the sentence. Come in immediately with: '*THANK GOD YOU'RE HERE!*' That deeply upsets intruders. 'What d'ye mean?'

This is when you give a rational answer. 'You'll never believe this – I was walking across the room when the biggest hairy spider you ever saw ran out from underneath the bookshelf. It was a HUGE bugger – the size of a soup plate! It came scuttling towards me and ran right up the leg of my trousers! Only last week I was reading that there's nothing tarantulas love more than to sink their teeth into people's testicles!!!! And I thought, "*That's* what the bugger's up to!!! It's away up the leg of my trousers to sink its teeth into the family jewels!!!" So, I whipped my tweeds down – and not a second too soon! It was raising its horrible hairy legs and its teeth were poised to bite, just as you walked in the door! So, I was desperately trying to shake it off! *Brush brush brush, jerk jerk jerk!!!* Get the fuck off me!!!'

———

When I was a boy, I thought confession was an extraordinary thing. I felt great afterwards. But it wasn't easy, deciding on the right sin for the occasion. My best friend at that time was Joe West. We met in the line to start primary school, and he was my friend for seventy years until he died a couple of years ago. When we were eight, we were comparing notes about confession and he came up with a great idea. He said, 'You can make it all up. As long as the last thing you say is "I've been telling lies", you can cancel what you've just said and still be forgiven.' I never tried it, but I think he did. He was braver than me.

It was generally understood that your confession would be confidential. But some priests – like Father Balducci – would throw discretion to the wind and yell, 'WHAT? You're a DISGRACE! That's DISGUSTING!!!' People nearby could hear it. The line outside his door was short compared to the long lines outside the other priests' doors. It was better to go to confession when you weren't in a hurry.

I always wondered why they gave you prayers as a punishment. Wasn't prayer supposed to be a holy and wholesome thing? But back then I believed much of what I was told – even when it didn't make any sense – and was happy in the Catholic religion. In fact, when I was a boy, I was enraptured by many aspects of the Church. I loved the music and the smells of incense. And the Lenten hymns. It felt good going to Communion, and I felt great afterwards. Sometimes I think I'd actually like to go to Mass now just to enjoy the service.

I was supposed to be following one narrow religious path, but just down the road in Stewartville Street there was a massive temptation to defect. Abingdon Hall, a bustling centre of evangelical activity, was at number twelve. Unknown to my family, I would sneak into meetings there with my Protestant friends. The leaders were very entertaining. They would tell Bible stories, present slide-shows, and I learned an excellent magic trick there where you fold and tear a piece of paper a certain way, then open it up to reveal the words 'heaven' and 'hell'. Some of the congregation had travelled as missionaries to Africa, and they would tell fascinating stories about villages and tribes. Towards the end of the year, you could put your name down to be given a Christmas present at a community party. They'd have a tinsel-encrusted tree with all the presents under it, and you'd get a jigsaw, a set of watercolour paints, or a toy gun. Best of all, at every meeting we were fed tea and buns. I'd do anything for a sticky bun.

———

I was drawn to many Protestant things. I liked the Salvation Army band and used to follow them up the street. I liked the Orange Walk too – it looked like such fun. They were probably all headed for hell, but then, absolutely everything I liked was headed for hell. I still enjoy the Orange Walk and the Salvation Army. The Orangemen have some good tunes. It's the only chance you get to hear a fife and drum band. I used to follow the Orange Band parade from Crawford Street all the way through Partick. I never crossed in front of them, though; people said the men protecting the parade at the side could legally beat you up with their truncheons if you did that. But Protestants generally seemed to have a far jollier life than us.

Anything that seemed like fun was frowned upon by my aunts. We never had parties. They considered any frivolous gathering 'common behaviour'. Joyless women. They had a bizarre, twisted view of many things. We were never allowed to go out for Halloween. Other people would have birthday cakes and make clootie dumplings at Christmas – that's a bit like a Christmas pudding, boiled in a cloth, with lucky charms or money wrapped in greased paper inside. My family treated it like it was black magic or something.

At least they let me go to the circus. You always knew when the circus was in town because there was elephant shit all over the high street. The police would put out public warnings: 'An elephant has shat in Sauchiehall Street. Drivers are asked to treat it as a roundabout.' I didn't really like circuses much and was especially wary of clowns. I liked the lion tamers, the trapeze artists and the horses, and it was a good way to see lions and tigers. But generally, I found the whole thing scary. I think you're supposed to. I think it relies on that childhood thing, where you like being scared. Your dad goes '*Whahhhh!*' And you scream: '*Ahhh!*' But as soon as he stops you go '*Again!*'

I first saw a clown at the circus at Kelvin Hall in Glasgow around Christmas time. His name was Jimmy. He wore a pale blue baggy suit with a bright-yellow shirt, and he was actually funny. He would pick boys from the audience and put them on a donkey. And as soon as he did, the donkey would go crazy and toss them all over the place. I remember sitting there terrified that he would ask me. Jimmy would always totter across the ring carrying a birthday cake with lighted candles, then trip and end up with his face in it. I didn't know what a birthday cake was at the time because I'd never had one. So, after my first circus I came home full of stories. I said, 'There was a clown called Jimmy – and he had candles in his loaf!' My family laughed about that for years, but that clown is the reason why, to this day, instead of a birthday cake I always have a loaf of bread with candles in it. People think I'm daft, but it means a lot to me.

Jimmy was the only clown I ever liked. Others I saw either bored or scared me. I especially despised the white-faced Pierrots . . . I never saw the point of them. They were always playing trumpets and trying to amuse the audience, but they weren't funny. I used to have a nightmare where somebody came to the door and it was a pale clown just standing there, silently looking at me. I would wake up screaming.

In reality, only priests came to our door in Stewartville Street. They were our only visitors. Our relatives all lived far away and could not afford cars. The priests never made an appointment; they just showed up. They would try to sound casual: 'Just checking to see how you're doing.' It was quite a nice thing. They were surveying the flock. Keeping you interested. They'd want to know that your kids were on the straight and narrow. The kettle would be put on to boil (it's always teatime for a priest) and they'd proceed to quiz the adults. 'How are you doing?' 'How are your relatives?' 'Any problems with the intermarriage?' They'd dole out advice in the form of a parable. Then they'd get to the point: 'Have you been attending Mass regularly?' The most important question seemed to be: 'Have you been paying your quarterly collection?' That was the percentage of your income you were supposed to give the Church. It was a sin if you didn't.

———

I'm still very conflicted about the Catholic Church. Despite the awfulness, it's kind of a loss, not to have Catholicism any more. A feeling of spiritual bereavement came upon me in my late teens or early twenties, when it dawned on me that I no longer believed it all. I tried to make those heretical thoughts go away – it felt sinful to even think like that. After a lot of consideration, I continued to believe that Jesus was an important leader in his time, but I could no longer relate that to Rome, to all the money, black clothes, gold shepherds' crooks and pointy hats.

A lot of the beliefs still make me angry. I wish I'd been at the meeting when the concept of original sin was put forth. 'How shall we go about making people feel so rotten that they feel the urge to go to Mass and give their hard-earned money to the Church?' 'I know! We'll give them a sin as a starter!' 'Yeah, that's good! And let's make masturbation a sin – we all know people can never avoid doing that . . .' Much later, I discovered Buddhism. There's a sense of goodwill in that philosophy. You start out good. They wish you the best – and presume that you are trying your hardest – which I find very attractive. And when the best is thought of you, you naturally feel like doing your best.

I know I've been going on a lot about Catholicism, but I would like to personally thank the Catholic Church for the rhythm method of contraception that my father used diligently, and without which I wouldn't be here at all. The rhythm method: now *there's* a great idea if ever I heard one. My father used to have a metronome on the sideboard. Tick-tock-tickety-tick. 'That's the stuff! Here we go!' *Shaggity shag, shaggity-shag.* And who came up with the line: *'At the point of ejaculation, withdraw'?* Oh, is that right, Father? Let me tell you something, Father, and I'm only going to tell you the once: at the point of ejaculation there isn't a herd of wild horses that could make my arse go in the opposite direction.

6

PLOT YOUR ESCAPE

ONE OF THE best moments of my life was when I played my banjo on the stage of Nashville's Grand Ole Opry, the famous country music concert that has been operating weekly since the nineteen-twenties. It was stunning, although it wasn't on the original stage – the concerts were moved from the Ryman Auditorium in the mid-seventies – but they cut out a circular, central area of the original main stage and put it in the new Grand Ole Opry House. So, I got to play my banjo standing in the exact spot that my heroes like Hank Williams and Johnny Cash stood playing their instruments. I kept thinking, 'Name a country star – they've played right here!'

But thrilling as it is to remember playing my banjo in the Grand Ole Opry House, it doesn't beat the feeling I get when I think about playing in Arran with my pals Geordie McGovern and his brother, Mick Broderick and others. It was something that just . . . came to be, over many years. At first, we were pals who used to go camping together on the Isle of Arran – a really beautiful, typically Scottish island in the Clyde. As I grew a bit older, I'd escape to Arran with them whenever I could. We'd sit around in the pub and pull out our instruments – banjos, guitars, mandolins and fiddles. Eventually, those guys I used to play with bought houses there on Arran and stayed. So, I'd go back time and time again to see them and play more music. It was simple, yet one of the most delightful musical experiences I've ever had. I miss it.

———

When I was a boy, my father would take us to the Barras market-place on a Sunday and, on the way, we would stop off at Glasgow Cross. There was a store there called Jack's Doll Hospital where they repaired and restored broken toys. The window was creepy – full of legs, arms, eyes and hair for dolls. But adjoining the shop was a music store. I can't remember the name of it, but they had guitars and banjos in the window. I used to linger there. They had lovely old Martin guitars, some decorated with evocative outdoor scenes, such as cowboys around a campfire. But of all the instruments in that window I was mostly drawn to the banjos.

One evening, my father said to Florence: 'Would you like to learn to play the piano?'

'Yes!' She'd already made it known that she would.

He said, 'Well, we'll sort out lessons for you.' We didn't have a piano, but she knew where your fingers should go, so she used to play on the sideboard. She wasn't the only one; Ian Meikle, who lived through the wall, played the drums on a sideboard in his house.

After my father asked Florence about piano lessons, he came over to me. 'What about you? Would you like to play the banjo?' He must have seen me looking at the banjos in the window at Glasgow Cross. But I said 'No.' I was embarrassed, I just . . . I didn't want him to know that I liked something, to admit that I wanted to play the banjo. I regretted it for years.

I never thought the same way as everybody else. I never felt the same as everybody else. But I always had a yearning to be 'somebody'. And although I wasn't ready to admit it to my dad, in my mind becoming 'somebody' involved playing a musical instrument. It was comforting to have a wee secret plan, an unlikely dream that might eventually come true.

The other reason I said 'no' at the time was I knew it would be used against me. By then Mona had started torturing me every day. Whenever there was nobody around, she would nag me and hit me. She was like Bette Davis in *Whatever Happened to Baby Jane?* When I saw that movie, I immediately thought of Mona, feeling that youth had slipped by her. Yeah, I think that was the reason for her sadism. She had been left with the housewifely job of the family when her parents had died, and then in the Stewartville Street house she was again the designated caregiver. This happened to a lot of older sisters in those days. She had a motherly role in our household – although she wasn't really anybody's mother until her son Michael arrived.

———

Michael mysteriously appeared when I was six years old. Mona had become pregnant and, although I knew things were strange from the beginning, I just chose to accept that Michael was my brother. Close to his birth they made the formal announcement: 'You have a new wee brother coming.' I thought it was a good thing that Mona finally had something in her life to take the focus off me. Nobody mentioned Michael's father, although just after he was born a local man turned up in Stewartville Street with a rocking horse. A big, expensive one. There was a heated conversation that turned to shouting, then as he made his escape downstairs Mona threw the horse at him, right over the banister.

Florence and I took care of Michael sometimes. But Mona made a big mistake in asking me to take Michael with me when I was on my way to hang out with my pals in the park. At the entrance to the park was a telephone box, and the door was known for jamming. When Michael was six – and I was twelve – I used to lock him in there. I'd go off and play, then pick him up on the way home. In 2010 I received the tribute 'Freedom of the City' from Glasgow City Council. It's a wonderful honour, and there are great perks attached to it, like being able to graze my cows on Glasgow Green, fish in the Clyde, and have the right to my own cell if I'm ever flung in jail. At the ceremony I told the audience, 'My brother Michael's here. I used to lock him in a phone box.' Everybody laughed. Maybe they thought I'd made it up. But I really did that. Even though I know it was a terrible thing to do, I'm afraid I still think it's funny. No doubt my resentment of him and Mona was behind it, but at the same time it wasn't his fault. He was vulnerable. When he was a toddler he became seriously ill – pneumonia, I think – and nearly died. I remember a terrible darkness about the house, and weird smells. Doctors and priests showed up at all hours.

Michael was a decent enough boy, but I felt he received special treatment by Mona and Margaret. He was very kindly looked after by them, received constant praise for everything he did, and got everything he wanted. By comparison, it seemed to me that Mona set out to make my life a misery – and succeeded. She bullied me mercilessly. Hit me, played games with my mind. Even when I was very small, she used to leave notes in the biscuit tin: *'thief!'*

This all started when I was in primary school. I was okay before she started picking on me, but then my schoolwork fell away. I felt I was on my own. Between Mona and Rosie I knew I had no allies – even Florence couldn't protect me. One afternoon I left school at the normal time, but instead of going home I just went in the opposite direction. I walked all the way to Hamilton, which is about twelve miles away. I stopped to watch a funeral procession going into the crematorium, then slowly walked back. I came in late for my dinner and there were all sorts of 'woe betides', but I felt strangely elated. I did always know there would eventually be something else for me. Somehow, I knew very early on that I was living somebody else's idea, that when the time came, I could create my own life the way I wanted and be okay. I surmised that following *their* rules is all right if you want to be like *them*. And I certainly didn't. Far from it.

———

At least I could be myself with the boys in my class. They found me funny, and I enjoyed making them laugh. They didn't know what my life was like at home, and the people at home didn't know what I was like when I was out. That suited me lovely. It was hard to focus on schoolwork, though. I didn't see the point when I was constantly being told I was useless.

But for one short period – when I was eleven – I became motivated to succeed at school. They had an exam called the Qualifying Exam, the results of which decided your future secondary school: senior secondary, junior secondary or a modified education. I failed it mightily and was headed for the modified. But I had really wanted to be with the kind of guys who were on track to attend St Gerard's secondary school. I could see they were winners. Guys with ambition. They were good fun to be around in primary school and I didn't want to be the duffer left by the wayside. Luckily, the first time I took the eleven plus I was only just eleven years old, so I was eligible to retake the exam without losing any ground. This time I really tried hard and managed to get myself an S2 (Senior 2), which is the second-highest result. That meant I was qualified to go to St Gerard's, and wear a green blazer, a tie and grey flannels. And I was okay when I started my new school. In my first result I was tenth in the class – I knew I could do it if I tried. But after a while, my resolve started falling away again.

There were some good teachers at St Gerard's, and some not so good. Our geography teacher was Mr Costello. He smoked in the classroom. He was hoarse and constantly coughing, but his lessons were brilliant. He was funny too, and everybody passed his class. He used to come into the boys' toilet in the playground and ask someone, 'Here, give us a light!' It was forbidden to smoke in the toilet. He was a hero.

There was a woodwork teacher called McGarity, whose opening line was: 'The boys call me "Faith, Hope and Charity" – it's up to yourself.' And Mr McNab the maths teacher made an unforgettable entrance. On the first day he walked into the classroom and fixed us all with a steely gaze. He strolled across to his desk, leaving the door wide open. Everybody got quiet. There was a metal waste bin beside the desk. Without looking down, he put his foot in the bucket and kicked it sharply backwards. *Whooooosh!* It landed exactly in place to hold the door open. '*Oooohh!!*' we thought. 'This is a serious one.' 'You!' he barked. 'C'mere!' Somebody was tasked with handing out the books. McNab started explaining geometry, using the hands of the classroom clock. We had to guess whether the angle between the hands would be acute or obtuse in three hours' time. When Philip Moore got it right, McNab reached into his pocket and pulled out half a crown. Flicked it to him. 'There you go.' Gave him a prize. Everybody loved him.

Barney Hill the English teacher tried to put life into Shakespeare. He was a middle-aged guy with white hair and moustache who always wore a tweed suit. We all thought the way he sounded reading Shakespeare was nuts, acting out *A Midsummer Night's Dream* and *The Merchant of Venice* with all the passion he could muster. Even at that age, I knew bad acting when I saw it. He was terrible. But he was also fun – and brave. He would say 'This is excellent, boys . . .', launching into a scene. He would play Titania at the drop of a hat, waving his arms in a hilarious, feminine way. He could be all bashful and taken aback: 'Ooooohhhh!' – and did his best to swoon convincingly. Willie O'Carol, the other English teacher, was handsome and flamboyant, and floated around the halls in his academic gown. If you got something wrong, he'd turn his face upwards: 'My GOD! Did you hear what he said? I'm being punished. This is for bombing those cathedrals in Germany. THIS is my punishment! I've been sent *YOUUUU*!!!'

I could always focus on lessons when there was a bit of drama involved. Big Bill Sheridan was an engaging science teacher. For our lesson about air pressure, he clamped a U-tube onto his desk and put mercury inside. Then he stuck a rubber hose over the top and invited each of us to blow into it and see how far we could get the mercury up the leg of the U-tube. *Pssffffsss!* It was heavy. Then he got another U-tube set up, but this time he put water inside. 'Hey, Connolly! C'mere!' The water shot out. Whoooshhhh! I was soaked.

Once, after seeing a variety show, I stupidly confessed I would like to be a comedian. At least the class tittered. When Mr Sheridan fixed his gaze on me, I instantly knew he was about to make me cringe. 'Well, Connolly,' he smirked, 'I saw you playing football at lunchtime, and I think you've achieved your ambition . . .'

Marist Brothers sometimes turned up to replace absent teachers. We used to make their lives a misery, throwing things at them when they were writing on the board. I remember one turning round, all flush-faced. 'Who was that???!!!' Lots of snickering. Folded-up paper on the end of a ruler being flicked in his direction. *Shwoocchhh!* It was wonderful. I was always very good at that sort of 'saxophone fart' noise. *Bhhhheeeuurrrrr!* It starts high, goes low and then steady: the changing tone is totally believable. He'd be writing on the board . . . *Bhhhheeeuurrrrr!* He'd look around, look back, resume writing. *Bhhhheeeuurrrrr!* We drove the poor guy insane.

I travelled to St Gerard's by public transport. It was a short tram ride to Partick Cross subway station, five minutes by train to Govan Cross, and from there to the school it was a short walk. The Glasgow trams were known as 'The Caurs'. They were wonderful things, and everybody loved them. They didn't go very fast, but they were efficient. Best of all, they always seemed to be approaching when you needed one. They were colour-coded so that, even from a distance, you could tell where they were going. Inside they had a peculiar smell from the electricity and metal, but you could open the windows and inhale Glasgow street smells instead. The drivers operated them from both ends; they just drove to the terminus then shoved the seats of the cars back and walked to the other end to drive back. The conductors were fabulous, pushy women with snappy answers. Their one-liners were famous at the time:

'Does this tram stop at the Renfrew Ferry?'

'I hope so. It cannae swim.'

Yeah, the caurs were brilliant. They ended up in the streets of Hong Kong. I saw them when I was there in the eighties.

———

Oooh!! I nearly forgot Heggarty the history teacher. He was one of the teachers who would take us on our annual summer holiday camp. One day he announced, 'Tomorrow we're going swimming!' And we did. We went to Aberdeen. Now, Aberdeen is a beach because it's got sand . . . but there the similarity ends. It's on the *North Sea.* On the horizon there are oil rigs, on which there are regular announcements: *'Now hear this. All employees must wear a survival suit at all times. You wouldn't last two minutes if you fell into the North Sea. Failure to wear the survival suit will result in instant dismissal.'* Forty miles away, there's women taking their children's clothes off. 'In you go, ya big numpties!'

My swimming costume had a belt and a pocket – the reason for which escapes me completely. And it was made of knitted stuff. A big woolly number. If you were stupid enough to go in above your waist, it grew. It was so absorbent it could drag you to the bottom. We arrived at the beach in the early afternoon.

'Connolly – in the water!'

'I'm going, I'm going!'

'Come *on*, you big bloody Jessie, get in there!!'

I ran down, put my foot in, and my heart stopped. I'd never felt cold like that before. *'Whoouaai!!'*

'Go in further, you big Jessie!'

I went up to my knees and lost the will to live. *'Ooouuaahhhaaoo!'*

'Billy!'

'*Uhaaaooah???*'

'Look over there.'

There was a bastard in a speedboat, making a big wave that was coming right for me. I didn't want to run, in case I fell in. '*Uuaahuuhooohh!*'

It inexorably slid in my direction, getting bigger . . . and bigger. '*Uuaaaoooohh!!!!*'

As long as my arse looks south, I will never forget that wave going up the inside of my thighs! '*Uuhoooaaaaaahh!!!!!!*' And it kissed the underside of my scrotum! '*Aaaaaaaaaaaaa-aaarrrggghhh!!!*'

———

I learned to swim in warmer water. When I was about ten years old, I used to go with my friends to the public baths in Whiteinch. It was cheap, and it made you nice and clean. They had huge showers where you could wash yourself before swimming. The boys and girls swam together in the same pool. I was too young to be interested in girls, but you could splash and annoy them. There were no actual swimming lessons; we just learned from watching others, clinging to the side and flailing around until we got the hang of it. We tried to impress each other with underwater swimming, and there was a platform from which you could dive or jump. Some guys could dive backwards – even somersault. Not me.

My father gave me flippers for my Christmas. And goggles. I couldn't believe how nice it was to swim with goggles. You could see all the underwater tiles. I didn't have a snorkel, though; I just held my breath. And my friend Nino Monibli gave me a really fancy swimsuit. He had been given a new, super-satiny one, with laces at the side, so he gave me his old one. I wore it proudly. It was stylish – red, white and glossy – and, more importantly, it did not become waterlogged like the knitted one.

My friends and I had a disgusting grooming routine. There was a Brylcreem machine in the changing room. You put a penny in, and when you heard a tap, you'd push the button, and it went '*PFFFT!*' A blob of Brylcreem shot onto your hand ('*A little dab'll do ya*' was the Brylcreem radio jingle) and you'd rub it straight onto your hair. But we never had money, so we used to clamp our mouths around the metal spout and suck the Brylcreem out of the hole.

––––––

Oooohh!! Here's the best one: the maths teacher at St Gerard's! On his first day, he stood in front of the class displaying an elite instrument of torture. 'My name's Campbell,' he said, 'and this is Pythagoras! You will get used to both of us.' Pythagoras was his 'tawse' or whip. It was thin, black and shiny and when he waved it in the air it went '*whhhishhhh*'. And, whereas most of the other teachers' tawses were thick and beige and went '*duffff*' when they hit you, Campbell's went '*cuackkkk!*' He was really proud of it.

My cousin John was a class below me at school. He was my father's brother's son. He was bright, funny and rebellious – and always in trouble too. One day John stole Pythagoras. He cut it up, then returned it to Campbell's drawer in little pieces. I couldn't believe he'd been so brave. He never confessed and was never found out – so everybody got punished. When Campbell got a new Pythagoras, he presented it to the class. 'Anyone like to try it?' Everybody put up their hand. So, the whole class went out one by one to get a maiden thwhacking by Pythagoras 2.

Campbell was a good laugh, and his canings were more token than serious. But there were other teachers who really hurt you. I got regular beltings for not doing my homework. Six of the best. Doing my homework would have meant sitting in a house with Mona giving me pelters, so I preferred to get belted next day instead. Occasionally I would consider doing my homework, but I'd weigh it against getting out of the house. I was punished for not doing homework all the way from St Peter's through St Gerard's. Quite an achievement.

My teachers at St Gerard's were decent educators and tried their best, but I just wasn't . . . receiving. I was lost. Maybe I was depressed, maybe I had Attention Deficit Disorder – I've learned they can appear similar. Part of me wanted to be better; I often knew the answers to questions, but I couldn't bring myself to give them. I often thought of myself in the third person. I could see myself sitting there, getting everything right. I told myself: 'You could have done it easily. You could have gone into the higher classes.' But there was another voice in my head saying, 'You don't belong here. You're not like everyone else.' When teachers would berate me, I'd sit there thinking, 'Yeah, it's okay for *you*. *You* don't have to go home to Mona.' Sometimes I think I was lucky to survive it. I thought a lot about drowning myself in the Clyde.

———

Mona's abuse increased as I got older. She'd smack me in the face so my nose bled. She whacked me with wet towels, kicked me, battered my head with her high-heeled shoes. But her speciality was humiliation – grabbing me and rubbing my dirty underwear in my face. I never fought back. Didn't think it was an option. She would embarrass me in front of others. When my cousin John came by Mona would say, 'Why can't you be more like John?' He'd be standing there. 'You could take a page out of his book. He's good at school – does his homework. Not like you.' Later, John would say: 'I hate it when she does that. I wish she wouldn't.'

Luckily, I had friends who had great parents. This helped me to see how deranged Mona was. I could see what was normal and what wasn't. I sort of knew it was nothing to do with me because their parents liked me. John McNab's parents even took me with John on holiday to Blackpool. They found me really funny. Mrs McNab used to piss herself laughing at me, and I loved making her laugh. One day John and I cycled to Edinburgh Zoo. When we got back, I described it all to Mrs McNab. I told her about the mating baboons, and about the way the female's arse is like wax – all shiny and tied in knots – and how she kept flashing it to the guy who was intent on giving her one. As I was describing it all, Mrs McNab just lost control. She went completely wobbly and fell on the couch.

And John's father also found me very funny. He would play with me: 'You're a noisy bugger and a nuisance. As a matter of fact, I'm going to fling you out of this house!' And he would grab me and throw me onto the street. I'd be in hysterics. They were such a happy family. They all loved each other, and that helped assure me that my family was cruel, bizarre, and that it was nothing to do with me.

———

Years later Mrs McNab came to see me perform at the Theatre Royal Drury Lane. She came backstage afterwards to see me and told me she loved my show. A lot of people had crowded into my dressing room. Mrs McNab was sitting beside me, marvelling, 'Is that Donovan? You know these people??'

Mona hated her. Called her by her maiden name. 'Lizzie O'Hara!' she would scoff. 'Common!' But I thought she was brilliant. A good laugh and a good cook. And sympathetic. When John had a girlfriend, she said, 'Oh she's a lovely girl.' She was interested in a nice way. For me, she was a great example of a kindly mother.

I was just thinking last night that my aunts would probably be horrified to hear me talking like this about them. They probably thought they were doing me a huge favour. Florence was the only one who knew what Mona was doing to me. Michael says he had no idea, never saw it. But Florence did. She saw the nagging and the hitting – she'd freeze in horror. Margaret knew, but she was a coward. As soon as she saw it starting, she'd leave the room.

My father eventually learned something of it. Once when he was sitting at the dinner table with me and Florence, he lifted his arm to scratch his head – and I flinched. Dived out of the road. He said, 'What the hell's wrong with you?' and Florence said, 'It's Auntie Mona. She's always hitting him.' He was horrified. I'm sure he had words with her, but he was rarely there so she just carried on.

But my father was the worst sort of hypocrite. Because Mona wasn't the only perpetrator in the house. My father sexually abused me for years. Six of us were crammed into a two-bedroom flat. Mona and Margaret were in one bedroom with Michael, and Florence had the living room alcove, so my father and I had to share a bed in the second bedroom. My father's abuse was a horrible, secretive routine that I had to put up with from when I was about ten years old until fourteen, when we moved to a bigger place. And for the following twenty years – until my father died – I just buried all that shame.

7

NEVER CHANGE PLANES TO WASH YOUR SOCKS

———

I DON'T LIKE going on holiday. Travel reminds me of work. After all the touring I've done in my life, I'm tired of it. It's a weird thing about showbusiness – what other people consider holiday we consider work. Getting on planes, going to hotels – that happens every other day if you're in showbusiness. And the endless laundry challenge . . . I fully understand Buddy Holly's doom-laden choice to change seats and buy himself some time to wash his socks.

Pamela used to have to trick me into going on holiday with the family. She'd know when I needed a break, so she'd make up something, like, 'You're filming with Paul McCartney.' I'd get on a plane and find myself in some Robinson Crusoe-type hut in the Seychelles surrounded by giant tortoises that wouldn't stop shagging. Big monsters, clattering against each other. I never knew they made so much noise.

I'd always enjoy the holiday eventually, but just *thinking* about it put me off. I prefer sitting in front of the telly, watching football and drinking cups of tea. The Covid-19 lockdown suited me just lovely.

When I was a boy, I loved a holiday. I was always ready to get a wee break away from my family. Whenever I could, I'd go camping with my pals. We'd cycle to a village called Bowling on the north bank of the Firth of Clyde, and camp nearby. Later, when I was a teenager, I'd go to Millport, a town on an island in the Clyde. I always liked the Clyde – the sea, the waves. But I didn't swim in it – we'd just try to catch a wee fishie to cook on a fire. We didn't have real camping equipment – a cheap tent, a few blankets, sandwiches and bottles of water. We'd usually last one night, then return home the next day, horribly cold and hungry.

It was always wet when we were camping. On one occasion we decided not to put up our tent. Instead, we slept underneath the arc of a bridge over a river. But it had a tunnel on each side that turned out to be some kind of storm drain. It overflowed during the night and washed us out. Yeah, we weren't very good at camping. We weren't country boys – we were city boys with no clue. We'd had very little experience outside central Glasgow. We were occasionally taken on school day trips to the country-side. It was supposed to do us good. They'd put us in a bus and wheech us out there. We'd all get off the bus and the teacher would say, 'Okay, boys, pay attention! Right. See that *green* stuff over there? Grass. Okay? See the *brown* and *white* things walkin' about on it? Cows. Don't break them. I'll be back here in half an hour.' Then the teachers would all shoot off to the boozer.

––––

There were houseboats on the Clyde. We used to 'borrow' sleeping bags and other stuff from the houseboats, then put them back when we were leaving. It was great fun, lying there at night, talking around the fire. When we were a bit older, we had more sophisticated camping, with a proper tent and a groundsheet. But my favourite was to go up near Aberfoyle and find a cow field. We'd move the cows along and put our sleeping bags where they'd been lying. It would be warm in that spot. You'd be in your sleeping bag, looking up at the stars. If you looked long enough you got scared at the sheer size of the operation. Some of the happiest nights of my life were spent just lying there, talking to my pals.

Considering parents now, how they want to know where their children are every second of the day, it was extraordinary that at around twelve years old I could just take off with my friends. If you'd asked my father or anybody at home where I was, they'd say, 'He's away camping.' And if you asked 'Where?' they'd say, 'I dunno.' That was normal then. We just went as far as we could cycle. They didn't have to worry too much about our safety. There were no drugs when I was a boy.

We had family holidays too, when I was young. My father, my aunts, Florence, Michael and I used to go to the Scottish seaside town of Rothesay. We travelled there on paddle steamers that sailed via the Firth of Clyde, Gourock, then Largs and Dunoon. The journey was half an hour. On board you could view the steam engine – a giant piston pounding away. They had entertainers on deck – musicians who played the accordion and fiddle, and a singer. They played Scottish music, then went round with a black velvet bag for donations. I loved it. They would play 'Sailing Down the Clyde':

On the Clyde the wonderful Clyde
The name of it thrills me and fills me with pride,
And I'm satisfied whate're may betide
The sweetest of songs is the song of the Clyde.

And another of my favourites:

> *Roamin' in the gloamin' on the bonny banks of Clyde*
> *Roamin' in the gloamin' wi' your lassie by your side*
> *When the sun has gone to rest*
> *That's the time that I love best*
> *Oh it's lovely roamin' in the glooooooaaamin'.*

If it was a special outfit that really knew their stuff they would sing 'Rothesay Bay'. That's a beautiful old ballad. You could learn your Scottish while singing that:

> *Fu' yellow lie the corn-rigs*
> *Far down the braid hillside;*
> *It is the brawest harst field*
> *Alang the shores o' Clyde,*
> *And I'm a puir harst lassie*
> *Wha stands the lee lang day*
> *Among the corn-rigs of Ardbeg*
> *Aboon sweet Rothesay Bay.*

One of the best holidays I ever had in my life was when I was around seventeen and went hitchhiking in France with my cousin John. John was a nutter like me – did things for the heck of it, just to see what would happen. He liked to startle people by wearing glasses with bullet holes on the lens. We were staying in a youth hostel in Dunkirk where everyone's food was kept in open cubbyholes in the kitchen. John would steal someone's banana and hold it vertically. Then he'd take a sewing needle and push it in through the skin near the top and use it to slice the flesh inside horizontally – *swish-swish-swish* – and then he'd pull the needle out, go down half an inch and do it again, continuing that process until he got to the bottom. Then he'd put the banana back where he got it. We'd wait for the owner to show up. He'd lift the banana and start peeling it . . . 'fuck's sake!'

And we'd say, 'What is it?'

'The banana was sliced inside its skin!!' We'd look at him like he was a loony, and the poor guy would spend the rest of his life trying to prove it to others.

John taught me wonderful, useless things. He would steal an egg and use the needle to put a hole in the top and a hole in each end. He'd blow the contents into a frying pan. *Phhhhhhhhhh*. Then he'd get a sheet of toilet paper. You know that hard stuff that hurts your arse? He'd write on it: '*Sorry, I was starving*', then he'd roll it up tightly, shove it inside the egg, and put the egg back where he got it. But my favourite of John's tricks was this one: for some reason he had a dislike of people who went to bed with their socks on. We'd lie in wait in the dormitory, watching people going to bed, and eventually John would see a victim.

'Billy, nine o'clock, blue socks . . .'

'Right, okay.' We'd wait until the guy was sleeping, then we'd creep up and gently roll the sheets back from his feet, take one sock off and put it on over the other one. You'd see the guy in the morning, looking for his sock. 'What the fuck? Has anybody seen a blue sock?' Eventually he'd put on his hiking boots with one bare foot and hobble off. I've always wondered what happened when he was undressing at home. 'Jesus Christ! How did that get on there??'

But my very best holiday memories are from when I was a child, going to Rothesay. It was the highlight of my year. We stayed in bed and breakfast digs, with several rooms between us. They wouldn't let you stay inside when it rained – you had to leave straight after breakfast. So even in miserable weather we'd play on the beach, go fishing off the pier, or kick a ball around on the grass. Putting was a great adventure too. The only time I was ever in a restaurant as a boy was in Rothesay when my dad would take us for high tea. We'd have fish and chips, bread with butter, and tea, in a simple cafe. It was delightful.

But in spending so much daytime with me, my father could easily spot my educational inadequacies. When I was around ten, we were at a cafe on a sloped road, looking down on a big clock tower. My father said, 'Billy, what's the time on that clock down there?' I said 'Errr . . . the big hand's at . . . two and the wee hand—' That's as far as I got.

Whack!! 'Can't even tell the bloody time???' *Whack!!* 'You dooley!!'

I learned how the following day.

My father had a Brownie box camera that took black and white photos. Before we left for Rothesay, he would buy two Ilford film rolls – one for the first week and one for the second – then after we came home he'd send them away to England to be developed. That camera was the terror of my life. I could never work it. Once we were standing by Rothesay pier, and my father handed me the camera. 'Right, Billy – you take a picture of me and Florence.' I peered at the two little square glass windows but, to this day, I don't know what I was expected to see when you looked through them. All I could see was myself, upside down. I would try, though. My dad would get tired of me. 'Just take the bloody picture!!'

'*Awwwwweeeahhh* . . . I cannae see! I cannae see you . . .'

'Stupid boy! Pay attention!'

'*Awwweeeahhh* . . . I can only see me!! What should I be looking at?'

'Come here.' *Whack!!*

'*AWWWEEEAAAHHH-OWWWW!-OWWW!!!*'

'Now take the bloody picture!!'

Finally, I would just press the button and pretend it had worked, knowing full well it would never turn out. He'd send the exposed roll away to be developed. and I'd be terrified, knowing I'd be found out in a couple of weeks. *Whack!! Whack!! Whack!!* '*Awwwweeeeaaahhhh!!!*' 'What did I tell you . . . ????' One night when I was telling this story onstage I *actually* cried. The audience didn't notice.

Rothesay used to be a fishing port. In earlier times there were plenty of cod in the Clyde, but the large industrial boats came and cleaned out most of the marine life. It was a crime. But instead, this picturesque holiday place developed. Most people holidaying in Rothesay were working-class people – welders, joiners, plumbers and their families. It was lovely, mixing with lots of other holidaymakers. The girls got all done up on Friday nights to impress the sailors from naval ships and submarines out in the bay who came ashore on leave. One night we were sitting having dinner in the lodging house and some girls who were fellow guests were eating nearby. I said to them: 'You should go downtown. There's loads of sailors ashore.' The girls just laughed. 'Oooohhh! You're an awful one!'

But I was hastily shut up by my father. I had just innocently thought girls liked sailors, and sailors liked girls. I'd seen all those funny 'Jolly Jack Tar' postcards down at the seafront saying things like 'All the nice girls love a sailor' – so why not bring it up?

Much later, I discovered that blurting out whatever was on my mind could make people laugh. It's what I've done as a comedian since the beginning. I never wrote anything down, never prepared 'a show'. It's heart-stopping to go onstage without having much of a clue what you're going to say, but that's what I've always done. But as a boy, not having a filter often got me into trouble. People thought I would never achieve anything because I couldn't organise my thoughts, edit my remarks, follow a sequence or generally behave the way they wanted. I hope I've shown a few disbelievers that they should never discount those they think are different, disorganised or distractible.

Rothesay had a flourishing variety theatre. Entertainers like Jimmy Logan, Chic Murray and others would play the summer seasons. Chic Murray was my hero. God, I loved him. The guy was a genius. He used to have me crying with laughter. He'd wear a tartan flat cap and a lugubrious expression, and told hilarious stories. He wasn't just a great Scottish comedian – he was a great comedian full stop. It was through watching him that I realised that, if you talk about things people can relate to – recognisably Scottish or Glaswegian stuff especially – then they'll love it. He inspired me to do the same.

I still think of Chic now. I can still hear his voice. He would say, 'She opened the door in her dressing gown. I thought to myself, what a strange place to have a door.' Or: 'I met a cowboy once. He was wearing a brown paper hat, a brown paper waistcoat and brown paper trousers. He was wanted for rustling.' I loved the way he used language: 'I was looking for lodgings. So, I went up to this boarding house. The landlady said, "Do you have a good memory for faces?" I said, "Yes, why?" She said, "There's no mirror in the bathroom."'

There was all kinds of entertainment in Rothesay. To amuse

the tourists, local people had trained blackbirds, crows and jack-daws to talk. One morning my father sent me to the corner shop for milk and bread rolls. The milk was kept in big metal milk churns. You dipped a ladle in and filled your own jug. I bought a bag of rolls and filled my milk jug and headed up the road. Halfway home a jackdaw landed on my head. 'Hello!' it squawked. I nearly shit myself. Everything went up in the air. Big claws gripping my head. I thought I was going to pass out. Everybody else thought it was a scream.

Some nights we would all go to the movies and have chips on the way home. And I used to enjoy the day outings – traipsing up and down hills or walking through the woods where you could see exotic wildlife like rabbits. You could take a bus up the hill and wander round the army barracks and golf course, then have tea and buns beside a lookout point with extraordi-nary views of the River Clyde. Once I even saw a double rainbow.

At the beachside Punch and Judy shows, boys and girls used to get up and sing. I was dying to do it too, but I never had the nerve. There was a little girl who used to sing . . . I think it might have been the famous singer Lulu:

Ma he's making eyes at me
Ma he's awful nice to me
Ma he's almost breaking my heart
I'm beside him mercy let his conscience guide him
Ma he wants to marry me be my honeybee
Every moment he gets bolder now
he's leaning on my shoulder
Ma he's kissing me . . .

I never got round to asking Lulu if it was really her. I will if I ever bump into her again.

—

Our annual trip to Rothesay always took place during the Glasgow Fair holiday, which was the second fortnight in July. It was traditionally stinking wet weather. I wore wellies and my cap on the beach. In later years Florence and I used to laugh at photographs of us shivering on the beach in our raincoats with our buckets. I used to talk about it onstage for the Glasgow audience – I'd say, 'How many of you have childhood photos of you standing in your raincoat on Rothesay beach?' A big roar would go up.

As inspired by Chic Murray, so much of my early stuff was rooted in identity. Making people think fondly about what others frowned upon. Like drunken singing – I like to think I helped people appreciate that. Yeah, I'm really proud of those early days when I was feeling my way onstage, awakening memories that turned out to be precious in the soul of the Glaswegian and other Scottish people. It had become fashionable to go to Spain for your holidays and to frown upon the basic nature of the Rothesay holiday. I'm glad I reminded people about the joy of the Scottish break. To this day, when I go to Rothesay, I get overwhelmed with nostalgia.

8

SEEK WISDOM AT THE
FONT OF SNAPPLE

———

I JUST GOT a fortune cookie with my Chinese takeaway. It said, '*Although it feels like a roller coaster now, life will calm down.*' Tosh. I'm stuck in the house. I don't trust any kind of soothsayer. The most roller-coasterish event in my life these days is reading a biography of Donald Trump.

At school they made us read Sir Walter Scott. Shite. I hated *The Black Arrow* and all that pish. I thought it was stultifying. But on my own, I found my way to books I loved, like *Lord of the Flies*. Then I found all those adventure books about hunting and surviving in the Yukon – Jack London's *White Fang* was one I loved. I found *Seven Years in Tibet* by Heinrich Harrer. Wonderful. The writer spent time there when it was so different it was akin to being on the moon. That led me to books about Japan, which were on the same library shelf. I read a lot about Japanese culture. I was educating *myself* – which I much preferred to school learning.

I have continued my self-education. Did you know that only

female mosquitoes bite? And that every hour more than one billion cells in the body must be replaced . . . so Billy at 2 p.m. is a different Billy from Billy at 3 p.m. or 4 p.m.? I learned those pieces of wisdom from the lids of my bottles of peach Snapple. It's my beverage of choice these days, along with Irish Breakfast tea. I learn a great deal from Snapple lids – *'The mummy of Ramesses II has a passport.'* See? You would never learn that at school.

I left school suddenly, at fifteen. A year earlier we had moved outside Glasgow to a new housing estate in Drumchapel, eight miles away. This move was the result of a scheme dreamed up by Glasgow Council to reduce inner city overcrowding. At first we thought it was great, because we had an extra bedroom and a better bathroom, but when we arrived there was bugger-all in that horrible wasteland – no shops, no cafes, no cinemas. They sold food out of vans. We did have a bath, which I thought was very exciting until I found out I wasn't supposed to use it; it cost too much to heat the water. We moved twice in Drumchapel and the second place was a stand-alone unit in which I had my own room. Finally, I could sleep soundly in my own bed without interference.

I was becoming more independent and wanted to earn money to buy things: fancy clothing, and an upgraded bicycle. So, I managed to get a job delivering milk six days a week. It meant getting up at 4.45 a.m. and working until 8 a.m. on school days and Saturdays. First, I cycled to the farm where the milk was processed. When the manager wasn't looking, some of the boys would grab a cow's udder and squirt milk at their pals, but I never did. I was too scared. You had to be pretty brave to do that. When you tried to get under the cow it could turn and get you with its horns.

We'd load up the milk crates on the electric milk float, then Tom Sweeney would jump in the driver's seat and we'd take off on our rounds. We each had a hand crate that held eight pints. You filled it up, jumped off the float and delivered the milk to people's doors. Tom would direct the operation. He knew his subject very well – how many bottles we had to leave at each house. We had to be quick. We'd run fast to leave the bottles and retrieve the empties, and by that time the float would have moved on, so we'd have to run after it. A crate of eight full pints was heavy. Running with it made you strong. And it was good money – a pound fifty for the week.

Mark Knopfler – from the band Dire Straits – was on my route. I met him in Australia a few years ago, and I asked him where he'd lived in Scotland. He said 'Bearsden.' When he told me the address, I surprised him with: 'I used to be your milk boy!' Mark and I were staying at the same hotel in Sydney, the Sebel Townhouse. When he and his band came to see my concert at the Sydney Opera House, he joined me onstage and played the famous Aussie song 'Waltzing Matilda' on his guitar – I was on autoharp:

Waltzing Matilda, Waltzing Matilda,
Who'll go a-waltzing Matilda with me?

I like that song. I used to perform it in French as well. I'd remind the audience that a French explorer – Lieutenant La Pérouse – was the second famous European explorer to arrive at Botany Bay. History books tell you that Australia was 'discovered' by an Englishman, Captain James Cook, but there was this Frenchman right behind him. Of course, there were many indigenous people already living on the Australian continent, but the British barged in and claimed it as their own. I used to say, 'If Cook had been a bit slower, Australia might have been colonised by the French. It would have been a very different place. "Waltzing Matilda" would have sounded like this:

'Qui viendra danser la valse Mathilde avec moi?'

I taught myself to speak French from audio tapes. I enjoy the language, and learning it was another wee unschooled triumph of mine. But by the middle of my third year of formal secondary school I'd fallen so far behind in my lessons I knew I'd never catch up. And during my milk run, I tripped over a low fence and fell on glass milk bottles that shattered and cut me badly. I split the tendons in my finger and was in the hospital for several weeks while they transferred a tendon from my toe to my finger. When I returned to school, I was thrashed on my injured hand for letting off a stink bomb in a bus headed for the sports ground. The stink bomb was a beauty. It came from Tam Shepherds Trick Shop in Queen Street, where I bought all kinds of paraphernalia for playing practical jokes. They had reasonably realistic plastic vomit, and a fantastic bandage with a nail attached designed to convince people you'd been impaled in a carpentry accident.

While I was in hospital having the tendon transplant, I fell even further behind in all my lessons. I was nearly fifteen and considered a bit of an academic no-hoper, so I just waited till my birthday, then left school permanently to look for a job. Pretty soon I found employment at John Smith's bookshop in St Vincent Street. I was in the dispatch department, delivering books, magazines and repaired fountain pens. I loved being surrounded by books and began to read everything in the shop.

I grew very fond of Nevil Shute's books. They sat next to the dispatch department, right at my eye level, so I grabbed them when I wasn't busy. I thought *A Town Like Alice* was written by a guy who knew what he was talking about, even though he didn't actually live that life. I found that impressive. And he wrote about people who, for no fault of their own, were in a world in which they didn't belong. That theme resonated with me.

———

Meanwhile, I was under pressure from my father to read *The Thirty-Nine Steps*. In fact, I was open to anything. I even walked those thirty-nine steps from Waverley Station in Edinburgh to Princes Street. One big favour my father did was introducing me to P. G. Wodehouse. His books made me laugh out loud and I loved the way he built scenes. There would be a gathering at Blandings Castle and a group of unlikely people would all be thrown together. They'd be having gin in the afternoon, and there would be, say, a con man among them, an explorer, a Church of England minister – all giving their ninepence worth. It was wonderfully ridiculous, and the language made me scream so much my legs would stop working. I didn't know people could be as funny as that on paper.

One of my favourites was *The Clicking of Cuthbert*, a collection of golf stories. I adored reading about such wonderful nonsense as the 'mashie niblick' golf club. But even Wodehouse couldn't make me like golf. For me, golf was always something done by pricks who dressed like tourists in their own homes. The golfing cliques didn't allow Catholic members. Much later on I used to listen to 'the golf set' in the pub – all waxing liberal. I always thought, 'You're a golf club member, and you know they don't allow black or brown people in, and you come in here and waffle away about fairness!' I've always had a beef with the unfairness of society – people going on TV and pontificating about democracy as if they knew what it meant when all the while they're doing deals under the counter. Bastards.

My father used to read Agatha Christie. Her mystery novels were all over the house, but I never read one. He followed a certain literary path, whereas I just put my hand out and grabbed any book. When I was about eleven my father bought us *The Children's Encyclopaedia* – ten volumes, edited by Arthur Mee. We savagely read each volume from cover to cover. I acquired a good general knowledge from that. I knew the size of a giant clam, that grasshoppers listen with their knees, and how to recognise the flags of many countries. We had five green volumes of *Lives of the Saints*, where I learned that many of those revered people were nutters, fanatics and headcases. I read that St Teresa of Avila used to show up at hospitals and lick people's wounds. Others – like St Mary of Egypt – starved themselves in the desert or, like St Simeon Stylites, sat on the top of poles for decades, or hung out in freezing caves overlooking the Irish Sea. Some people call them 'extreme ascetics' but I say they were fucking nutcases.

———

I read a lot of autobiographies in my teens, like Douglas Bader's *Reach for the Sky*. They introduced me to the idea that what you do with your life is pretty much up to you. That was a new concept for me. It was a long way from what I was hearing at home. I liked reading about people like Florence Nightingale who didn't actually choose to be famous – it just happened because she followed the path *she* chose. To this day I love biographies – learning wee interesting things about people. For example (Snapple fact), *The twenty-ninth American President Warren G. Harding lost White House china in a poker game!*

I read *Little Women* when I was a boy. And I read the Brontë sisters' books. In fact, when I was on tour in West Yorkshire many years later, I had the pleasure of going to the house where the Brontës lived and wrote their novels – The Brontë Parsonage Museum. It wasn't the season for tourists, so I was alone in the house, and naturally took the opportunity to sit on the furniture. It was very loosely roped off, and more than likely there was a sign saying, *'Don't sit on the furniture'*, but I cared not a jot. Being a Windswept and Interesting showbiz personality, I thought I'd get away with it. And I did. I lounged on the chaise longue where one of them had died – I think it was Emily. I wondered if her ghost would appear and frighten the bejesus out of me.

In Haworth, the village where the Brontës lived, there was an interesting little store called Spooks of Haworth that sold things like oracle cards, crystal balls, mythical pendants and books about dowsing. They offered a test to see if you were psychic. You had to hold a 'terminal' in each hand, with some kind of current running through the whole contraption. I was so disappointed to learn I'd failed the test. Apparently, I'm not psychic. I'd been looking forward to a life of metaphysical mumbo-jumbo. If I was psychic, I could wear a satin turban with a peacock feather, predict the future and truly astound people.

———

At John Smith's bookshop, I swept the floor in the morning, then made the deliveries. I would read Robert Burns when nobody was looking. The music of his language was lovely. You can almost sing his poems. Well, people do; the most famous song in the world is 'Auld Lang Syne' by Robert Burns. My favourite of his poems is 'Holy Willie's Prayer'. It's just so observant about hypocrites who go to church and profess piety. Holy Willie thinks he's got the world sorted out and is asking God to strike down sinners. He thinks he's got a one-on-one with God, and that God's going to see him right. I like seeing people performing the poem as Holy Willie, wearing a long nightshirt, a nightcap with a tassel on it, and carrying a candle in a holder: '*O Lord, who ken's aw things . . .*'

I read that Abraham Lincoln knew some of Robert Burns's longer poems off by heart . . . Snapple fact.

———

Do you know that man – they call him 'the father of documentary film' – a Scotsman called John Grierson? He did a famous film called *Night Mail* about the train from Glasgow to London and won numerous prizes. When I worked at John Smith's I used to deliver periodicals to Mr Grierson. He was one of the few adults I ever met who seemed interested in my career: 'Oh hello, son! Sit down. So – what are you going to do? You're not going to do this for your whole life are you?'

I said, 'No, I'm going to be an engineer.' I had already failed to achieve my Engineering Certificate.

'That's good. When are you gonna do this?'

'Before I'm sixteen, I'll have to get into the shipyards because the apprenticeship starts at sixteen.'

'Aye. Well, good luck to you.'

They fired me at the bookshop. There was a little scam going on in the dispatch department, where guys would steal books and put them out in the rubbish bins in the lane, then retrieve them after hours. I got the blame for the missing books, because I was the lowest common denominator. I wasn't involved; the scheme was way too complex for me to have dreamed up. I'd seen them throwing parcels into the garbage, but it never dawned on me they were stealing. I didn't try to protest my innocence. I just left. When I told them at home that I'd been fired from my first full-time job the reaction was 'Typical. Bloody typical. I knew you'd never succeed at anything'.

———

Did you know the most shoplifted book in the world is the Bible? I want to read the Bible. It's daft that it's been there all my life and I've never read it. The Catholic Church doesn't bother with it much; the Old Testament is fraught with danger for Catholics. But so many decisions have been made based on what it says. People get their ideas of right and wrong from interpretations that, over the years, have been changed to suit political desires when nobody else could read. Poor Mary Magdalene was made out to be a hooker when she was anything but. We learned about another woman – Veronica. She's not in the Bible but her story had a profound effect on me when I was a wee boy. Miss Gleason told us about her in primary school. I loved the drama of it all, Jesus coming up the hill carrying his cross to Golgotha, his face all bleeding from the thorns, and Veronica gives him a piece of white cloth from her outfit to wipe his face. When he gave it back to her there was an imprint of his face on it – that struck me as being brilliantly dramatic. I think I even believed it then.

Later, after I became a welder, I read whatever I could get my hands on. I especially loved George Orwell: *Animal Farm, Down and Out in Paris and London, The Road to Wigan Pier*, about the pre-war living conditions of the working class in northern England, and the essay 'Down the Mine'. I found 'Shooting an Elephant' truly moving as well. It's an anti-imperialist story, narrated by a policeman who was ordered to shoot an aggressive elephant in Burma. Through books like those I found proof that you can think for yourself, that you don't need to fit into 'the system' like a piece of Lego. That you can change the Lego pieces to suit yourself. All you need is the nerve to admit that you think differently from everybody else.

After I was fired from the bookshop, I got a job delivering bread at Bilsland's Bakery. I loved being a van boy. The driver Tony Roper, who became an actor and is still my friend, was a big shot. We'd all gather down at the depot in the morning, and he was in charge. We'd talk about football, and have a good laugh. The other employees were mostly Protestants – Rangers supporters – so when Bilsland changed the uniform from a knee-length brown industrial shop coat to a green coat with a yellow half-belt (green is the colour of the other football club, Celtic), the Rangers supporters went crazy. It was great fun mixing with the drivers and delivering the bread and cakes. I only left because it was time to start an apprenticeship.

———

The other day, someone asked me to nominate my favourite book of all time. That's a difficult one. It's like being asked what your all-time favourite song is. Dostoevsky's *The Brothers Karamazov* would definitely be in my top three, along with that trilogy by Lewis Grassic Gibbon, 'A Scots Quair', that is such a brilliant portrait of a woman living in the north-east of Scotland during World War One. And *A Confederacy of Dunces* by John Kennedy Toole. That made me howl. The main character is just such an awkward big guy with so many hilarious imperfections. His pyloric valve needs constant loosening, so he rolls about in his bed. When he farts it reduces the pressure, so he feels better. He has a lovely outlook on life – takes the world as he finds it. He's useless; made an arse of school and college, lives with his mother, gets everything wrong. It's hysterically funny. He wears a duffle coat and a hat with ears and bumbles his way through life with his prophetic girlfriend. The writing is perfect. It was published ten or so years after Toole's suicide. His mother discovered a beaten-up copy of the manuscript and did everything she could to get it published. I love that. It ended up winning a Pulitzer Prize.

———

Just before my sixteenth birthday the management at Alexander Stephen and Sons at Linthouse on the River Clyde took me into the shipyard. I was to be a tea boy and help out in the electrical drawing office. I also helped Willie Bain, the one-legged store man, give out the screws, nails and padlocks in the joiners' shop. When I turned up there on my first day, Willie said, 'Come with me.' He took me up to a strong-smelling shop where a man was making glue for the joiners. Willie Bain said to him, 'I've got one for you here!' The glue man turned round and peered at me. He said to Willie, 'Turn him to the left.' Willie turned me to the left. I said, 'What's this?' They ignored me. 'Turn him to the right. Now turn him round . . .' There was a brief pause, and then the glue man gave his verdict. 'Catholic!' He'd never been known to be wrong.

That was my first experience of the shipyards and of the people who worked there. They were to become a second family to me, the best people you could ever hope to meet.

9

CONSIDER YOURSELF LUCKY

—

I'VE GOT PARKINSON'S disease, and I wish he'd fucking kept it to himself. As a matter of fact, I got diagnosed with Parkinson's disease AND prostate cancer the same week. Holy Mother of God. It wasn't too bad, though. I got treated for the cancer and now I seem to be okay. The Parkinson's just rumbles along, doing its thing. It bothered me for a while but when I think about it, I suppose I'm lucky I didn't get something worse. Because I was a welder.

———

The diseases they talk about now due to welding weren't known when I was in the shipyards. They didn't know about the hazards of asbestos. And men were always dying in accidents too. I was in an accident myself. I fell off the ship into the Clyde. Dropped forty feet into three feet of water and broke my ankle. It was in the newspaper: *'Lucky Bill Falls 40 Feet, Breaks Ankle'*. That's what they called me after that: 'Hello Lucky Bill!' It happened when I was pulling on my welding cable. It had joints in it that screwed together to make it longer, but I hadn't fastened them properly. It snapped apart and I catapulted backwards and fell over the side of the ship. Dropped the whole height of the hull, from the deck into the River Clyde. I was exceptionally lucky. I landed in a ten-foot space between two cranes. It was the day before my eighteenth birthday.

———

I remember the day a guy was killed while painting the anchor well. The anchor is supposed to be secured, but something wasn't in place, so it suddenly whooshed out of the well and drove him into the Clyde. You could see the drips of paint he'd made all the way down the hull to his death. The workplace at the shipyards wasn't like construction workplaces today – not nearly the same consideration for safety. It was a dangerous place to be, and you were constantly told that. But we didn't really care much. A welder would be forty feet up balancing on a narrow beam and we'd go and jump on it. *'Whooooahhhhh!!!'*

There were two planks going across the mouth of the deep cargo hold. One day I saw a welder trying to inch his way across with a roll of cable on each shoulder and a bunch of welding rods. Halfway across, the dark visor of his helmet came down so he couldn't see. 'Help!!! *Heeeeeelp!!!'* We thought it was hilarious. 'Away, you prick, what d'you think you're doing?' He was balanced there, blind. Too scared to move. Someone did help him eventually . . . once we'd all had a good laugh.

Our humour was dark. Frequently cruel. There was an older guy, a plater-carpenter called Coley. He was really funny. He was in an accident one day in the tank. I'd gone for a piss and was on the way back when I saw that a rescue operation was in full swing. They'd called the ambulance room for help, and responders had come to look after him. I can't remember exactly what had happened – something fell on him, or maybe he'd fallen off something – but when I got there, he was being pulled out with a crane. They'd wrapped him in a swaddling of bamboo mat, and he was being lifted out head-first. Everyone was standing about gawking.

As soon as his head appeared out of the tank I said, 'Coley, what happened to you?' He said, 'I was putting the chalk line on the deck and I knelt on my prick.'

———

The main killer of the shipyard workers was asbestos. Just like coal miners got silicosis – black lung disease – shipyard workers got asbestosis. We'd be working in the double bottoms of the engine room – deep penetration welding – and our lips would become all black and yellow. We'd come out for a smoke and they'd be cladding the pipes around us so it would be snowing asbestos. I remember it being in my hair. The place was a death trap. I was very lucky that after I did my apprenticeship for five years I only stayed on as a welder for two or three more years and left the shipyards in my early twenties, but many men were there much longer and got asbestosis in their forties or fifties. I remember older welders spitting up all kinds of nasty black stuff.

As an apprentice I got up to a fair amount of mischief. It was really inspired by the older guys, who would take the piss as soon as new apprentices arrived. They'd send us on nonsensical errands for things like 'a long stand', a 'sky hook' or a pot of tartan paint. But after a while we got wise and started playing pranks ourselves.

I used to give people electric shocks in the rain. One of my accomplices was Alec Mawson, who has since become the Lord

Provost of Glasgow and all kinds of grand and important things, but back then he was just a nutcase like me. When it rained, we'd go onto the ship's deck and look for puddles. If we found a nice big one, we'd nod to each other and I would go down underneath the deck to lurk directly beneath that puddle with my electric welding gear. Meanwhile, Alec would remain above, holding a metal rod. He'd wait until someone walked through the puddle, then he'd quickly knock twice on the deck with this rod, and I'd go: *fizzzzzzzzzz*. The victim would go flying in the air. '*Aaaagghh!*' We used to swap places, taking it in turns to electrify the puddle. Up they'd come – *knock knock* – *fizzzzzzzz* – '*Aaaagghh!*' We'd try to guess how high they'd jump. We were going for world records.

Strangely enough, the prank I liked the best was the simplest. When workers were drawing guidelines for the superstructure to be laid against, they would highlight them with paint. We'd take a bit of their paint and find an excuse to walk behind someone. When he stopped, we'd surreptitiously bend down and paint his heel as he was standing there. So, people would be wandering around with white or pale-blue heels. It became awfully funny – to us. We used to roar about it, and yet it was nothing. Just a guy walking along with white heels on his boots.

We used to bend welding rods into an 'S' shape and hang them onto the little half-belt at the back of people's boiler suits. A bit later it became cool to dangle your sandwich paper from it as well. People would be walking along, oblivious to our merriment. Another trick was nailing a man's tea can to the work bench. We thought it was a scream when he tried to lift it. And we used to sneak paper inside people's sandwiches, along with the cheese and other fillings, then watch them taking a bite: 'What the fuck's this?'

Teatime in the shipyards was a joy. We used to sit by the fire to have our sandwiches and tea. People brought all kinds of sandwiches. Some guys even had steak as a filling, while others never liked their sandwiches. The first thing they ask you when you're an apprentice is: 'Who makes your sandwich?' 'My mother.' 'Don't tell her you liked it! Never say that you enjoyed your cheese sandwich because you'll get it for ever. That'll be you – chained to cheese for the rest of your life.'

I used to work with a couple of stagers. They're the guys who put up the planks that you balance on to do your job. When I was working with them, assisting as a welder, I was struck by the elaborateness of their sandwiches. They had spaghetti from a tin on them, sausages and beans together, and eggs – real luxury sandwiches. I was jealous. Then I found out they'd both been in Japanese prison camps, so they knew all about starving. This was their life now – eggs and beans and spaghetti sandwiches. They ate with such relish – I loved watching them.

There was a shipyard workers' lunch canteen for those who wanted it. It was cheap, but you didn't always have any money. There was a blonde woman working there. She looked like Myra Hindley, the Moors murderer. She had the same sort of vacant eyes, and big lips, and she always had love-bites on her neck. She would put her pinkie in the pie to see if it was hot enough. Big red nail plunged through your pie. 'There you go!' And she would try to be posh. You'd say, 'Mince, please.' And she'd call 'One gent's mince please!' The mince pie would arrive. 'There you go. Two gents' mince, one apple pie.' We were 'gents' all of a sudden. She was lovely. I used to fantasise about her.

———

The characters I met in the shipyards were endlessly fascinating. There was a guy called Joe the Blow who could get sparks out of your eyes. A little hard bit of metal would sometimes fly into your eye – they called it a 'fire'. You could go to the ambulance room and they would fart about with cotton wool on a little stick to try to get it out, but your best bet was to go to Joe the Blow. 'Ah c'mere, son. You got a fire in your eye?' He would get a match and delicately twirl it on your eyelid, so it rolled up like a venetian blind. Then he would put his tongue on your eyeball, slurp the metal piece into his mouth, then spit it out. 'There you go.' He was a godsend. And there was a welding inspector in the shipyards called Hot Lips. He had the strangest big lips. He used to say: 'Here, son, give us a swallow of your tea.' You'd offer him your boiling can: 'Sure – here!' You'd be thinking it would scald the face off him, but it never did. '*Slurp slurp slurp slurp slurp.*' He was the talk of the place, Hot Lips.

Men weren't too subservient to the managers. Bunny Patterson had slacked off work one day. The manager marched up to him. 'What do you think you're doing?' Bunny said, 'I'm having a smoke.' The manager said, 'Do you know who I am?' Bunny turned to the guys around him: 'This joker doesn't know who he is!'

Another day, a guy called Willie McGuinness was trying to escape from work without being noticed. He had figured out a secret route – there were sewerage works next door, so instead of going through the shipyard gates, he jumped over a hedge, found his way past all the shit-filled lagoons and out onto the road. But one of the foremen had heard about his scheme and was hiding in some bushes. He leapt out, catching Willie in the act. 'Aha!' But Willie was unfazed. 'Ah, Mr Johnston! – The very man I'm looking for! Could you kindly give me a pass-out?'

The sewerage works had a boat for transporting sewage down the Clyde to dump it. At the same time, they would take elderly folk aboard on day trips. There's a song about it – 'The *SS Shieldhall*':

We're the crew of the SS Shieldhall
Pull the chain and we'll answer your call . . .

There would be nurses on board to look after the people with disabilities. When the boat passed our ship, the guys would shout to the nurses, pretending to be in pain: 'Ohhhh . . . oohhh my heart! Come and see me, I'm not well!' We were eager for any distraction – and always looking for a way round the system. The best excuse I heard for lateness was: 'My wife was lying on my shirt tail and I didn't have the heart to wake her up . . .'

———

The shipyards were full of patter merchants. That's where I first really understood that you could be incredibly funny without telling jokes. Those guys were extremely quick off the mark – and so were the women, although the only women who worked in the place were French polishers. They were gallus – tough women, and very funny. Two of them were hurrying past us one day and this guy Cami called after them, 'Don't run, dear – you'll heat your water!' And one of the women shouted back over her shoulder: 'Well *you'll* no' scald your cock in it!'

There was a guy, I can't remember his name, but he was famous for being really tight with money. He smoked a broken pipe he'd found in the Clyde and, to make his tobacco go further, he would rub his bus ticket into wee pieces and mix it in with his tobacco. One of the welders had gone away for the weekend to Wemyss Bay, which was thirty miles away. He brought back the bus ticket and presented it to the cheapskate: 'Here's a very expensive smoke for you. Keep it for your birthday.'

After I'd been working at the shipyards for some time, I started to risk trying to make the older guys laugh. We'd be around the fire, and I'd sing like a drunk man. They liked that. 'Eh, Big Yin, give us one o' them gallus songs . . .' It was wonderful to find my place among them. But the hysterical things *they* said often played with your heartstrings as well. I learned in the shipyards that you can be funny *and* profound.

The patter merchants would use any situation to make onlookers scream, but during tea breaks around the fire they had a captive audience. There were shipyard tea breaks at ten o'clock in the morning and three o'clock in the afternoon. They were unofficial, but everybody took them. When I was a tea boy, six guys paid me five shillings a week each to make their tea, so I got thirty bob a week that paid up my motorbike. Like all tea boys, I made the brew in a big National Milk tin – one that had held food the government gave out for babies. You'd poke two holes in it and make it a handle out of two welding rods. Then you'd use the oxyacetylene torch to boil the tea in the can. The men brought their own loose tea in little tins with two lids – tea in one end and sugar in the other. After I made the tea in the big can I poured it into their own little cans. At three o'clock on a Friday afternoon, the shipyard men would play cards and gamble, and as the tea boy I was brought in to bang things and make industrial noises in case the inspector was passing. Sometimes people would deliberately scare you. They would show up shouting, 'Hey, the manager's coming!' Guys running in all directions, cans flying. But the manager would just make a pass to let everybody know he was there. Then we'd all just finish our tea and get back to work. I learned a lot in my tea breaks.

I even learned sign language. Patting your head was a sign the manager was coming. Patting your left shoulder warned that the foreman was coming. If the chargehand was coming, you'd pat your left bicep. There were all sorts of signals. 'What time is it?' was miming taking out your pocket watch. 'Quarter past' you drew your hand across your throat. For three o'clock you'd pat your forehead three times. This visual paging system was essential, because the noise was deafening: riveters with their guns – '*didididididididi! dididididididi*', platers and carpenters hammering at the deck and bulkheads, welders crackling away, and caulkers with their air-pressure chisel guns that could cut through metal – '*aaaaahhhnnnnnnngggg!*' That's where my deafness started. We didn't wear earplugs or anything. Most of us were actually glad to lose some of our hearing; it made working in that environment more comfortable. Between the shipyards and touring with rock 'n' roll bands I'm lucky I'm not completely deaf.

———

The old guys would sit there by the fire, endlessly coughing. I once said to one of them – a guy who chain-smoked as well – 'That's some cough you've got.' 'Och rubbish!' he said, 'There's men in the graveyard would love to have my cough.' That was the attitude. If they made it to sixty-five, you'd see them retiring. A note would come round – a sheet of paper asking you to give fifty pence to the fund for Harry or whoever was retiring. In those days it usually totalled about ten shillings – quite a lot of money. Then a couple of months later there would be a little ceremony down at the paint shop. A little circle of five or six guys would gather out of the rain under a corrugated plastic awning. There would be a manager there to conduct the affair. 'Well, Harry, you've given us some great years of service. I suppose you'll be pottering around in your garden now . . .'

Harry probably lived in a high-rise: 'Garden? What are you talking about?'

'Good luck to you, Harry, and here's something from your compatriots . . .' He'd pass on a wallet containing the money we'd given, and a big, gold-plated watch.

'Hurray!' Clap, clap, clap.

———

We used to go for a pint at lunchtime. Just one. With working up high on planks of wood it was too dangerous to drink more. And Harry would come into the pub from his retirement. At first, he'd come in two or three times a week, then it would fall off to once a week. After a while he wouldn't come in at all, and eventually the word would come that he was dead. It usually took eighteen months. He probably just died of nothing to do. I often thought about those men. Sixty-five, retirement age, seems young nowadays, but back then they were old, wizened men. They'd come through the Depression and World War Two and unemployment and the shipyards. It made them what they were.

A huge number of them were alcoholics. They'd drink before coming to work. They'd complain about the bastard who was supposed to open the off-licence at seven in the morning but was late. They needed a drink before coming to work. Some of them worked on a Sunday, so first they'd go to Govan Cross, where the moneylender's table was set up next to the guy selling cheap wine. These men would go to the first table and get a loan, then take the loan to the wine-seller and pay for booze at grossly inflated prices. Then the loan shark would appear at the shipyards at pay time on Friday to get his money.

———

I'm dead lucky to have known those shipyard men. Great guys. I love them to this day. They looked upon me warmly. I felt accepted by them – I could tell they liked me by the way they looked at me, the way they talked to me, the way they found me funny. And to be found funny by them was gold. I owe them everything. They saved me. They made everything better for me. After all that shit I'd been through, to then be befriended by them, and considered one of them – that was a gigantic step to getting over it. And what man wouldn't take pride in being one of the guys who worked on a great ship's superstructure? After all, we were known as 'The Erection Squad'.

10

TAKE YOUR KNICKERS DOWN AND DANCE

———

I HAVE A close personal relationship with my willy, but still I never minded sharing it with strangers. When I was about twenty-two, I was up at Loch Lomondside with a bunch of hippies, getting up to mischief. We were camping there, and somebody said, 'I bet you a fiver you can't run along the pier naked, and dive into the water.' And I did it. It was fucking freezing. When I got home that night, Florence said, 'I saw some of your friends up at Loch Lomond making a nuisance of themselves. Long-haired types. They were running around naked and diving off the pier!'

She'd been on a bus run with her friends. I didn't own up, and I didn't get the fiver. Those things always end up the same: the bastard won't pay.

I think that was the first time I was naked in public since I was four. My striptease career had only just begun. I liked the feeling. I knew at that very moment that the Dance of the Flaming Arseholes awaited me; that happened when I was in the Parachute Regiment.

I joined the Paras because I met a fellow welder who told me all about it. He talked about the fun of jumping out of aeroplanes and going on exercises to Germany, France and Cyprus. I thought, 'I could use a bit of that!' I was desperate to see other countries. It was my father's influence really – he'd brought back all those wartime photographs from Africa and India, and could even speak a little Urdu. He'd occasionally meet lost Indians off the ships and give them directions in their language. I'd be suitably impressed.

I wanted to join the merchant navy, but my father was horrified. He said, 'It's full of homosexuals!' I went along and joined the Parachute Regiment, part of the 15th (Scottish) Parachute Battalion (Territorial Army). I was still working full time in the shipyards, just attending army training sessions on weekends and Wednesday nights. As you'd probably imagine, it wasn't a natural fit for me. There were a lot of rules. And you had to pay attention to details. Even just getting kitted out was complicated. First, you got your uniform from a storeroom, but you were best off getting it adjusted by a tailor, because otherwise you'd look like a right dork. You had to sew your badges on yourself – I learned there and then how to sew. It wasn't so difficult. I had watched people sewing, and I had fished. Threading a needle and attaching a fly to a line are similar operations.

When you sign up for the Paras, you have to start by going through basic training. We were taken to a chemical dump and ordered to run through mountains of ash carrying a telegraph pole. Then we had to learn to shoot a rifle – a Lee-Enfield 303. We were taught to strip it down, clean it and put it back together again. We learned to do the same with the Bren gun, then after a year we progressed to a more modern SLR – self-loading rifle. We learned to march, too. Learning how to turn corners and how to stay in line was surprisingly complicated, but I rather enjoyed it. It was like dancing.

———

I was no stranger to combat. In Glasgow, you learn the rules of street fighting very early in life. The first rule is 'Hit him while he's talking.' There's nothing worse than getting a fist in the mouth when you're halfway through a word – especially if it's a word of warning. 'Watch it, pal, you better—' *Boooffff!!* Doesn't half stop you in your tracks. Another street rule is: 'Don't look anybody in the eye. If you do, you'll hear: "Who're you looking at?"'

But most Glasgow street fighting is a shambles. People try to land a punch, but miss and spin out of control. Men topple over while trying to headbutt their opponents. Usually, one or both sides are drunk, making it more likely they'll stagger and fall. And they quickly get out of breath. Street fights usually last about thirty seconds – although when you're engaged in one it feels like for ever.

When I was little, we used to wait outside the pub at closing time, hoping to witness a fight. It was great entertainment. Hyndland Street and Fordyce Street meet at a place we called 'The Hot Corner'. It was opposite a pub called the Hyndland Bar. 'The Hot Corner' was so named because the paving stones would be warmed by an underground baker's kitchen. We used to sit there with our backs to the wall, sing songs and wait. After a while, men would come pouring out of the pub and there'd be all kinds of exciting skirmishes and scuffles. We'd see people getting flung out. We'd see them fighting. We'd see them trying to stand up, vomiting and pissing themselves. '*Ooooooohhhh!*

D'you see *thaaaaat!!???*' 'Here comes another one . . . awwwww, he fell flat on his nose – brilliant!!!' In those years before television, it was the best entertainment you could get. That's where I learned to perform my 'drunk walks', acting like a man trying to stay sufficiently upright to walk home, or a man trying to prove he's not smashed. People would scream because it was so accurate.

There is a pub in Govan called Brechins Bar. People used to call it 'The Black Man Pub' because a dark bronze statue of a famous Govan shipbuilder and MP, Sir William Pearce, stands nearby. The pub lies in a 'gushet' – a triangular piece of land at a fork in the road, so it had two doors on Govan Road and two on Burleigh Street. One evening, a man who'd had too much to drink was thrown out one of the Govan Road doors by the owner. He went staggering along and nipped in the next door he came to. The same owner spotted him right away: 'What've I told you? Get out of my pub.' The man careened round the corner and tried to enter the first door on Burleigh Street. *'Bifff!!! Booof!!'* When he got in a tussle with the owner for the fourth time, the drunk guy became irate: 'D'you work in every fucking pub in this toon?'

———

Glasgow street fighting is more entertaining than lethal. But in the Paras, we learned proper fighting. They even gave us precise information about how to kill people and get away unscathed. The most important part of the Paras training involved going on a two-week parachute jump course to Abingdon in Oxfordshire. You were allowed time away from work for that. My daughter Cara has a photo of me on a bit of equipment known as 'The

Knacker Cracker'. You stood ready in the doorway of a very high tower with your parachute equipment on, hooked onto a rope that was hung between two turrets. On the signal 'Go!' you'd jump out as if you were jumping from an aeroplane, and bounce along the rope to the end. There was a strap at your crotch that tightened up as you bounced – that's why they called it the Knacker Cracker. *Achhhhaaa!! Ooophh !!! Ouuuuucccchhhhhaaa!!!!*'

We did a lot of exercises along those lines – jumping off platforms onto mats to practise landing and so on. Then the great day came when we got to jump from a cage suspended from a military barrage balloon at 800 feet. There are supposed to be two jumps from the balloon: one from the door, and one from a hole in the floor. Four or five of you wait inside the balloon with the instructor, and when you're summoned to the door you place one foot inside and one over the edge. The instructor shouts 'Go!' and you jump – using your hand and foot to propel you out so you plummet straight down from the balloon. My first experience was more mysterious than scary. When my feet came up, I wondered what they were. Then my parachute deployed, and I floated down, guiding myself. The thing I most noticed on the way down was the ambulance waiting below, with a big red cross on the roof.

After you've completed the balloon exercises, you can finally jump out of a plane. You have to be extra-alert for that. We were told to exit the door very fast, one after the other: 'Go! Go! Go! Go!' in a line, doing a sort of march. Forward together, forward together: 'Go! Go! Go!' Your parachute was deployed by a static line you hooked onto inside the plane, and your weight flying through the air pulls it out. I was scared, but afterwards it was a great feeling.

My last training jumps were from the kind of cargo plane

that carries tanks and jeeps. The parachutists jump through a hole in the floor. It's the most extraordinary feeling. The air whooshes past you, and you fall straight, facing the back of the plane. Once your legs hit the slipstream, you're wheeked into a sitting position, and almost immediately afterwards, the slipstream hits your parachute. Then you go *Whoooossshhh!!* Down. It's very exciting. You're trained to such a pitch that the possibility that it might not work never crosses your mind. Even so, nervous people sometimes behave in a strange way. The guy in front of me suddenly refused to go. They started pulling him out of the road, but he suddenly changed his mind and jumped. I was thrown off my guard and looked around: 'What the . . . ?' So, when they told me 'GO!' I was angled sideways, and after I went out the door I started spinning. My helmet hit the side of the plane – that's called 'ringing the bell'. '*Ooooooocha!!!*' Then you get a thing called a 'blown periphery', when you've spun so much that your rigging lines get twisted into a coil above your neck. '*Fuuuuuuuckkkk!*' Luckily, I managed to disentangle them. To complete my course, I did seven jumps – two from the balloon and five from planes. Some people I knew thought I was off my head. They thought that to jump out of an aeroplane – when you could take a flight, sit in a comfy seat and land normally – was insane.

———

I was just thinking the other day that I never showed Pamela the Big Sui and the Wee Sui in Partick. They were my first jumps – aged eight or nine – the kind of daredevil stunts kids attempt all over the world. 'Sui' is short for suicide, which gives you an idea how dangerous it was. The Wee Sui was a jump from a ten-foot-high rectangular air-raid shelter to a six-foot-high midden with a concrete roof. The Big Sui was similar, but there was a much wider gap – six or seven feet – and it was a short landing. You didn't have much time to get your balance back, so you could easily shoot off the other end and fall to the ground. Older boys did the Big Sui. I did the Wee Sui lots of times, but I never ever attempted the Big Sui – I was always too scared.

I've still got a scar under my chin from doing a jump called the 'White Patch'. The roof of the midden had been repaired, and there was a square of white cement on it that gave the jump its name. The 'White Patch' was preceded by a jump called the 'Shelter to Shelter', which is exactly what it sounds like. So, you jumped from one air-raid shelter to another the same height, and then you had a short run before jumping onto the White Patch. The first and only time I attempted this, I misjudged it. I landed with my toes on the edge, overbalanced, then slipped and fell vertically, hitting my chin on the way down. I didn't mind so much. As far as I was concerned, three stitches was a badge of honour.

Fordyce Street had the best jumps. They were like a mountain range. The boys who lived there were very good at the jumps because they'd had years of practice. Even so, many got fractured ankle bones, broken legs and worse. I remember when Gerald McGee attempted the Big Sui. He fell onto the rubbish cans and sat there totally stunned, eating tea leaves out of the garbage. Everybody thought it was a scream. That kind of attitude prepared me well for the Paras.

———

After I finished my Para training and got my wings, I was finally one of the boys, ready to be pulled into combat if the country went to war. But even in peacetime, having your Para wings meant you could go abroad on exercises. I was given time off from the shipyards to go on three trips, to France, Germany and Cyprus. I was pleased as punch, because that was what I joined for – to go abroad, see exotic places and have adventures. We'd go out every morning and parachute into a particular region, where our job was to find and 'take out' various companies of 'baddies' – other territorials from different regiments.

The Cyprus trip was the best. We parachuted in at night. We'd been told to look for a spinning green and white light indicating the position of the troop, but I couldn't see a thing. I seemed to have landed in an orange orchard. I wound up my parachute and made my way up a short hill, but pretty soon I came to a sheer drop and realised I was on top of some guy's house. After an hour or two, I found my group and we marched through the night to the Kyrenia Mountains that lie in the tail of Cyprus. But we were actually fired upon one night by a group called the EOKA. The Ethniki Organosis Kyprion Agoniston was a Greek Cypriot nationalist guerrilla group that was desperate to get the British out of Cyprus. We took cover and returned the fire, but it was as dark as shoe polish and neither side could see a thing.

For training purposes in Cyprus, our nemesis was a group of infantry soldiers called the Green Howards. We were supposed to hunt them down, but they were tough to locate. We had to trek for six days, wading through mud and sleeping in ditches, before we spotted the first Green Howard man, hiding in some trees. I went over to take a look at him. He was sitting on the ground, smoking and, when I approached, he grinned at me: 'Eh, Big Yin! How ya doing!' It was an electrician I knew from the shipyards. 'Fuck me, Tam,' I said. 'I didn't need to come all this way . . . I could have captured you last week in the canteen!'

————

In 1990 when I was living in Los Angeles, I saw combat on live television during the Gulf War. I couldn't tear myself away. It was a totally different kind of action. Smart bombs? Those fucking things arrive in your street in a taxi. They ask people where you live. You're reading the Sunday papers. *Knock! Knock!* 'Who is it?' 'Bomb-a-gram!' *Boom-whoosh!* It was extraordinary. Like a video game. In four weeks, I didn't see one bandage. And 'friendly fire'? What's that? The guy who shoots you has a big smile on his face. *Boof!* 'Nice to see you . . . *Boom!*' It's such a consolation when you're lying on the stretcher and your bollocks are missing, and there's an ugly gaping wound where they used to be – at least you have the consolation of knowing that your *friend* did it to you!

I was in the Paras for about three years, and it was good for me. It made me clean up my act: be reliable, be on time and look after my friends, as well as shave regularly and maintain my gear. Para training also teaches you some things that I didn't agree with, like being blindly obedient to people above you in rank. That was irksome. I'm not really cut out for that kind of thing. Even now, my wife says, 'You're being oppositional.' I say, 'I disagree.' Then she says, 'See??!!'

One of the best things about the Paras was that it launched my lifetime habit of public nakedness. I turned twenty-one while I was in Cyprus and we had a party on my birthday. That's where I performed the 'Dance of the Flaming Arseholes'. It's a long-established ritual in which a birthday boy is expected to strip, stick a rolled-up newspaper in his bum, and light it. Then I had to dance on the table, to see how long I could stand it, as the flame got nearer to my arse. Meanwhile, the guys were singing: 'da da naah naah naah' . . .

Oh, the girls in France
Take their knickers down and dance
Singing Nelly keep your belly close to mine . . .

It was a great laugh. I kept my socks on, though. Times may change, but standards must remain. When I got home, I told my cousin John, who promptly came up with an even funnier idea – 'The Dance of the Seven Army Surplus Blankets'.

———

That first public naked performance had only a few spectators – but, over time, my audience for bare-arsed dancing has grown to millions. It started when I was filming on the Isle of Orkney at an ancient ring of standing stones called the Ring of Brodgar. I didn't really know what to say about the place, apart from, 'Ooh, look! There's a big stone!' And: 'Ooh, there's another one!' I was trying to work out what they were for. So, I said to the camera: 'Nobody knows what these stones are for, or what they represent. Some think they might be calendars, or altars where people watched the sun's movements on holy days. But the fact is – they have no clue. They should just have a sign that says *"We have no idea what this is. Try to leave it as you find it"*. But apparently some hippy types have been spotted carrying out strange rituals when they think nobody's looking.' Then the camera moved, and I came out from behind one of the stones

My mum and dad on their wedding day. My dad looks as if he's been strong-armed into it. Best man looks like a gangster, doesn't he?

My dad holding Florence. As usual, there's only one leg on his glasses.

My default position: clinging onto Flo.

Me at Granny MacLean's house in Stobcross Street. I loved being there.

Florence (*middle*) with me and a friend outside our close in dingy Stewartville Street. After the war, the world was black and white. There was no colour until the sixties…

Day out with my guardian Flo at the Botanic Gardens in Kelvinside.

Me in unbelievably itchy grey flannel – proving I'm a man who knows a jerkin from a gherkin.

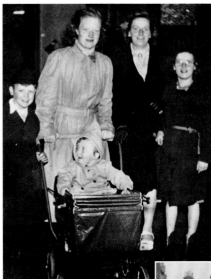

Me, Margaret, Mona and Florence with baby Michael. No idea where we were going in the dark…

The Partick gang in 'Bumbee Park'.

Back row: Gerald Magee, Frankie McBride, Tom Laurie, me.

Front row: Johnny McBride (Frankie's brother), my brother Michael, and Tom Laurie's cousin.

Me and Mona on holiday by the Rothesay promenade – snapped by a passing tourist photographer.

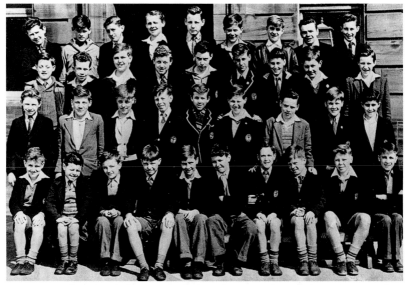

St Gerard's School photo at thirteen – I'm second right from the second bottom row. I recently met Dezzie Herron (*top row, second from the left*) at Celtic Park. He was the school's star football player who later played for Aberdeen F.C. Bastard didn't remember me from school.

Posing at Arbroath in my knitted swimsuit, wishing I had tits like the guy next to me.

Britain was safe in the hands of Private Connolly.

Suffering the 'Knacker Cracker' parachute practice jump.

Me and Uncle James having a laugh, with Margaret looking on. The two women on the couch are (*left*) my Uncle Charlie's wife, and (*right*) James' wife Peggy.

All Three Govan Teams Beaten

-TOMORROW IS SCOTTISH CUP DAY

Govan's three main football teams -Rangers, St. Anthony's and Benburb - were all defeated in league games last Saturday. Rangers were trounced 3-0 by Hearts at Ibrox; St. Anthony's were beaten 5-2 by Yoker Athletic at Moore Park in Copland Road and Benburb went down by the odd goal in three to Vale of Leven at Alexandria.

Tomorrow is Scottish Cup day for the Juniors. St. Anthony's have Whitburn as their guests at Moore Park. This is the team that gave the Ants their walking ticket in the Scottish last season.

There is a touch of history in the Newtongrange Star versus Benburb game. Twenty-eight years ago Newtongrange Star were the guests of Benburb in a Scottish Junior Cup tie when they opened their present Tinto Park. Newtongrange won this tie with the only goal scored in the game.

When Benburb visit Newtongrange tomorrow they will play on the first football ground in Britain to have floodlights installed.

Yard Meeting Votes Yes

APRIL

M	T	W	T	F	S	S
					1	2
3	4	5	6	7	8	9
10	11	12	13	14	15	16
17	18	19	20	21	22	23
24	25	26	27	28	29	30

Me at a Trades Union anti-Vietnam demonstration. Tam Harvey is on my left.

We were singing 'LBJ, LBJ … how many kids did you kill today?'

Cara calls this photo 'The Chosen One'.

Me in Biafra. We were in a bucket being lowered down by a crane after a day working on the leg of the oil rig.

Me cycling from London to Brighton for charity. It was very hard – and very good.

Me and Gerry playing live as a duo in The Humblebums in 1969.

Me and Tam onstage at the Kelvin Hall. That's the 'gay pirate' shirt I was wearing when my mother turned up after my show.

Tuning up backstage – that's my roadie Jamie Wark caught in the mirror.

With Iris, Cara and Jamie at the Hyndland Street flat.

In one of my stage shows I did a piss-take of BBC TV's nightly closer; 'The Epilogue'.

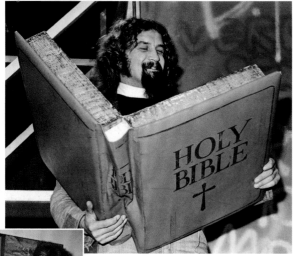

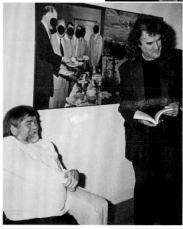

Me and Danny Kyle when I was playing in The Fruit Market – a live music and exhibition venue in Glasgow.

in my birthday suit and did a sort of magical fairy dance around the circle. It just seemed the right thing to do.

After that, I always did a naked dancing bit in my travel shows. I did one north-west of Perth, Australia, where they have extraordinary limestone pillars – probably once seashells – in Nambung National Park. They call them The Pinnacles. I danced naked round them, as was my wont, for my *World Tour of Australia* TV series. When I got back home, a letter arrived with a photograph of children dancing naked around the same pillars. In the accompanying note, a woman had written: '*These are my children and their friends. They loved it when they saw you dancing round The Pinnacles on television, so we let them copy you.*' I thought it was great, and I put the photo in my autoharp case. But shortly after I was getting ready to go away on tour, and Pamela said, 'What's that?'

I said, 'Oh, it's naked kids dancing.'

Pamela said, 'Are you seriously taking it with you? Through customs?'

And I said, 'I've had it in my case for a while.'

She said, 'Give me that.'

I'm awful naive sometimes.

———

I bungee jumped naked in New Zealand when I was filming there. I found the thought of being naked while bungee jumping exceptionally funny. It was some crazy bastards in New Zealand who invented the bungee, and the highest one in the world is the Nevis bungee near Queenstown. You jump from a cable car into a gorge. It costs about two hundred dollars, but if you do it naked it's free. It was seen as a mental thing to do, but I'm glad I did it. It was lovely, and I saved a few bucks. People thought my willy would have got a bit of a thrashing, but it was bearable. It's always embarrassing after you've done something like that, though, because everybody's dressed and you're not.

———

I danced naked round the Eros statue at Piccadilly Circus for Comic Relief. There were hordes of people there, and buses and taxis around me: *Beep! Beep! Beep!* 'Connolly, you're mental!' First of all, I sussed the area with my clothes on, so I'd know where to run. Then I went away to get ready, came back out without my kit and ran all the way round the middle of Piccadilly Circus. It was brilliant. And the Comic Relief people had arranged for twenty or thirty naked people with purple beards to follow me, doing the same circuit.

A drunk Irish guy kept yelling at me on the street: 'That's a fucking disgrace. You're – *hic* – offending the children!' He was puking all over the place. After the run, I went into the theatre to put my clothes on, and he tried to follow me inside. The television crew was standing in a line so he couldn't get near me, but he kept on: 'It's fucking disgraceful!' *Blah blah blah.* I said to the crew, 'When I say FIVE, separate . . . One, two, three, four – FIVE!' On five, I shot through and smacked him in the face. 'Take that, yah bastard!!!' *'Aaaaggghhh!!!'*

A couple of hours later, I ended up in Savile Row. I must have been going to Vivienne Westwood or something. A policeman came out of the police station, and said, 'You're . . . Billy Connolly?'

I said, 'Yeah.'

He said, 'I'm looking for you.'

I said, 'What for?'

He said, 'You punched a guy.'

I said, 'And he fucking deserved it too.'

He said, 'On your way.'

———

When your knickers are down, you're funny. Dancing naked on film was always a joy. It's a bit like being in an accident: everything goes into slow motion. I usually sang 'Christmas Day in the Morning' to myself while I was dancing, so it was easy to add music when they edited it. The trick about dancing naked on TV is, you must be out of shape. If you look like a normal guy, then it's funny. But if you're in good shape it's not funny and you're just showing off. Luckily, I have the physique of an overripe banana. I'm all squidgy. I was always planning to order one of those contraptions people use to try to get six-packs, but I never got round to it.

I think my favourite naked dance was in the Arctic Circle. I was in Baffin Island, which is just to the left of Greenland, at the top of Canada. I was doing a BBC documentary film there, camping alone on an iceberg. I wanted to build an igloo and sleep in it, but you can't just build one with any old snow that's lying around. You need a special kind of snow that you saw into rectangles. It's not easy. My igloo was a disaster. I sat on it to talk to the camera, and it collapsed beneath my weight.

While I was there, some local Inuit people took me out on a twelve-dog sled. Those dogs fart non-stop, in unison: *Pppbbrrrrriiittt!* Holy Jesus! *Pppbbrrrrriiittt!* Lumps of dog shit in it. *Pppbbrrrrriiittt!* It's not surprising they fart like that. They lie out in the snow and people throw them bits of frozen walrus and seal. They lick it until it thaws and then they eat it. I was sitting up at the front of the sled, and a big Inuit guy was standing at the back with a whip, going, 'Ka-tyakakka! Tyatta Akayakka!'

I said, 'Oh, *come on!*'

He said, 'What?'

I said, 'Whatever happened to "*Mush!*"? Everyone knows you're supposed to go "*MUSH MUSH MUSH!*"'

He said, 'No, that's Hollywood. *We* say, "Ka-tyakakka! Tyatta Akayakka!" Roughly translated, it means: "Who cut the cheese?"'

I had a rifle just in case, and a guy from the SAS – Paddy – was camped a couple of miles away from me, watching to see that polar bears didn't emerge from the sea and eat me. Paddy liked to take the piss. He would phone me on the walkie-talkie and hum 'The Teddy Bears' Picnic'. Great guy. Those SAS guys have an amazing grip on things. They see life differently from other people.

The film crew came every day for just a few hours, then again next morning to see if I was still alive. It didn't get dark until about four in the morning, and the night lasted half an hour. I stank most of the time because I didn't wash. I had a ground-sheet made of uncured musk ox, and it stank too. But it was lovely to be left to my own devices like that. If I took off my glove, miniature snowflakes landed on my hand. Billions of them. Up there in the Arctic Circle, the air freezes and starts to sparkle. I remember thinking, 'My girlies would love this sparkling air. They'd call it "fairy dust".' One night I was wandering around all alone, and the aurora borealis appeared. There was no one beside me to see it; I was the only man in the world.

I was secretly dreading my naked dance there in the Arctic, because outdoors the temperature was minus several squillion. But I dutifully stripped in my tent, then emerged and danced gaily in a circle, waving my arms, kicking my legs and swishing my willy around in the frozen air. I had my locally made boots on to avoid frostbite on my toes. They have fur inside and skin outside, and you wear them with bare feet – no socks. The whole thing wasn't as bad as you'd think. In fact, it was quite exhilarating. The trick is to go into something like that imagining that you're going to have a good time – with optimism and joy and a certain degree of lunacy. I wanted people to enjoy it. I wanted people sitting at home in front of the telly to have a great laugh: 'Look at that big nutter! What will he think of next?'

11

LEARN TO DO THE MOONIE

IT CAN LEAD TO WINCHING

—

———

A FEW YEARS ago, when we were still living in New York, Pamela – who'd read that Argentine tango was helpful for people with Parkinson's disease – found me a lovely French tango teacher at Triangulo, a specialist dance studio on Twentieth Street. *Voulez-vous danser avec moi? Mais OUI, ma cherie!* I got special shoes and everything.

I would go along every week for my private lesson. They had a beautiful, smooth floor, and a mural on the walls depicting dancing *tangueros* from the school. My teacher was very encouraging – so much so that after a while I began to think I was something of a tango star. I even fantasised that the students who came into the studio for their lesson after me would be so struck by my dancing *savoir faire*, my creative *je ne sais quoi* – not to mention my fancy fucking footwork – that they'd stand there transfixed and forget to change their shoes in time for the *milonga*. To be perfectly frank, I did hear them applaud – just the once – but that might have been when I tripped and would have plummeted to the polished sprung hardwood had not *ma cherie* caught me halfway. Those tango divas are stronger than they look.

I first learned dancing at school. They taught us Scottish country dances – the Gay Gordons and Strip the Willow, which I have continued to enjoy – plus really rotten jiving. There was a school dance in the gymnasium every year. We never normally got to mix with the girls at St Gerard's, but at Christmas they opened up the dividing wall of the gym and held a dance for everyone. You weren't allowed to go to the Christmas dance until the third year. It was awful being a little third-year guy at your first dance, because you'd quickly learn that those dances they'd taught us in class were useless. Instead, the older boys would put on records and do some serious moves you just wished you could do. I desperately wanted to cut a serious dash but that was not to be. I was a dead loss.

I asked Rena Connell if she would come with me to the third-year school dance. When she said 'Yes' I was so surprised I just stood there, not knowing what to say next. I hadn't practised any follow-up line. As the dance drew closer, my anxiety mounted. I couldn't remember whether I'd agreed to meet Rena somewhere first, but it eventually came back to me that I'd mentioned the subway. To my surprise she actually showed up there, and I walked her along to the school. She was beautiful in her dress. I was in my school uniform – I didn't have a suit – and on the way I tripped and fell on my face. I guess Rena thought that was a long way from a suave move, because when we got to the school, she shot inside to join her trendier friends and avoided me for the rest of the night. I didn't even get to dance with her.

Rena Connell ended up marrying a policeman. While she was still at school, she became pally with my sister, and their friendship continued on. In 2014, I was on the phone to Florence, and she mentioned that Rena had been round at her house. I wished I'd been there. I wanted to see what Rena looked like now . . . and I rather fancied having the chance to redeem myself as a successful guy who's not afraid to ask anybody to a dance. But in any case, Rena was with her sister-in-law, Anne, who was quite unimpressed by me and my celebrity. Florence reported that Anne had huffed at her: 'You know your brother wrecked my bike . . .' I did. I crashed it and, even worse, I told her it wasn't me. Sixty years had gone by, but my name was still mud in that family.

———

At the third-year dance, the girls would line up on one side of the gym and the boys on the other. The teachers would say, 'Come on, boys! Take your partners! They won't bite you!' Easy for them to say. I wouldn't have dared approach a girl if I could get out of it. It was embarrassing. But after I'd left school, I found that going to the Glasgow dance halls was a great way to meet women. I used to go with my best friend Joe West. This was when I lived in Drumchapel, so I had to take a bus into the centre of Glasgow. We'd be broke all week, but on Fridays we'd get paid, so we'd slap on the Old Spice and come into town. I'd meet women at the dance halls but, even if they showed interest in me, it was difficult to walk them home and hopefully engage in a little winching (courting, kissing), which I was only too desperate to do – because they always lived the other way – fucking *miles* to go home.

There were special Drumchapel buses at around midnight, so people who lived there would all gather at the bus stop

– drunk guys, waifs and strays, scoundrels and vagabonds. The drunks would be singing: '*Oh-ohh-yehh-ehhhh . . .*' Four pairs of trousers, all with the fly open. '*Ahhh-ee-ayyyy . . .*' A big dark cave. You could see somethin' jiggling around in there. You didn't know where to look. Loonies would come on the bus. One had been a boxer. Every time the conductor rang a bell he got up and battered somebody, then when it rang again, he'd sit back down and fan himself. Another loonie would come on:

'*Ayyyuu-ayhollllll . . .*'

There's one seat, beside you: Oh, no!

'D'ya wanna sweetie?'

'No, thank you!'

'Take a fuckin' sweetie!!'

'Ah. I'll, er, have it after.'

'You'll have it *noooooow*! Eat it!! Fuckin' *nooooooooow*!!'

'Okay, okay, take it easy!' *Gulp.*

'That's been up ma BUM! *Ha-ha-ha-ha!*'

———

Dancing in Glasgow would start about eight in the evening. First, we went to the F and F dance hall in Partick, which was open until eleven. Other options were the Barrowland Ballroom in town, the Locarno in Sauchiehall Street, or the Dennistoun Palais, which was the trendiest. The Barrowland had a big band, and a star MC who told jokes and guided the dances. They had a rock 'n' roll band you could jive to. In the middle of the evening they'd have ladies' choices, but I wasn't usually asked. They tended to ask the trendier, handsomer guys to dance, which I took very personally, but in fact most of the time it ended up with girls dancing together.

There were two dances you had to know: a slow one called the Moonie, which was *step, two, three, together; step, two, three, together*, and the other was a kind of quickstep called the Glide that was more complicated; I never got the hang of that one. It was dangerous too. There was always the chance you'd bump into someone and get into a fight. I was in loads of skirmishes at dance halls, and they usually started because of a dance-floor collision. 'Watch where you're going!' 'See, you, who you talking to? You talking to me?' *Biff!!!* A rumble would erupt. Girls would shriek, and bouncers would grab the ringleaders and fling them out. They occasionally had old-time dancing like the waltz, and Scottish country dancing, which was taken as a laugh – as it should be. That's when crashing into each other was allowed. *Yeeeehahhhh!* Good fun.

You had to take big risks in order to invite someone onto the dance floor. The girls would stand against the wall, and the guys would stand on the edge of the dance floor looking inwards. So, you'd have to look over your shoulder to try to spot a willing partner, and you had to be quick. There were no guarantees she'd dance with you, so you had to get up to all sorts of dodges to try to save face. You'd walk over this no-man's-land towards the girl you fancied, and if she said 'no' you daren't ask the one next to her. That was a big mistake for newcomers. 'What about you?' 'No.' 'You?' 'Nah.' The refusals would be repeated right down the line and you'd be done for. You might as well just leave.

On my first night at the dance hall, Joe West – who was far more confident than I was – said to me: 'I'll show you. Get ready.' He'd wait until two women came dancing up together, then he would saunter out onto the floor and grab the one he fancied most. I'd be stuck with the other one but at least I'd have someone to practise with and, invariably, she wasn't very good at the quickstep either. I didn't have any idea of the kind of girl I would like – and I had no idea how to socialise with women. I just wanted one that showed up. Anyone would do.

If you could get a girl to dance with you, she would normally stay for two dances, then say 'Thanks', and you'd take her back to where you found her. But if she stayed with you for a third dance it was a good sign. You could keep dancing with her for a few more songs. You could even whisper in her ear while you danced the Moonie – as long as you didn't count out loud. You'd pray that the slow music would continue. The Twist came out when I was in my late teens. It would spoil the mood. You'd be getting all close to the girl during the Moonie or the Glide, and then 'Let's Twist Again' would burst in and ruin everything.

The last dance was usually 'Only the Lonely' by Roy Orbison – a great Moonie. If a girl stayed for the last dance, oh, Jesus! It meant you'd probably be allowed to see her home. You could get all romantic during the last dance – they called it 'fanny dancing'. You'd take her hand in your left hand and your right hand round her waist. Next, you'd put her left hand on your neck and put your two hands on her bum and pull her in. Dance cheek to cheek. They didn't dim the lights though.

One night Violet Johnson stayed with me for the last dance. Everything was right for a nice wee kiss and cuddle when I walked her home, and I was already resigned to having to walk back to Drumchapel. But while I was waiting outside for her to get her coat, another girl passed by and vomited on me. *Bbbllouggghhhh!!!* It was running all down the backs of my trouser legs. I just left. Got the bus home to Drumchapel. I was a simple soul. The following week I went along to dance and there she was again, the lovely Violet Johnson. I said, 'Violet! I'm—'

'Fuck off!' she hinted.

———

There was no way to get drunk at the dances in Glasgow. They didn't serve booze, so we drank Coca-Cola. But the older guys would drink alcohol before they arrived. People were always being thrown out of the dances for being drunk, for fighting, for messing about, or for bothering women. There was a famous uniformed bouncer with a big scar on his face. In Glasgow they call a scar a 'second prize'. This man and his sidekicks once threw me out of the Barrowland Ballroom. They were trying to clear the entrance but couldn't move people along fast enough, so they started randomly flinging people out – 'Right, you! Out! And you! And you! And you!' In Scotland they called bouncers 'chuckeroots'. There were very steep stairs from the door down to the street. Two guys had me – each one had an arm. I could look back and see my feet coming down the stairs. They threw me out along with some other guys. I protested, 'What about my coat?'

'Give us your ticket.'

I gave him my ticket. The style of coat at the time was a 'white shorty' – like Detective Columbo's coat. He retrieved it from the cloakroom and threw it after me into the street: 'There's your fucking coat!' White coat, big brown puddle. Bastard.

———

You had to look good at the dances. 'Going on your own can' meant that you gave your father your rent money and kept the rest for clothes and other necessities. I had a suit made for me at Jackson the Tailor that I paid off every week, after my father signed a guarantee. We wore Italian-style Perry Como suits, usually in narrow blue stripes. The boxy jacket had three buttons at the front and folded-back cuffs with an inch vent and a button on each side. Some people had custom features – six buttons, or three buttons. I used to get a link button on my jacket. I was quite the fashion maven.

At one point we wore collarless shirts with separate paper collars. Some guys would draw on the points of the paper collars to make them look round – or squiggly, just to be different. I wore tight trousers that had one-inch side vents with a white button at the top. My feet had an 'Aladdin' look about them: I wore 'winkle-pickers' – narrow shoes with pointed, turned-up toes. At one point I had basket-weave winkle-pickers. They were brilliant. I was wearing them on the bus and the woman beside me said, 'You're very neat about the feet!'

My ties were one colour and dead skinny, with a tiepin. The final touch was a pair of huge, gaudy cufflinks – an eagle standing on a ruby. Thirty bob a pair, and I looked as if I owned South Africa. I got a brutal Perry Como haircut, and shaved round the acne – no mean task. I looked like a butcher's window. My father would think I'd been slashed. 'What happened to you, son??'

When we were old enough to enjoy going to pubs, we'd start the night in Gallowgate at the Sarry Heid – otherwise known as the Saracen Head pub. Angus the barman would pass pints over the heads of everybody who was standing at the bar, thus spilling beer and cider all over his patrons. Most people tolerated this, but we were all dressed up for the dancing and preferred not to arrive with a soggy arse. My pal Hughie Gilchrist came up with a novel solution: he started coming in with a pac-a-mac, a plastic raincoat that folded up into an envelope. He'd put it on and button it right up to his neck, so that he could stand at the bar and drink away without spoiling his clothes. We regarded Hughie as a natural leader.

The dancing itself was obviously secondary to the business of trying to attract women, but I did love the way the good dancers moved. As soon as I saw the jive, I was crazy about it. The couples who did it at the dance halls in the early days were looked upon as rebels. People criticised them because they didn't follow the circular line of dance – jive is the wrong shape for that – and they were always bumping into others. Eventually they had their own section: 'the jivers' corner'. Once I really got the bug for jiving, I started going to lessons in a smaller, clubby place. It wasn't that tricksy American jive – lifting girls and swinging them through the air – that wasn't popular then. It was closer to the floor. You didn't even move your feet much, just shifted your weight. I haven't forgotten how to jive. It's like riding a bike – you don't forget.

After I met Pamela, I tried to teach her how to jive in our kitchen. She wasn't a good student. She kept saying things like 'How come you never do that break step on the other foot?' I had no fucking idea. She improved when she did *Strictly Come Dancing*; in fact, she did rather well. I really liked the way her legs moved – it was different from when she walked. Impressive.

I got the giggles when I first saw her rehearsing with her partner James in New York. It wasn't actually funny – I just got nervous seeing her in that romantic position with another guy. When you see something like that, you're either going to get angry, or laugh uncontrollably . . .

___

At one point, dancing actually lured me into a holy phase. On Saturday nights they held dances at St Laurence's in my cousin John's parish so Catholic youth could meet each other. They would test you at the door. You'd have to say a prayer to prove you were Catholic, so we'd teach our Protestant pals the right prayers to get in. We taught them the Catholic version of the Lord's Prayer, which has 'forgive us our trespasses' rather than 'forgive us our debts', and we'd teach them the Hail Mary. Protestants rarely know that.

One night the leader of the dancing at St Laurence's came up to me. He said, 'You come here every Saturday?'

'Yeah.'

'Have you ever thought of joining the Children of Mary?'

I said, 'No. I never gave it a thought.'

He said, 'You should come along.'

So, I did. Joined the Children of Mary, a group of children and teenagers who used to go around people's houses to say the rosary with whoever was there. This was based on the story that Mary, Mother of Jesus, had appeared to St Catherine Labouré and said that the world would be saved if only people said the rosary.

We had an Our Lady of Lourdes statue in a shoebox – I used to talk about it onstage. We'd put it on the mantelpiece in people's houses, and we'd kneel down with the family to say the rosary. Sometimes when it got close to a certain hour you could see the family getting itchy. And then, from next door, you'd hear '*dooo, do do, dododoo . . .*' – the *Coronation Street* theme. We'd be kneeling there: '*To thee we cry, poor banished children of Eve, to thee do we send up our sighs, mourning and weeping in this valley . . .* Christ! Them bastards all fucked off and left us . . .'

———

I've never lost my curiosity about dance. Our apartment in New York was close to the Joyce Theater, so every month I saw fantastic dance companies – mainly modern ballet and contemporary dance. My favourite was a wonderful piece by Dorrance Dance in which spectacularly good modern tap dancers riffed with a blues band.

When we lived in London, Pamela took me to the ballet. It was a performance by the Bolshoi. It was the first time for me, and I loved it. A bit later I saw *Cinderella*, and that ballet about pirates – *Le Corsaire*. Brilliant! I was first introduced to contemporary dance by David Bowie – he took me to see a Canadian group called La La La Human Steps that blew me away.

But I wasn't just a spectator of dance; I had my Argentine tango experience in New York, of course, and I tried clog dancing in a town called Floyd in Virginia when I was filming a TV series called *Billy Connolly's Great American Trail* in 2019. There was a Friday Night Jamboree with country music in the Floyd Country store. I loved it. When the band started up people immediately went to the floor and started this kind of skipping dance. I said to my daughter Cara who was with me: 'I'm gonna try this!' I got up and joined them all. It's not hard to get by in that dance. It's like *diggy donk, diggy donk, diggy donk* . . . I was struck by the joy of it. Everyone joined in, just like they do in Scottish country dancing – children, adults, old people – nobody gave a shit, they just got right into it. There was a friendliness about the whole thing that was lovely. The dance had a basic step, but you could improvise so anybody could do it. There was even a guy there wearing tap shoes. The people there originally came from Ireland and Scotland. There were even people in the audience playing spoons . . .

The most enjoyable dancing I ever witnessed was in Los

Angeles. Every year we'd go along to see our girls perform at their ballet school's Christmas show. It was absolutely wonderful to see all the little galumphers trying their very best to remember their moves. The stage was full of puffy tutus, saggy tights, tiaras falling off, five-year-olds missing their entrance then scooting onstage behind everyone else with big smirks on their faces. They'd be sliding into the scenery, pouting, having wee fights onstage . . . it was the entertainment highlight of my year.

12

IF YOU ARRIVE ON A MOTORCYCLE, YOU'LL HAVE A BETTER DAY

—

IN MY LATE teens I became desperate to be part of a group of leather-clad, motorcycling guys I'd noticed about the place. I really fancied being that kind of rebel, and I thought it would make me attractive to women. I started saving in earnest and by the time I was about nineteen, I had managed to put a down payment on a BSA C12. It had a 250cc engine and I loved it, although it wasn't long before I craved a more powerful one and traded it in for a bike with a 500cc engine. My new BSA Shooting Star gave me the edge I craved; anything less than 500 cc was looked down on by the leather tribe. We poured scorn on motor scooters. A guy once called his scooter a 'bike'. 'It's not a fucking bike, it's a hairdryer.'

The motorcycle crowd all wore black leather jackets, Levi's, white T-shirts, fireman's boots and a white silk scarf. Marlon Brando's movie *The Wild One* was popular with the bikers. He influenced our style of dress, and our choice of riding machine. We wore aviator-style sunglasses, a red and black striped cotton cap with a buckle at the back (known as a Milano), and our hair was short, like Eddie Cochran. I would stash a bottle of cider down each sleeve of my leather jacket and ride up to Aberfoyle with my pals.

There, on the banks of Loch Ard, we'd light a fire and lie around talking and drinking. Somebody would have a guitar and we'd all sing songs. I would try to make them laugh, and sometimes succeeded. By then I knew that was the key to popularity.

The motorcycle crowd didn't go to pubs. Instead, we used to ride to the Hillfoot Cafe on Milngavie Road in Bearsden. We'd drink Cokes, chat up women, and play records. There was another place we used to ride to in Balfron where they had dancing on a Friday night, upstairs in the McLintock Hall.

———

That reminds me of the first girl who ever kissed me – it was Gracie McLintock, and we were both five. It took place behind an air-raid shelter. No one had ever kissed me on the lips before – in fact, no one had kissed me much at all. It was lovely. A year later Gracie and her family emigrated to Canada. I don't think it was anything to do with my kissing her, but I did wonder. They settled in Toronto. I've thought about Gracie over the years, especially when I was becoming well-known in Toronto, and doing concerts there. I thought, 'I wonder if she realises that I'm Billy Connolly? The guy from the kiss?' I was imagining we might meet in the street or something, and it would be nice; I would ask her how she's getting on, is she married, does she have children, what does she do, blahdy-blahdy-blah. As the years went on, it became even more of a fantasy. These days it has reached ridiculous proportions: now I see her running towards me in slow motion, her breasts slowly bouncing, crying, 'Billy! *BILLEEEEYYY!* (echo effect) Finish what you started!!!!!!'

———

I created an entrance for my arrival at the cafes. It was designed to make me appear Windswept and Interesting and amuse the women. I'd walk in and stand posing at the door, slowly surveying the room. I'd take my cigarette pack from my right pocket and put one in my mouth. Then I'd pull my matches from my left pocket and slowly light up. I'd throw away my match, but it didn't end there. In slow motion, with the same suave attitude, I'd throw away my whole matchbox, then I'd chuck my whole pack of cigarettes, and finally take the one from my mouth and toss it too. I did this act every time I went to that cafe. People found it awfully funny (many years later, I tried it in my local cigar store in New York – it worked just as well).

I discovered that I liked telling the cafe crowd funny stories and making them laugh. I learned there that I could entertain a small gathering. It felt so nice when people would scream at something I said that I started trying to *think* like a funny guy. I was always trying to find a humorous way to talk about football, politics, work and life in general. It made me more popular, and I liked that. I wanted to be a treasured member of the team, always invited to things. When people laughed at me, I felt really worthwhile.

I started trusting that I didn't have to try too hard, I was just *going* to be funny. I realised that you can't plan to make people laugh, but if you do it right, it just happens. Trusting myself to always produce comedy was an essential part of my self-education. People think I learned to be funny when I was an apprentice in the shipyards, but it was the older men who were funny there. I only started feeling like a naturally funny guy when I was with my motorcycle tribe. It grew over the years, until I found myself walking onstage for a three-hour concert not having the faintest clue what I was going to say. It has become my well-established way of doing things – both my path to becoming known and appreciated as a comedian AND the best laxative known to man.

The motorcycle guys I mixed with were different from the friends I'd had before. It was a diverse group of about eight of us. Some had tattoos, and we all wore leather and chains. Jimmy Hogg had a beard and long hair, which was really unusual at the time. People used to call him St Peter. There was Mick Quinn, Jimmy Dinny, Freddy Wallace . . . they were all from different parts of Glasgow and had a variety of jobs. Sometimes we went to England on camping holidays, usually to Blackpool. We'd go out at night to the seaside entertainment places, visit the sideshows and give the machines a serious workout. We'd go crazy on the dodgems, hanging on the outside – general showing off.

It was a stark contrast to my home life. I was still living with my family at Drumchapel. They never approved of anything. My aunts hated motorbikes and hated my having one. As far as they were concerned, motorbikes were not only noisy but, worse, they denoted a wild type of person of whom they disapproved terribly. I imagine they were jealous of my freedom. I used to whoosh past the house with a girl on the back.

———

I was thankful that my motorbike afforded me an escape. Even when I was at home I could get outside the house and tinker with my engine. Mona was getting worse and worse. She had found all kinds of new ways to torture me. When I became an apprentice she would call me 'Willy the Welder' as an insult, as though it was something beneath her. 'Here he comes . . .

Shipyard Willy!' Once I said, 'But your father used to work in the shipyard!'

'Don't you talk back!' And she'd hit me again. It was hell.

When I got to nineteen or so, Mona excelled herself in hideousness. Once I made the mistake of bringing a girlfriend home. We were sitting talking in the living room when I heard the door opening behind me. Mona had sneaked in, slyly waving my dirty underpants at us with a scary smile on her face.

I tried not to be alone in the house with Mona. She found all kinds of nasty ways to torture me. My room was on the top floor. When I was going out dancing, I would press my trousers on the floor with a blanket. I was doing this one day, and the iron suddenly stopped working. I went downstairs to where the power point was and saw that it was switched off at the mains. So, I switched it back on and climbed back up the stairs, thinking, 'Wonder what that was?' I continued ironing but it went off again. I traipsed downstairs, and again it was switched off. This time I only went halfway up. I hid round a corner of the stairwell and my suspicions were confirmed: I heard Mona going into the cupboard where the switches were. I came down the stairs and said, 'Are you enjoying yourself?' She went crazy. Lunged at me. She was unspeakably violent. I just slithered out of her clutches and went back upstairs to finish ironing my trousers and my shirt. It was always like that. By contrast, Michael was very well-treated. 'Oh Michael, let me press your suit for you!' There I was, upstairs on the floor trying to press my own trousers, with that bastard playing tricks on me.

I used to work on my motorbike behind the building. One day I was changing the clutch. I had all my tools laid out, but I had to leave them for a moment to do something else. When I came back, my tools were scattered. Mona had kicked them all over the yard. I gathered them up and went back to work, but again I had to nip upstairs – and she did it again. This time I challenged her: 'Did you do that to my tools?' She went, 'Don't be ridiculous, I wouldn't lower myself to touch your tools.' Then she said something that made it obvious it was her. I got so angry I shoved her, and she fell on the floor. She got up and went to hit me the way she'd always done. But this time, something snapped in me. I stood up straight, tensed my muscles and clenched my fists. 'Go on, hit me! *Fucking hit me!!!*' She hesitated, and that gave me the courage I needed. *'You hit me again and I'll fucking break your jaw!'*

That was the end of Mona's physical violence towards me. It was over. Finally, I was powerful enough to stand up to her.

Pamela says she must have suffered from paranoid schizophrenia, but to me she was just a bastard. I suppose there must have been something terribly wrong with her because she changed all of a sudden. One day I came in from work and saw her sitting down quietly. Usually, she'd be in the kitchen preparing food when I came in, but this time she was just sitting. She said 'Hello', which was weird. I wasn't usually greeted politely. Then she said, 'What's the time?' The clock was beside her. I said, 'Half past four.' She said something else, and then she said, 'What's the time?' again. I answered her again. When she asked me the time for the third time I thought she was playing with me. But then she told me that the McKees – a family that lived four or five houses along the road – were listening to her with a tape recorder under the floorboards. When Florence came home, I said, 'There's something wrong with Mona.' She noticed it too, and we told my dad when he came in.

Mona ended up in what was then known as Woodilee Asylum in Kirkintilloch, where she remained for the rest of her life. We had to go and visit her in the hospital. It was awful. She would just sit there, bewildered. I'd talk about whatever I could think of to say to her. Then she would piss herself, so I'd have to go and get the nurse. She became genuinely pathetic.

———

All I ever wanted was to be left in peace. To go dancing and ride my motorbike. Escape. Once I rode up to see my granny in Eastwood. She wasn't home, but my granddad was. He said, 'Your mother's here. She's seeing some friends.' That was a shock. It had been fifteen years since I'd last seen her. He gave me the address, in a place called Kelvinhaugh, and I decided to go along to see her. A strange woman – my mother's friend – opened the door and let me in. My mother was waiting for me – I guess my granddad had phoned ahead. I knew her immediately by the way she smiled at me. I said, 'Hello.' She said, 'Oh hello, Billy. You've grown so much! You're so changed . . .' I don't remember the rest of it, but it was just a bit of light chat. Mainly, I remember that she was nice to me. That was it. It took about ten minutes and then I rode away. I felt pretty good though, because it proved me right. Mona had always said what a bastard she was, but I had refused to accept that. Now I had seen the truth for myself: my mother was pleasant.

———

These days I often see groups of bikers and trikers riding around the Florida Keys. Many of them have stunning machines with handstitched saddlebags and are all kitted out in custom leathers. Some ride in groups of ten or more, roaring up Interstate

Highway 1 across the Seven Mile Bridge towards Miami in the blazing sun, surrounded by turquoise water. People say it's a cliché to retire and grab yourself a snazzy 1200cc Harley, but I envy them. There are no helmet laws here, which gives my heart a wee jolt.

———

After having my Shooting Star for a couple of years back in the sixties – great days of speeding, being with women, and generally being a nuisance – I crashed it. I came off the road on a corner and ploughed through a fence into a field. People on a tourist bus stopped to help. They climbed into the field and sent for an ambulance. At the hospital, the doctors patched me up, but I took quite a while to heal – my elbows still have the scars. I was wearing a helmet and leathers, but I still got a fright.

My bike was all bent up. It was salvageable but it was going to cost a fortune. I got it repaired eventually, but I'd started to lose interest in biking. Things were changing for me. The banjo had come into my life. I became interested in the folk scene and I wanted to go to bars where you could drink and hear music. It was a whole different culture. I was about to disappear into the hairy wilderness.

GROW YOUR HAIR

—

I'M QUITE HIRSUTE about the head. I keep waiting for it to get thinner, waiting for my hairline to recede – but it just continues to sprout pretty much like it always did. My hair was always a bit on the untamable side. Once a guy yelled at me in the street: 'Eh, Big Yin, did you glue your heid and dive into a barber's midden?'

I'm not really into haircuts. I couldn't be bothered. When I was doing movies, I would just grow my hair before I started a shoot, and when I arrived on the set on my first day, they'd cut it to suit the person I was playing. For years that was the only occasion I'd ever have a haircut. I don't do movies any more, so I'm just letting it grow. I'll get it cut when I have another good idea.

The first time I'd cut my hair and shaved my beard since the seventies was twenty years later, just before I did a movie with Liam Neeson called *The Big Man*. It had been so many years of hairiness the result was startling. Frightened the life out of my family. I got my razor and went to the mirror, leaving the door open so my kids could watch the process. Amy called her sisters. 'Come and look! Daddy's in the bathroom scraping off his fur!'

I was shocked too. I'd forgotten my face. I never knew I looked like Mr Potato Head. It wasn't all bad, though – people could finally see the Kirk Douglas dimple in my chin. Some Americans even mistook me for John Cleese. The first time I performed without my beard I screamed at the audience: 'It's ME!!! Isn't it fucking awful? All those years of looking like I'd swallowed a bear and left its tail hanging out . . . THIS was underneath!'

I've had a few hairstyle changes over the years. I became a blond for the movie *Gabriel & Me*. I once had a white skunk stripe down the middle of my head – I just fancied that. It was some time in the nineties, when I was touring Britain. A lot of my hair experiments have been 'ain't dead yet' moves. I was just thinking that I'm about ready for another change. I fancy a bit of mohawk . . . but that would expose my hearing aids.

———

I first saw a mass of hairy heads when I went to a live Pete Seeger concert in Glasgow in the early sixties. I was blessed to be young in the hairy sixties. I was The Chosen One! The whole hippy thing created such optimism – a thing they knew fuck all about here in the western world in the years before that. Everyone was shuffling about in drab overcoats and hats. The sixties was such a breakthrough. You looked different from the soles of your feet to the top of your head and scared the shit out of everybody. Frightened the life out of your parents. Bob Dylan going: '*Everybody must get stoned!*' I remember it with such joy.

I grew my beard in the sixties, as well as my hair. I was still a welder then, and the shipyard guys started calling me 'Ho Chi Minh' (at the time, the Vietnamese revolutionary had a similar straggly chin-decoration). Once a tipsy woman in the street badgered me to let her give it 'a wee tug for luck'. I bent down and obliged her, but once she'd had a yank she wouldn't let go. She called out to her friend Betty to come and have a tug, but Betty was nowhere to be seen. So, she pulled me by the beard all the way round the corner until she found her. 'Look what I found, Betty! D'you want a wee tug for luck?'

My beard has been all different shapes, from goatee to wild mountain man. I had a purple beard in the nineties. I'd really wanted a green one, though. I saw a guy in France with an emerald-green moustache that looked amazing, so I had my beard dyed green for Celtic. But I looked as if I'd just vomited, so I went back to the hairdresser to try purple. It was a disaster. The dye didn't take. Then somebody told me it had to be bleached first, and that I should go to the places where punk rockers went. That was the breakthrough. I found a product called Purple Haze, which was excellent, although in summer it caused my beard to veer towards the aubergine.

The best thing about having a primary-coloured beard is that it's the perfect arsehole detector. There was a lot of head-shaking from beige people in the street. But in the USA I went on Bill Maher's programme *Politically Incorrect*. He said to me: 'Connolly, you look as if you've been going down on Barney!' That's the purple dinosaur on children's TV. I said, 'There you go – racism raises its ugly head again. It's a Scottish thing. I've gone prematurely purple.'

———

In the sixties, being hairy was only one part of my evolution to Windswept and Interesting folk singer. I got my first banjo because of Pete Seeger. The moment I saw him I loved the look of his instrument, and the noise it made just had me hooked. I thought, 'That's what I want to do.' His concert was one of the great moments of my life. He played the first Bob Dylan song I'd heard: 'A Hard Rain's A-Gonna Fall'. And he also played a Tom Paxton song, 'Ramblin' Boy'. I immediately went out and bought the records of both. When I came out of the concert, I knew every word of 'Ramblin' Boy'. That song had a profound effect on me.

My main aim in life became to be a real rambler – a bum. A hobo. A loner. I had a childhood reading book with a picture of a 'tramp' in it. He was a nice-looking guy. His coat was closed with a rope instead of a belt, and he was eating a sandwich outside a picturesque cottage. There was a wee smiley woman standing beside him who'd obviously given him the sandwich. I thought, 'That's a nifty thing to do. Just wandering about on your own with people giving you sandwiches.' I may have been alone in my ambition – my schoolteachers didn't have too many other students who aspired to being a tramp – but when I took on the folk scene, I almost achieved it.

Once I discovered Hank Williams, I started seeing myself as his alter ego 'Luke the Drifter' – the character he created for his 'talking blues' recordings. I was desperate to be like him – a lonely guy with a guitar, walking into the sunset, a 'ramblin' man' full of yearning and wanderlust. The difference was, in my fantasy I had a banjo. My first banjo was a terrible old thing, but I loved it. I bought it at the Barras, which was a weekend street market in town underneath the Barrowland Ballroom in Gallowgate. My father used to take us there on a Sunday when I was a boy. We would wander around the stalls, then eat hot peas and vinegar with a hot orange drink before we went home.

The Barras was an amazing place, like a medieval fair. Aside

from second-hand stalls there were dozens of interesting characters, all competing for our attention – sideshow artists lying
in broken glass and throwing knives at people in bags. One of
them was a tipster, dressed up like an Indian prince with a
feathered turban, yelling, 'I got a horse! I got a horse!' And Chief
Abadu was a snake oil salesman – he used to let me try his
potion for stuffed-up noses . . . it made your eyes and nose
stream.

The men selling goods from the backs of trucks tried to give
you the impression the stuff was stolen. 'We've only got six of
these . . . (*wink, wink*) – keep them well-covered 'til you're home!'
Those men were funny. Bennet was the best. He'd give out free
samples of items from his 'job lots', like really rotten-coloured
pens. He'd say, 'A green yin for a Fenian, blue yins for blue noses.'
He gave me a sandwich once. He was eating his lunch and said
to the crowd, 'Look at that boy watchin' me eat this sandwich.
D'you want a bit?' I said 'Yeah' and he tore me off a bit of his
corned beef. I was well pleased.

The Barras was noisy. Everyone was shouting and bawling to
try to sell their stuff. The fruit salesman would sing, 'Come oot,
come oot, we're selling froot, the juice is runnin' down the legs
of the barra.' Some vendors would attract your attention by
rattling two plates together. There was so much variety. You
could buy old 78 LP records of blues singers and jazz musicians.
They had coffee tables with little glass panes with the Pope on
them, or Jesus, or King Billy (he's the hero of the Orangemen
who defeated King James at the Battle of the Boyne and thereby
gave Protestants the royal line). They had seafood stalls too, with
clabbydoos for sale. A clabbydoo is a delicious big mussel that
grows in the west of Scotland. Great word, clabbydoo.

There was a photography booth, with a wall outside displaying customers' pictures – some of the best 'Teddy boys' you ever saw. That casual pose in their long jackets with one hand inside their lapel – that was a great 'Teddy' stance. I've often wished I could see those 'Teddy boy' pictures again. I wonder what became of them? Probably flung in a bin somewhere. Lately, I've started to draw Teddies, leaning against lamp posts.

Straight after I bought my first banjo at the Barras, I looked around to find some lessons. I wandered up to George Square, where there was an Inquiries Office – the kind of general advice booth where you could find out where to get the bus for Oban or the train for Edinburgh. I said, 'Where can I get banjo lessons?' The woman looked at me kind of askew, but she brought a shoebox from the back with business cards in it. She rumbled around for a minute or two, then said, 'Ah, here we are! The Glasgow Folk Centre.' It was only two blocks away. I went straight up there and was delighted to find there was a banjo class in progress. I got started right away.

A fellow called Harry Campbell went to banjo lessons with me there. He was about seventy, and he was trying to take it up as a hobby. He'd been a miner, and his fingers were very stiff, so it wasn't easy for him. After a couple of weeks, he stopped going to the lessons and disappeared. I assumed he'd just given up. But a couple of years later I was having a pint in a pub in Anderston when I heard – *ding-dong-ding-ding-ding* – this banjo noise coming from the lounge. I got up to take a wee look inside, and there was Harry Campbell! He was the cabaret, sitting with his banjo in the spotlight. I seriously thought he was a comedy turn. He was doing very odd things and I thought he was really, really funny. I was laughing very loudly, '*Ha-ha-ha!* That's magic, that! *Ha-ha,* that's . . . oh.' Then I realised I was the only one laughing. All these hard men were there, friends of his, probably ex-miners like him. Guys with broken noses and big hands. They were turning round to look at me. I became terrified because they were a seriously rough crowd. I mean, if they don't like you, they don't do simple things like punch you on the nose. They ambush you when you go for chips. The reason I thought Harry was so funny was because when he came to a bit of the song he didn't know – which was all-too often – he'd just stop playing and sing until he knew the chords again. But he didn't even know the lyrics, so it wasn't the most brilliant of schemes – he just had to sing noises instead of words. So, he'd play his banjo – *bing-bing-bong-bing* – and then he'd have to stop and go – 'Dah-de-dah-de-dah!' – and then a bit more playing – *bing-bing-bong* – and then he'd have to stop again – 'Dee-dee-deedle-eee-ooooo!' Every song was like that! It only made sense to him. God bless Harry. He had found his own style, and if you didn't like it, he always had the heavies there to change your mind.

——

The lessons at the Glasgow Folk Centre were very basic, and pretty soon I needed more complex licks. I had talked to one of the guys in the Paras about country music, and he'd said, 'There's a pub in Clydebank where they play folk music.' So I went along there, and immediately met a man called Danny Kyle. He played guitar in the resident band, and also ran a folk club on Sundays in an RAF Association place in Paisley. He was brave and funny, and told his audiences wild jokes people wouldn't normally get away with. He became my best friend.

After the first show I saw in the Clydebank pub I went up to Danny and said, 'Where can I get good banjo lessons?' He said,

'Ask Ron. He'll do it.' Ron Duff was in Danny's band. I went to his house and he taught me some more advanced picking. After only two lessons, Ron invited me to play a gig with him. 'Come on, you're good enough!' We played in a workers' canteen, and the banjo took the trick. People hadn't heard picking before.

I eventually got a lot of gigs like that, because there were a number of musicians around who could play a bit of banjo but preferred to play other instruments – mandolin and guitar for example – so when they saw I was keen on the banjo they'd bring me into the band for a night or two.

I knew the banjo wasn't considered the sexiest instrument around, but I didn't care. I practised really hard. I became very good at obscure stuff that nobody else could play, simply because they didn't want to learn it. I found my own audience. Banjo players are weird, they just . . . like it. Everybody gives them a hard time because a banjo's skin moves and it's hard to keep it in tune. So it's easy to get the impression that a banjo player can't tune his instrument. They are a much-maligned group. There are plenty of banjo-player jokes:

What's the definition of perfect pitch? Throwing a banjo into the dumpster without touching the sides.

Expressions you'll never hear: 'She's shagging the banjo player!'

———

The Glasgow Folk Centre wasn't pretty. It looked like they'd hastily converted offices into a small concert hall. But I saw some fantastic artists there. I liked them as much for their rebelliousness as for their musicianship. They were mainly British folkies, but sometimes, if a bigger group like the Dubliners were in town, they would play there on their night off. Best of all, there was a record library at the Glasgow Folk Centre. I borrowed *Lester Flatt & Earl Scruggs – Songs of the Famous Carter Family* and learned all the songs. It pretty much became my folk act.

I practised my banjo endlessly in the living room at White Street, where my family had moved after tolerating Drumchapel for far too long. No one else ever went in there. In Scotland, many people keep a room pristine for visitors. If they don't have a living room, they'll keep the kitchen ready for visitors at all times – even if someone sleeps in there. That's where the expression 'all done up like a kitchen bed' came from. The bed would be turned into a day couch first thing in the morning.

I practised on the banjo a lot because I was desperate to be good. I also learned to play the autoharp – I bought one at Biggars Music in Sauchiehall Street and I really liked it. The Carter Family played the autoharp in numbers like 'My Dixie Darling' and 'You Are My Flower', but very few people I knew played it. It was largely considered an instrument on which women played things like 'Plaisir d'Amour'. It was frowned upon because the chords were marked on the bars, which was regarded as 'playing by numbers'. I didn't care about any of that. I just loved the noise it made and adored the sound of guitar and autoharp together.

I met a guy called Jimmy Steel who played banjo in a band. He taught me a couple of licks. Then he said, 'Do you fancy performing? I've got a gig at the Paisley Folk Attic.' That was the place that Danny Kyle ran. I said, 'I've never played in a club before.' He said, 'Oh, you'll like it. You're good enough.' Jimmy had a stammer. Audiences used to laugh at him – they thought he was putting it on because he didn't do it when he sang. And despite his stammer, he still insisted on introducing everything.

He brought me onstage with him, and I played a banjo tune. Then he said, 'Sing that song . . . !' I'd sung 'St Brendan's Fair Isle' by Jimmy Driftwood for him in the pub. It's a song about St Brendan sailing to America from Ireland on a leather-bound boat. He comes to an island and steps on the shore, and then he notices the island's moving along – because it's actually a whale. Halfway through the number I got lost. I said to the audience, 'Oh, I've forgotten the words – but here's what it's about . . .' And I started telling them the story. To my surprise they found it very funny. They were roaring, and it went down a storm. That experience was an epiphany. I thought, '*Oooohhhhhh!*' A big lightbulb switched on in my head. Jimmy Steel said, 'You should do that with all the songs!'

After that I played in various bands as a guest from time to time, even doing a little solo now and again – which scared the life out of me. I wasn't the best musician in the world, but people liked me because I was funny. I would look at people in a weird way, and capture their attention through my attitude . . . I was really just experimenting with different ways to approach and talk to the audience. I would make fun of the music I was playing. I'd say, 'There's a murder in this song. A guy called Robbie gets killed. But you'll find in most of these kinds of songs a guy gets murdered.' It wasn't true, but people laughed. Some performers create a stage persona that's different from who they are offstage. I didn't really need to do that because people just seemed to find me funny as I was. I was never completely sure why.

I wanted to be fully part of the folk scene as a hairy, banjo-playing guy – but the rest of my life didn't match that plan. I had left the Paras about a year after my apprenticeship ended, but I was still working in the shipyards as a fully fledged welder. Welding – and the Paras – had been very good for me. Until I was about twenty-one though, I was prey. I was picked on mercilessly and it was unpleasant. As I grew towards my twenty-first birthday I felt more like I belonged in the world, that I wasn't prey any more. Becoming a welder and getting my Para wings helped because I had attempted and completed things that were my own idea. Being a person in a trade and regiment that were looked up to – that gave me an adulthood that the Church hadn't given me, school hadn't given me, and my family life hadn't given me. I felt like I was a successful human. A man.

But now I felt restless, ready for a new challenge. I became more and more of a dreamer, spending an inordinate amount of time imagining what my first album cover would look like. This daydreaming began to interrupt my workday at Stephens shipyard, and pretty soon my lackadaisical attitude began to be noticed by my manager. One day he said, 'I've had enough of you and your slacking off. You'll have to go.' It was fair. I was malingering. I just couldn't be bothered any more. My aim had been to wait until the 'Fair Friday'– the first fortnight in July when all the heavy industry and factories closed down for a holiday – then walk out and try to become a professional banjo player. Due to my 'fly by night' attitude my manager had taken it out of my hands. For that I'm very grateful.

My dream of becoming 'Luke the Drifter' was coming closer to reality. I wanted to just quit welding altogether and become a banjo-playing, folk singer kind of guy, but I was nervous about taking such a big step. Entirely turning my back on welding seemed reckless. The guys who played the folk clubs were as close to my 'hobo' fantasy as you could get, but at the same time there was a pragmatic side of me. I knew it wouldn't be easy. I was trying to separate the fantasy from the reality. Real hobos lived on trains in America, slept in hobo wastelands and had to live on their wits. But when I saw Alex Campbell and Josh McCrae and others like them, I thought: '*Ahhh!!! That's* the kind of hobo I should be – the kind that travels to different towns to play in folk clubs, gets paid and leaves.' I could picture myself in that life, wearing cowboy boots and earrings, having long hair, being Windswept and Interesting and popular with women!

When a welder is leaving a job you always know because he'll have his leather jacket tied up under his arm. The day I was fired from Stephen's shipyard I was walking out with my jacket when I was approached by a guy called Bill Shankley. 'Where are you going?'

I said, 'I've been fired.'

He said, 'Did you deserve it?'

'Yeah.'

'Where are you going?'

'Somebody told me that Wessel were building tanks in Renfrew. I was going to have a look-see.'

He said, 'How do you fancy Nigeria? My friend is hiring welders – why not give him a phone.'

So, I did, and was invited down to London for an interview. I passed the welding test and was soon off to Biafra to help build an oil platform.

This was in the mid-sixties. For six weeks I worked all day on an oil rig out at sea. There wasn't much else to do. At the end of my stint in Biafra I returned to Glasgow and immediately got a job at John Brown & Company shipyard. They built some famous ships – the *Queen Mary*, the *Queen Elizabeth* and the *QE2*. I've scored a lot of points over the years saying I worked on the *QE2*. It's true – but it was only for a few seconds. I was on my way to take a piss when someone called: 'Hey, welder! Gonnae do this?' It was just a washer he wanted welded to the deck.

———

A year after I started at John Brown, I got a message from my pal Joe West, who had also become a welder. Joe had been working in Jersey for a while, and they needed a welder, so he sent for me. 'Come on over! The money's good, the laughs are good, the pubs are great!' So I went to Jersey to work for a local firm, welding the freshwater tanks for the new power station. Jersey was great for me. Not only was it good fun and good money with low tax, but I took my banjo and played the folk clubs there and did well – which ultimately led to my decision to go professional.

The Jersey folk clubs were very good. The standard of the guests was excellent, so to get onstage you had to be good. I would work as a welder from eight in the morning until half five at night, then two nights a week I would go onstage as a folk singer in two different folk clubs. Joe came with me when I performed. He was delighted about my progress and encouraged me. I wasn't a headliner, of course. I just filled the spaces between the more established performers, maybe twenty minutes at a time. But I was funny, and there weren't any other funny guys around. I gradually became popular, which was a real boost for my confidence.

Not surprisingly, I was fired from the Jersey firm. By then I had become a thoroughly lazy welder. My heart wasn't in it. I was always going for walks and talking to people when I was supposed to be working. I deserved to be given the boot. Joe had already left to work in Liverpool, where his girlfriend lived. I returned to Glasgow and made a big decision. I had a wee drop of money left from Biafra and some more I'd saved in Jersey, so I thought, 'I'm going to try it. I'm going to go professional until my money runs out.' It never did.

14

STAY CLEAR OF MUSICALS, MOHAIR SUITS AND MORRIS MINORS ON FIRE

———

MY BODY NEEDS a wee massage. Every week a man called Stephen gives my back a severe rumble-pumble. I call it my Pitch and Toss. Stephen, who wrestles me to the ground with great dexterity, is a smashing guy. He plays bluegrass music for me while he works. We both join in the choruses of John Denver's 'Rocky Mountain High' and the Carter Family's 'Wildwood Flower'. He didn't know them before, but he does now. I had to introduce him to my musical tastes. Couldn't endure another back rub with *Phantom of the Opera* wailing in my ear.

I hate musicals. They're so phony. People suddenly bursting into song. If you did that in the street, you'd get a smack in the jaw. The last good musical was *Singin' in the Rain*. Most musicals just seem to give people an excuse to say obtuse or ridiculous things. Like in *Seven Brides for Seven Brothers* when they sing, *'Gotta get me a woman before the snow comes.'* You should have your arse kicked for that. What's that musical about two gangs in New York? Yeah, *West Side Story*. Crap. All that clicking their fingers while they're walking on the streets – you'd be battered if you tried that in Glasgow. The guys look like they've decided to form a gang on the way to dance lessons.

We W & I's prefer more highbrow entertainment. I was in *Die Fledermaus* once. I played Frosch, the drunken jailer, with Scottish Opera at the Theatre Royal in Glasgow. It was great to be among such talented people. But they're a noisy bunch. They would warm up in the corridor outside my dressing room, and the volume they sang at was ear-shattering. I saw great opera in London, L.A. and New York when I lived in those cities – and also came to love good plays: *Death of a Salesman*, *Copenhagen* and *The History Boys*. I loved *Dancing at Lughnasa*. I've written a few plays myself: *An' Me Wi' a Bad Leg, Tae*; *When Hair Was Long and Time Was Short*; and *Red Runner*.

———

The first time I ever saw a play, I was in it. This happened by chance, after I returned from Jersey and was trying to get work playing my banjo. I managed to land some gigs here and there in some of the smaller clubs, and I was doing quite well. Then I became friendly with Tam Harvey, an experienced musician I met in the Scotia Bar. He seemed like a nice bloke, and he was a brilliant guitar player. He said to me, 'Come up to my house. We'll practise.' He lived with his mother in Knightswood. I'd never practised with anyone before, but it was pleasant. He would say, 'I know this song . . . can you play that?' So, we'd work on that. Then I would say, 'There's one I'd like to play . . .' and he would support me and make it sound good.

One day a theatre director called Keith Darvel came into the Scotia Bar. He said to me, 'Are you Billy Connolly?'

'Yeah.'

'I've been given your name. I'm from the Citizens' Theatre.'

He had written a play called *Clydeside* about a radical socialist movement known as 'Red Clydeside' that took place in areas around the Clyde River just after World War One. There were songs in this play, and Keith wanted a musician to accompany the actors. He said, 'I hear you're good. You play guitar and banjo?'

'Yes, and a wee bit of harmonica,' I said, 'but I know a guy who's better than me. His name's Tam Harvey and he's a great guitarist. He's good at finding the keys people can sing in and arranging music – stuff I'm rotten at.'

He said, 'Well, bring him up to the theatre this afternoon.'

So, Tam and I went along to the Close Theatre, which was a very trendy small venue next door to the big, well-known Citizens' Theatre. The actors were there. Keith the director said to me, 'Why don't you play along with Tam?' So, I did. They were World War One songs, which suited us lovely. We accompanied the actors, trying out the songs, and at the end Keith said, 'That's great! Could the two of you do the show?' Neither Tam nor I was doing anything else at the time so we both agreed.

I didn't have a clue about plays or the theatre. I kept missing my cue. I didn't realise you had to follow the play along and come in at a certain time. Over a cup of tea with Keith I said, 'Listen, I've got this idea. I'm going to mark my script with bits of sticky paper, so I won't miss my cue.' He said, 'Watch it – don't talk too loud or the actors will all be copying you.' Taking the piss. He said, 'You're a stranger to this, aren't you?'

I said, 'Yeah, I've never seen a play before.'

'Get out of here. Even at school?'

'No – we didn't do plays. We just read them.'

Clydeside was a big success, and Tam and I were quite the hit. If you don't count a few wee one-nighters for a fiver, that was my first professional gig. After that, Tam and I started playing on the folk circuit and gradually became quite well known in the Scottish folk scene. But we needed to name our duo. At a party after one of the gigs, a guy called Walt Nichol said, 'Stumblebum's a good name.' I said 'Yeah, it is. Or Humblebum.' That was it. We became The Humblebums.

———

Tam and I needed reliable transport to get to our gigs. At that point I had bought another BSA motorbike with a sidecar in which I could stick my guitars and banjos. I toured around like that for about a year, but that sidecar kept breaking down, so I got a solo bike, an Ariel Leader. At first, I had panniers that we'd settle the banjos and guitars in, but they used to stick up quite high. So Tam Harvey had to sit behind me holding the instruments. He thought it was funny.

Sometimes we'd get a lift in a car, which was far more comfortable. I was travelling to England to do a gig with Tam, and Hamish Imlach was driving us in his car. I was reading the paper, the *Glasgow Evening Times*, and noticed an advertisement for an Indian restaurant. It said they had a folk group playing there certain nights – at that time *everyone* was getting in on the popularity of folk music. It said, '*Eat traditional Indian food and listen to traditional Scottish music*'. Not exactly catchy. I read it out, and Tam Harvey to his eternal credit said, '"Chapati's over"!' We all tried to come up with song titles where we could substitute the names of Indian dishes. I came up with 'Standing on the korma watching all the grills go by'. The best one was 'I Love a Lassi'.

Eventually, I bought a car. I didn't learn to drive; I just got a car. It cost me forty pounds. It was a yellow Morris Minor with an electric vase of flowers stuck to the windscreen. I've always loved Morris Minors. It was advertised in a newspaper shop window along with other adverts: 'Home Help Wanted'. I had a friend called Billy Johnston, who became my roadie. He had a licence, so I could drive with my provisional licence as long as he was there. Now, this may seem like a step up from motorbikes with or without sidecars, or bumming lifts – but it was a terrible car. Lasted a day. It did one gig, then burst into flames on the road to Fife. I managed to pull over into a sort of housing estate and escape it. There were clouds of smoke coming out of the exhaust and burning material falling onto the street. I said to Billy Johnston: 'What's the hand signal for "We're on fire"?'

Despite our transport issues, those folk days were wonderful. We got to ride out of town, do the gig, then stay in people's houses. We'd be paid a fee for the evening plus bed and break-fast, so the organiser of the club would usually put us up in his flat. I loved that. I got to know people south of the border – especially in Lancashire and Yorkshire. We played in little towns with quaint names – like Oswaldtwistle, the weaving town. It was lovely hearing all the different accents, and meeting so many different people who were nevertheless just like me – coming from one background and trying to live in another. There were musicians playing ragtime guitar, country music, traditional folk. It all worked brilliantly. Their humour was lovely, their accents were lovely, and their songs were great. It gave me a love of England. I became an Anglophile – although I was one already because of my reading. In those early folk days, I was perfectly happy just wandering from town to town with my banjo. I had actually achieved my goal of becoming a drifter. I slept on so many floors I could tell Axminster from Wilton just by the taste.

The folk audience at that time was very dedicated to the genre.

Tam and I played traditional tunes like 'Cripple Creek' and 'Home Sweet Home' that worked well on banjo, as well as folk songs about ordinary things like working on the land, fishing, hunting and animals. I liked playing those simple songs – and still do. They seemed comforting and real – a far cry from some of the commercial entertainment on offer at the time: the blue mohair suit guys. Our audience was all ages, and they were mainly left-wing politically, so you could talk to them about unions, laws and unfairness of all kinds, and they'd be on the same page. I'd talk about Harold Wilson: 'The prime minister says he's going to halve employment tax. You know how he's going to do that? By halving employment.'

Tam and I didn't only play traditional songs, though. I discovered our audience also liked funny lyrics, so I began to sing parodies. I sang Roy Rodgers's song 'A Four-Legged Friend' as 'A Four-Letter Word', and 'Living Doll' by Cliff Richard & The Shadows as 'Dribblin' Doll'. Eventually I would take the piss out of well-known American country songs with talking sections, like Ray Peterson's 'Tell Laura I Love Her'. And the Irish songwriter Shay Healy wrote smashing parodies for me including 'The Shitkicker's Waltz' and 'The Country and Western Supersong' – a sick song about a blind orphan. Shay was a great guy. Crazy man. The day he died in April 2021, I sent him an email he would have enjoyed:

Dear Shay,
Apparently, you died this morning. That was a bit inconvenient of you – leaving without saying goodbye. I'll never forget how kind you were to me in America when I was out of my depth. When we meet again, we'll have a good laugh about it.

Bon voyage my dear friend. It was a pleasure making you laugh, and you left the world in better shape than you found it.

Love Billy

Most of our early Humblebums performances were not in theatres. They were in lounge bars, so we would hang around in the bar after the show and people would come up to say 'Hello'. Best of all, I'd occasionally meet women who – despite the jokes – let me know they actually wouldn't mind 'shagging the banjo player'.

When I was playing with Tam in Dunoon, my mother came along to see the gig. She lived nearby. She turned up after the show and approached me: 'Billy Connolly?'

'Yeah.'

It was only a couple of years since I'd seen her, but it was so unexpected that at first I thought she was a fan. Instead, she delivered the heart-stopping line: 'I'm your mother.'

We hugged, and I knew her smell. I remembered the writer Peter McDougall's line, 'You never forget your mother's smell.' I buried my face in the back of her neck and something inside me went 'Ding!' I felt very moved, but uneasy too. I had a lot of conflicting feelings . . . and a load of unanswered questions. Seeing her now I was a successful guy was pleasant, though. I fantasised that *now* she might be sorry. Maybe she would wish she'd stayed with me, or even taken me with her. Could my life have been different? And *why exactly* did she go? What was in her mind all those years ago?

I was wearing a puffy green silk shirt. I looked like a gay pirate. She was in an elegant camel-hair coat and her hair was shoulder length, brownish and wavy. She seemed like she wanted to talk. There was a lounge bar off the foyer, so I said, 'We'd better go in there.' She gave me a disapproving look and said, 'You don't drink too much, do you?' I was thinking, 'Really? A birthday card would have been nice.'

In the lounge we talked about her children and about Florence. I think she said she worked in a hospital. She'd had four kids with Willy, and some others who had died. She asked where I was staying, and I said, 'Here.' I was performing in the ballroom of the Glenmorag Hotel. She said quite casually, 'You can come back to my place if you want . . .' I tried to sound equally casual in my reply: 'Sure.'

It was very strange to see her new family, although they were extremely nice to me. Her daughters were there, and Willy. I had a bed in someone's room – I think it belonged to her son, who was away at the time. The bed smelled really good. It reminded me of the days when we used to hang sheets outside to dry.

Willy just sat quietly by the fire. We chatted in a superficial way about her family and their lives in Dunoon. I learned their son was in the army – in the Parachute Regiment. My mother mentioned she had once seen Florence in Dunoon and followed her along the street. Florence was on holiday, pushing a pram with one of her kids in it. I said, 'How did you recognise her?' She said, 'I knew the walk.'

I left my mother's house after breakfast next morning, feeling very strange. I had never expected to have so much contact with her ever, and I wasn't sure how I felt about it. I couldn't work out why she had come to see me now, after so many years – and this sudden insight into her life and family was a bit too much of a surprise. What made it even weirder was the way we had acted towards each other – with this hideous semblance of normalcy. I had just buried twenty years of longing and suffering and pretended to be a guest in her house.

When I told Florence I'd seen her, she was upset. She always took it worse than me. She didn't want anything to do with our mother. These things are so complex. I was so disappointed with myself. I'd had a chance to ask her some of our burning questions, but I didn't take it. Had she tried to get in touch with us over the years but was kept away? I should have asked her that, but I suppose I was afraid of the answer. I wanted to tell her about Mona too, but what would she say about it? Could she have protected me?

Years later, I did learn that shortly after she'd first left my mother had turned up a couple of times to see us at Stewartville Street but was refused entry by my aunts. The second time she tried to see us things got so heated my mother punched Mona in the face. Flattened her. My heart did a wee dance when I heard that, but that joy didn't last long, because it suddenly struck me that during all those years of suffering from Mona and Rosie and my dad, she *could* have been my protector. But she wasn't. Instead, she was sitting in a nice house in Dunoon with fucking Willie and her new weans, making sure *their* bedsheets had a nice fresh smell.

15

AIM HIGHER THAN
'STUPID BUT SAVEABLE'

—

I'M ANNOYED. I changed my phone recently, and I thought I'd ordered exactly the same kind, but it's not. I'd just managed to get on top of the old one and now that's fucked. My kids say, 'It's okay – Just swipe it, Dad!' But what the hell does that mean? The mystery drives me insane. I don't understand why they give you a phone and no instructions. You're just thrown ill-equipped into the world of technology to fend for yourself.

Mobile phones tame the wild beast in you. They pin you down. Before we had them, the answer to the question: 'Where's Billy?' would simply be: 'Where he wants to be. Now fuck off.' Since we got mobile phones, you can always be reached. You're always *gettable*. Now people can call you in your nice quiet moments that you used to love. I don't understand people who like that. Some people seem to be so afraid of being alone with themselves and their thoughts that they have to be constantly on the phone to someone else . . . and talking really, really loudly. 'HELLO? YEAH! I'M ALL RIGHT, HOW ARE YOU?' It's madness.

How do all those people get your phone number? Bastards trying to sell you warranties for your car. They should all be fucked and burned. When they phone, you should say, 'I'm a bit busy just now – can you give me your number and I'll phone you back?'

They'll say, 'I can't give you my number.'

'Why not?'

'Because it would be annoying, with everybody phoning me.'

'I couldn't agree more. Goodbye.'

Another thing . . . people keep saying, 'Email me.' I keep saying, 'No, I won't!' I don't know how to do it. I'm not 'computer literate'. I have no desire to be. Don't feel sorry for me. I write with a fountain pen. I'd like your address so I can write a letter on paper and place it in an envelope to post. I don't want your 'dot-com-double-you-double-you' pish.

———

Back in the sixties, when telephones had cords and there was no fucking swiping to be done, Tam Harvey and I did a charity concert at a hall in Paisley, and Gerry Rafferty was in the audience. I didn't know him then. He came over and said, 'You were brilliant, I've never laughed so much in my life.'

I said, 'Yeah?'

He said, 'I write songs.'

I thought, 'Oh no! Not another one . . .' Too many people were approaching me and Tam with terrible songs.

He said, 'I've got a few beers . . . do you want to come back to my place?'

I went back for the beer, and he played a couple of songs. I genuinely thought he'd learned them from some obscure LP. I said, 'They're amazing songs,' and he said, 'Yeah, they're mine. I'm looking for a band to join.' I said, 'Well, I'll ask Tam. See if we can get you in our band.' I was scared to ask Tam. I knew he would hate having somebody else.

After that, I kept running into Gerry – he was obviously stalking me. I gave him some money because he was broke. Finally, I summoned the courage to ask Tam. He shrugged and said, 'Well . . . let's give it a try.' So we had a little rehearsal, during which Gerry proved himself to Tam, so we became a trio. It really was a great combination. Gerry was an excellent musician. He sang and played his own songs, and he also covered numbers like 'Summertime'. People in the folk scene had never heard anybody that good before. He played a more modern style of guitar than Tam, who was an old-school plectrum guy. Gerry knew all the Beatles' music, and he had played in a band called the Mavericks who had been popular in Scotland until they broke up.

That new Humblebums trio – me, Gerry and Tam – were together for a year or two. It was a bit rocky. We tried to fit Gerry's material with ours, but it didn't always work. Eventually Tam became deeply unhappy with Gerry's being in the band. Maybe he was jealous of him. It had become very obvious that we were headed in a direction Tam didn't like, and he could see the writing on the wall. One of the hardest things I ever had to do was to tell Tam it was over. It was in the Kinema Ballroom in Dunfermline. We'd just ripped the place to bits and Gerry said, 'You better tell him.' I said, 'Do you not fancy telling him?' He said, 'No, it's your band.' So, I just told Tam the truth. He took it very badly. It was horrible.

We were quite good as a duo, Gerry and I. And we made decent money, playing Scottish and English venues. We performed songs written by both of us – and a couple of covers as well. We became big fish in the wee pond of the Scottish folk scene, and the feeling was colossal. When we played in Broughty Ferry, on the River Tay, there were so many people in the room we had to enter via the fire escape. It was obvious that we were 'hot'. Even Aunt Margaret and Michael came to see me when we did the theatres, and they were quite complimentary. My father came a couple of times, but he wounded me with his comments. At that time, even saying 'fart' onstage was startling, and I was up there swearing, and talking like people did in pubs, so of course my father disapproved. I imagine he would have liked to see me in a bow tie playing in variety theatre. I hoped he'd stay away.

Women liked us. They were mad about Gerry. I think they could see his future. It wasn't hard to predict that, with his musical talent, he was going places. Gerry came from Paisley. His father was a miner. He was Catholic too and spoke like me. In our own towns we'd even been in Scout troops with the same name – the Peewits. We both hated it because other boys were in troops with far more impressive names: Jaguars, Lions or Wildcats. Sharing the humiliation of having been a Peewit meant it was a match made in heaven.

Gerry hated performing – or said he did – but he loved what it gave him. I never understood why someone would not enjoy being onstage. I loved it. I made him comfortable up there. I would grab the audience and entertain them until they were red hot – and then he would play and go down a storm. We were odd together, but I knew it would work, and it did.

Gerry and I had fun together when we were travelling. We'd tie each other in knots inventing stupid games. Gerry was especially good at prank calling. He would phone people at three in the morning. It would be someone he'd found in the telephone book. 'Mr McFarlane.' 'Aye . . . aye . . .' The guy had just woken up.

'This is Workingshore Brickworks.'

'Whaaaa???'

'This is Workingshore Brickworks. You can expect six dozen well-fired bricks at half past seven this morning!'

'I . . . I never ordered—'

'Goodbye!' He'd just hang up. It always killed me.

———

One night, a Scottish nationalist guy called Alistair drove us home from Gourock. He was using the official car they'd been using for political announcements. It had a loudhailer mounted on the roof so he could drive through the town urging people to vote for them. We'd had a couple of pints after the gig, so it was after one in the morning when we set off. We were driving home through these little towns in Renfrewshire, and Gerry said to Alistair: 'How do you work that loudhailer?'

'Oh, it's dead easy. You just click that thing there and talk through the microphone . . .'

When we reached the town of Johnston, Gerry grabbed the microphone: 'Good evening Johnston! This is an important message! A terrible accident has occurred – a lorry carrying large venomous snakes has crashed. The snakes have escaped. They're running wild all over town. Do not panic! Come onto the street carrying your old folks. Gather at the square.'

By then we were out of the town.

Gerry's pranks were hysterical, but he was troubled. He could be unpredictable too and suddenly snap. He didn't invite me to his wedding, but I showed up anyway. I thought, 'I'll just go to the wedding. It'll be a good laugh. There'll be booze.' Gerry took it well. I think he was slightly embarrassed by me. He knew I was good; he told the artist and playwright John Byrne I was the funniest man in the world. Maybe he didn't want to be in my company in front of people he respected from the music world. I dunno.

Gerry was single-minded and ruthless about his career. I admired that, but we would make records and afterwards he'd go in and re-record my guitar part. Maybe he genuinely thought he could do a better job, but I was really wounded. Ouch! I've always been able to put up with anything for a quiet life. Mona taught me that. So, I'd always give in to Gerry's pressure: 'Okay, we'll do it your way'.

Strangely enough, in recent years people have been rediscovering The Humblebums and letting me know they like my stuff. They like 'Everybody Knows That'.

It only rains when clouds bang together
But everybody knows that.
And it's rockets and missiles that are causing this bad
  weather,
But everybody knows that.

Gerry was definitely an all-round better musician than me. He was extremely clever and wrote brilliant songs. And he was a great harmoniser; I was not. Florence had tried to teach me how to harmonise when we were kids. We'd be in bed and she would demonstrate the harmonies and expect me to repeat them. I was terrible at it. Years later, Gerry Rafferty would get just as angry with me when I was supposed to harmonise with the band. I think this fear of harmonising intensified in school. I hated music lessons. My music teacher was bloody terrible. Every single music lesson would be dominated by her favourite song:

'Marie's Wedding'. You'd be sitting there, your nose stuffed up with snot, singing, *'Step we gaily, on we go.'* Every damned time. She believed in all the modern teaching methods: like grabbing you by the back of the neck and smashing your nose into your desk. 'Come *on*, Connolly!' she'd scream. 'SING IT!' It was terrifying.

She used to divide the class into four sections, and each one sang 'Marie's Wedding' as a round, coming in at different times. We rehearsed for about a year, and then came the big day: performing at the school concert. It started with the row who sat by the window – that was the Brylcreem crowd, with the clean shirts – they were always top of the class – *'Step we gaily, on we go.'* Then the second row, who were also clever, but a wee bit scruffy. I was in the third row. We were 'stupid but saveable'. The fourth row was a joke. They were already singing something else when the song started. They would've beaten the teachers up if they'd tried to teach them anything. So, they were left alone to sit there and squeeze each other's boils.

The music teacher went, 'Right, class!' and the first row started off: *'Step we gaily, on we go . . .'* The second row got it right, because it's easy enough when you're coming in second. But by the time it came to our turn we'd forgotten who started the song. So we were looking up and down the line, starting and stopping, and by this stage the fourth row had come in, singing a completely different song. It was an utter disaster, and there were generous beatings all round, which really encouraged us all.

From then on, harmonising was beyond me. I was aware that the way others in the folk scene looked on The Humblebums was that, if the band broke up, Gerry would be successful, and I would disappear. But that wasn't the plan I had. They thought what he produced was more worthwhile – and they were right when it came to music. I was watching *Seinfeld* the other night and one of the cast said, 'It's like "Stuck in the Middle with You".' And I thought, 'My God – Gerry's dead and he's being quoted on *Seinfeld!*' Joe Egan – who became Gerry's partner in a band called Stealers Wheel after we split up – co-wrote 'Stuck in the Middle with You'. I'm sure he still makes a living from it. You hear it on American TV all the time. It was brilliantly inserted into Quentin Tarantino's film *Reservoir Dogs.* Remember where the guy's slashing someone to it? I love Steve Buscemi. He plays Mr Pink – 'Why do I have to be Mr Pink?' 'Shut up. You be Mr Pink.'

Gerry and I both liked hymns. We used to sing Lenten hymns like 'De Profundis' on the way to the gig:

Out of the depths have I cried to thee, O Lord
Lord, hear my voice
Let thine ears be attentive to the voice of my supplication
If thou, O Lord wilt mark iniquities
Lord, who shall endure it?
For with Thee there is mercy . . .

I know there's always tension among band members, and it's never easy. We had some mad times together. When Matt McGinn was performing in Ayrshire, Gerry and I went along to see him. While Matt was singing there was a heckler – a real troublemaker – shouting non-stop. Matt's solution was to ask him to come onstage and sing along with him. Of course, that just made him worse. Then Matt saw us in the audience. 'Oh! Gerry and Billy! Come on up!' So, there we were – singing along with Matt and the troublemaker, and every time we got to the end of a line in the chorus, this guy would shout, 'Fuck the Pope!' You could see the crowd turning. 'W*hooooahhhh . . .*'

I said to him, 'Cut it out!'

He said, 'Whaaa's wrong with it???'

I said, 'Somebody's going to throw a bottle and it might hit me.'

He said, 'Ah, fuck off!!'

So, I plastered him one. He flew over a drum kit onto the floor, and I dived after him to pound him some more. The organiser grabbed both of us and threw us out on the street. I said to the guy, 'Come on, ya bastard . . .', putting up my fists, but he didn't feel like fighting any more. Those idiots go all wobbly when there's no audience.

Another time, Gerry and I were at Rosyth Dockyard on the Firth of Forth, about to do a show. We turned up at seven o'clock, and we weren't on until nine. The guy there said, 'Sorry, we've got no dressing rooms, just use the office.' So, we're in the office waiting. Gerry goes over to the phone and starts thumbing through the phone book. The next thing I know is he's phoning someone called Joseph Johnson. The guy lifts the phone: 'Hello?' And Gerry goes, 'How you doin'?'

The person at the other end goes, 'Is that you, Willie Ferguson?'

Without missing a beat, Gerry says, 'Yes, it's me.'

'Well, you *bastard!*'

'Aye? What's wrong with you?'

He says, 'You said you'd be here tae sweep ma chimney at three o'clock this afternoon! We waited *all day*! I've had time off work!'

Gerry says, 'I'm sorry, Joseph. You'll never believe this: new government regulations.'

Now the guy's bewildered. 'What?'

'Took me by surprise myself. Tell me, do you have a safety net at home?'

'*What?*'

'The government has said we need a safety net in case we fall off the roof.'

'Oh aye? Well . . . I dunno . . . What would *I* be doin' with a safety net?'

'Well, have you got blankets and sheets and that?'

'Er, aye, I've got a few.'

'Put them in the garden – we'll *make* a safety net. Do you have any scaffolding there?'

'*What*?? What would I be doin' with *scaffolding*???'

'We need scaffolding. Safety measure by the government. I cannae leave the office without a guarantee of that. Er, could you get some furniture out the house? Put a chair on top of a sideboard, we could get away with that and call it scaffolding, along with the sheets and blankets.'

'Er, aye, I guess I could do that.'

'But look, the other regulation is: I have to have four other people. I could do you at ten o'clock tomorrow morning, but you'll have to provide breakfast. Nothing much – fried egg, bacon, sausage, you know the kind of thing, potato scones, maybe a couple of mushrooms, a wee bit of black puddin' in there, all right, Mr Johnson? Five breakfasts, furniture, a few sheets and blankets – oh, have you any ropes, we'll need some ropes, aye, a washing line, that'll do – have it all ready at ten. Okay? See you later, Joe!'

'Aye.'

Bam.

So then Gerry's straight into the Yellow Pages: 'Now: Ferguson . . . Ferguson, *Ferguson, chimney sweep* – got you!' Dialling. *Brrr-Brrr.* 'Hello?'

Gerry's off again: 'Is that you, Ferguson?'

'Aye.'

'Where the FUCK were you??? This is Joe Johnson! You promised three o'clock, I had a day off work!!'

'Oh, er, ah, ma diary's full, I've got it up tae here.'

'Well, look: I've asked for some time off tomorrow morning, can you be here at ten?'

'Er, aye, I-I . . .'

'You be here at ten, and I'll see you then!'

'Er, a-aye, fine?'

'Cheerio!'

Bam!

I think Gerry wanted to be that funny onstage but couldn't do it, and I wanted to be as good a musician as him.

———

Gerry passed away in 2011. When he was dying, I spoke to him a lot, and we had a good laugh. We talked about things we'd done together. I learned a lot from Gerry. He demonstrated how to fix your aim on something and set out to get it, knowing where you'd like to be by a certain point – and never losing sight of it. That has stood me in great stead over the years. We were very productive together. After a couple of years, we'd made two albums for Transatlantic Records – *The New Humblebums* and *Open Up the Door* – and we were doing very well on the concert circuit. But Gerry was getting better and better, and his music style was leaving me behind. He was developing as a musician much faster than I was, to the point where he was having to curtail his efforts to suit me. I knew our collaboration wasn't going to last because we were moving in different directions – Gerry into his individual music style, and me more towards comedy. So, we split.

GET YOURSELF A FIRE-BREATHING
HOOTCHY-COOTCHY DANCER

———

MY WIFE'S A sexologist – a rather limiting subject, I think. How can you study something that only lasts seven seconds?

I have always had a problem with sex. Not the sex itself so much – more the beginning bit. I was never any good at chatting women up. I don't know if I was lousy at it and saying the wrong things, or being too funny or silly, but I could never read the signs. I didn't know when it was working. When a woman was on my case, I didn't see it. I couldn't get the message. My friends used to tell me: 'She's MAD for you!'

'Who?'

'That one over there!'

'What one??'

Being a funny guy always got in my way. Women would laugh and laugh all night, and I wouldn't know how to make the quantum leap from 'ha-ha-ha' to getting into bed. They would say, 'Oh, you are so funny! You are my best friend!' I'd be thinking, 'I don't want to be your friend! I've got plenty of friends! And I don't want you to be my friend either. I want a fire-breathing hootchy-cootchy dancer!' Sex is a very, very important thing. Terrible stuff happens when people are fuckless. My own sexual demands are extremely simple: I like the missionary position – standing in a cook pot wearing a safari suit, looking towards Africa. Is that too much to ask??

———

I never really learned to be comfortable with women. Apart from my sister, the only women I knew well were my aunts, so I was afraid women would be cruel to me if I got too close. In my teens I would meet girls and take them to the movies, then go dancing, then go to the movies again – and then I would quit. I wouldn't know what to do next, or even where it was supposed to go. Anyway, I wasn't interested in going any further. I think I was afraid that if I got too close a girl might expect more from me – like being invited to my house. Bringing girls to the house had been proven to be a mistake. Neither Florence nor I wanted to bring a friend anywhere near Mona because she would humiliate us in front of them. But when Michael brought girlfriends to the house it was all very nice.

My social life was generally weird. I would go to parties and leave in the middle just because I needed to be by myself. I wasn't particularly uncomfortable with groups of people – I just got bored. And I didn't know how to extract myself from awkward situations. No one had ever taught me about that kind of thing. Social graces were never on the curriculum.

The first steady girlfriend I had was June MacQueen. I met her at the jiving lessons. She was a great dancer – way ahead of me. Once she became my girlfriend, we stopped jiving because couples didn't really go out dancing. June explained it to me: dancing was for people 'playing the field'. Couples went out for dinner and the movies instead. But I was used to being alone and had no idea how to be somebody's boyfriend. After about a year I broke it off. I could see she wanted to settle down, whereas I wanted to explore the wilder side of life – the hairy, banjo-playing, travelling existence. My explanation was: 'I want to be a beatnik.' I didn't know exactly what that was, but I knew I wanted to be free in the world without having to consider anyone else. The zeitgeist of the early sixties – free love, free self-expression – only reinforced my view.

A few years after I broke up with June, I met her by chance in Dunoon. I had spent the night sleeping on the beach with some hairy nutters – funny, wild people – drinking and having a great time. In the morning we were sitting around waiting for the cafe to open. We had a fire going – a bonfire of the insanities. I was wearing 'raggle-taggle gypsy' clothes and the fire had melted the soles of my green corduroy boots. June came walking along the beach and saw me there. 'Oh hello . . .' She was with a man called John MacLean and they were on their honeymoon. They moved to the Isle of Arran, where they raised two children – that's what she wanted. And I got what I wanted . . . to become Windswept and Interesting.

———

About six months after I broke up with June, I met Iris Pressagh at the folk club. I liked her a lot. She was very good looking, and reminded me of the American singer Cher, with long dark hair and a hippy-Indian style. She was attending classes at Glasgow School of Art, which is a famous place partly designed by Charles Rennie Mackintosh. Iris was on her own path to become a kitchen designer, and her classes were at night, so there wasn't the pressure for me to see her regularly – which suited me just fine. Even so, after a short romance I broke up with her for the same reasons I'd left June – I wanted to be a Ramblin' Man. Iris went off to pick grapes in France and Spain and was gone about a year. By the time she returned I was a little more open to having a steady relationship. I was getting into my twenties and maturing a bit, so I no longer saw closeness with a woman as being threatening to my rambling ways. I had finally reasoned that I could live with someone – and even have a family – and still be a rebel. Iris and I started seeing each other again. She was a sweet woman with an air of innocence, who tolerated the way I was – wanting to be off with my friends when the mood took me, playing music with the guys and not necessarily being too attentive to her. Her family wasn't religious. They were socialists who had been part of the trades-union, working-class, left-wing movement.

After we had been going out for a few months I gave her an invitation that represented a milestone for me: 'Come up to the house . . . see where I live.' I took Iris to White Street. Aunt Margaret and Florence were there, and they were kind and welcoming. Even my father was pleasant, and Iris got on well with him. I had talked to her about Mona's abuse of me, but not my father's, because I felt a lot of shame about it. The fact that Iris wasn't Catholic didn't really come up at that point; they were all pretty aware of the way things were going regarding my beliefs and they were no longer hopeful that I'd change my ways. But not long afterwards, my father kicked me out for not going to Mass. He said, 'Get out of my house, you communist poof!'

I moved into Danny Kyle's place. He lived in a nice Georgian terrace house in Paisley, opposite a hotel where he ran a folk club on Sunday nights. I was very pleased to be living at Danny's. He was protective of me, and very tolerant of my quirks. At that point I would still flinch whenever anybody made a sudden movement next to me – a reflex left over from Mona's abuse – and in fact I didn't like anyone touching me at all. Danny used to laugh about this in a kindly way: 'It's ME, Billy! No one's trying to hurt you! It's no good – you'll have to calm down.' He helped me to relax about it. I was afraid of the dark too and I used to sleep with the light on. Danny laughed at that as well. Once I became brave enough to switch off the light, Danny would sew a stitch at the corner of my sheet and wind the thread out of my room so, after I went to bed, he could pull the covers back remotely. Frightened the life out of me. And he would attach thread to a crucifix on the wall and make it quiver during the night. Crazy bugger.

After a while, I got wise to Danny's tricks. I noticed he was reading a book by Dennis Wheatley called *The Devil Rides Out* that had a picture on the cover of a sinister-looking black horse. A few nights later I was lying in bed and I heard the sound of a horse outside: *Clippity clop, clippity clop.* I thought, 'What the fuck?' and looked out the window. A black horse was passing by, running along the road. I went to Danny and woke him up: 'How'd you manage that?' I thought he had somehow arranged for the horse to frighten me. But Danny just said, 'What are you talking about?'

'Fucking black horse in the middle of the road!'

We phoned the police. 'Oh – so it's there, is it?' they said. 'Thanks. We've been trying to find it.'

———

Danny helped me understand how the folk scene worked. There was a lot to learn about performing in clubs – how you should approach people, and what not to do. He gave me hints about how to behave with the promoter, whom to watch, who was untrustworthy. He really put me right on a multitude of things. When I first moved into his house, I was just doing short sets at his folk club – never headlining. I was one of the 'floor boys' – just filling in whenever an extra act was needed. This was before The Humblebums. Geordie McGovern and I used to play each other's banjos simultaneously. We'd be side by side, with our arms crossed over our two banjos. I've never seen anyone else doing that.

Danny invited wonderful guests to play at his folk club, so I would meet all the top-of-the-bill folkies after the gig. Folk stars like the Incredible String Band, Josh McCrae and Archie Fisher would come over to Danny's house, and everyone would be talking into the night. I learned a lot. It was a sensational and formative time in my life. I met people like Tom Paley, the American guitarist, banjoist and fiddler who had made it big. Some of them lived abroad – Paris, Amsterdam and Denmark – and performed all over the world. They were raffish, bohemian people and I admired them. I fancied being like them. They made me want to radically change my lifestyle, and I did.

Iris eventually moved into Danny's house with me. I had already introduced her to things I liked, including country music. Iris had musical talent. She had learned to play the piano early on. After we met she took up the autoharp, and we played together in Danny's house. We'd go out together to the folk clubs, to the pub, and eat in cafes with folkie pals. Iris cooked at home sometimes. She was a very good cook, which was just as well because I couldn't cook, and Danny was the worst imaginable. He once made a Brussels sprouts vindaloo . . . ohh fuck!

Iris was a talented designer, and she made lovely, wearable

things too. She crocheted shoulder bags with floor-length beaded tails in various colours. My favourite was a black one with coloured beads. In time, Iris began to make stage clothes for me. She made velvet trousers from old curtains, and wonderful candy-striped ones.

———

I started to become adventurous in the wardrobe department when I was a novice folkie. I decided this was necessary because when I arrived at gigs wearing jeans and a denim jacket, nobody would know who I was. I'd say, 'Where's the folk club?'

'Upstairs.'

'Okay, thanks – I'm Billy Connolly.'

'Oh yeah? Didn't know what you looked like.'

I was fed up with this, so I started to dress in a way that would grab people's attention. Once I started showing up in, say, a pair of wild striped trousers with stars on my T-shirt, right away they'd say, 'Oh, you must be the guest!'

'Yes!'

From that point on I adopted an extroverted style of dress, and it never let me down. I've really had fun with it over the years. I was always on the lookout for sensational outfits. I was once walking home at night over a bridge in Amsterdam. A man came towards me, wearing fabulous suede flared trousers.

I said, 'I love your trousers.'

He said, 'I love yours!'

I said, 'I'll swap you.'

'Right,' he said.

We did it. Took off our trousers in the middle of the bridge and swapped them then and there. People walking by . . .

—

In keeping with Glaswegian culture at the time, alcohol began to play a central role in our lives. Iris and I were both drinking quite a bit – mainly in the Hangman's Rest near Glasgow Cross. I never drank in the house, although I noticed Iris did. And at that time I never drank spirits, only beer. I would never drink before a gig. Well, maybe a pint at the gig, but that was really rare. Neither of us could see that we were overdoing it – heading for trouble.

—

I remember my first drink. When I first got into the folk scene at about eighteen years old I was with a guy called Willie Kelly, a friend who lived close by to us in Drumchapel. One summer we were in a town called Troon for the day, headed for the seaside.

He said, 'Fancy going for a pint?'

I said, 'I've never had a pint.'

He said, 'Come on – you'll like it.'

I went with him to a pub and tried beer. I didn't like it but I thought the pub experience was rather good. I liked the camaraderie. People were chatting to each other and being funny, sometimes addressing the entire room. The atmosphere was a bit like when men congregated by the church wall after Mass. And it wasn't long before I changed my mind about beer.

Willie Kelly came to my show when I was touring Australia a few years ago. It was a lovely surprise. I contributed to his football team from the Collaroy Peninsula, and afterwards I received a 'thank you note' – a photo of the entire team with their shorts down, and 'T-H-A-N-K-S—B-I-L-L-Y' written across their bare bums.

———

A couple of years after I started going out with Iris, she told me she was pregnant and wanted to be married. I didn't want to get married; I just wanted to carry on the way we were. Iris got so upset I said, 'Aye, okay.' I went to Danny and said, 'How do you get married?' He said, 'It's seven pounds and six shillings. You go to the registry office. They'll sort it out for you.'

We got married at eleven in the morning on the 28th of June 1968. The service was very pleasant. Gerry was my best man – it was before we split up – and our wedding guests were Iris's parents, Danny, and various friends from the folk club. Nobody from my family came to my wedding – not even Florence – because I was marrying outside the Catholic Church. That didn't bother me. I remember Iris's mother caused a ripple in the room. The registrar asked, 'Do you take this woman as your lawful wedded wife?' and she gave a muffled laugh. Spoiled the atmosphere a bit.

Iris wore a white lacy trouser suit and hat. She looked great. She had bought herself a ring because I had no idea how to do things like that. But at least I had figured out my own wedding suit. I had bought two suit lengths – one fawn and one black mohair. I wore the black one to Gerry's wedding and the fawn one to my own. Or was it the other way round?

After the ceremony, a guy we knew from the Scotia Bar turned up with his horse and cart and drove us through Glasgow to the pub for a couple of celebratory drinks. I couldn't get blootered because we had a gig that night at Kilmarnock town hall. It was the only time in my life I performed in a suit.

Jamie was born a few months afterwards, on the 28th of December. We moved out of Danny's house to a little ground-floor tenement flat in Paisley. By then I had decided it was a rather good thing being anchored to a home life. I wanted to be an exceptional entertainer and to make a decent living. I wanted to live in a nice house with a wife and kids. Well, I wanted the woman and the children – I wasn't keen on the marriage bit. I had hoped to avoid the regular world, where you got engaged and then married. I wanted the more hippyish life, where you grew your hair and lived the way you pleased. I wanted a house decorated in our own style; to that end, I sawed the legs off our living room chairs so we could sit close to the ground, and I stuck polystyrene cut-outs in abstract shapes on our orange-and-purple-painted walls.

With all the wonderful things that were happening in the sixties in music and in fashion, it was a great time to design your life any way you damn well pleased. I sided with those who were advocating for different kinds of relationships, behaviour and lifestyles. We had friends who'd moved out of town and lived in a caravan in Glencoe. They had long hair and beards and made candles for a living; I considered that a great way to live. I thought if I could make a living playing the banjo and being funny that would be the icing on the cake. And once The Humblebums started making twenty-five pounds a gig it looked as though it was working out for me. The work was inconsistent but, as far as I was concerned, we were cooking on gas. Going up in the world.

But Iris begged to differ. I remember sitting by the fire with her in her mother's house. I said to her, 'You know, I think I'm going to make it.' She looked at me doubtfully. 'Nonsense.' Iris thought that to be really successful you had to be in the theatre, like Jimmy Logan or Chic Murray. She didn't think people like me could achieve that. To be fair, there was no evidence of people like me ever becoming big stars, because people like me hadn't existed before. I thought it was funny that I didn't have the approval of my wife, but it seemed pretty normal considering my background. Iris's mother was different, though. She thought I was the bee's knees. Her father used to collect newspaper cuttings about me and stick them in a huge scrapbook.

Despite my misgivings, we settled into a traditional type of married life where I played gigs and Iris kept things going at home. One day, Iris was wheeling wee Jamie in a pushchair around St Enoch's Square in Glasgow when a drunk man fell in the snow in front of them. He lay there with slush seeping all down his neck. Iris helped him up onto a seat and brushed him off. He said, 'Thanks very much, hen. You're a nice lassie! There's some horrible people about. I'm not used to being treated so bad. People just don't know who I am . . . See, I write Billy Connolly's material – and he never gives me a penny.'

17

FUCK POLITICAL CORRECTNESS

—

—

I SOMETIMES STRAY into political incorrectness, and I care not a jot. Comedians always walk a tightrope regarding political correctness, even more so in the era of so-called 'cancel culture'. When I played the King of the Dwarves in *The Hobbit* there was never any problem regarding the use of the word 'dwarf', because it was in the original Tolkien book. 'I am the King of the Dwarves,' I would say with great pride. But Pamela took exception to my using the word 'dwarf' onstage. I had heard a great story from Florence, so I said to Pamela, 'I want to tell this onstage. It's about a wee dwarf.'

She said, 'You can't say that!'

I said, 'What are you talking about? It's ABOUT a dwarf!'

She rolled her eyes.

Then I asked, 'Well, how should I say "dwarf"?'

She said, 'They prefer to be called "little people".'

I said, 'No, they're *dwarfs*. Little people are little people. If you get a little person and a dwarf standing side by side you can easily tell one of them's a dwarf. And they both know which one that is.'

We never resolved the argument. When it comes to comedy,

you can twist yourself in knots to avoid offence, but the thing just loses its punch.

———

The first time I went onstage without Gerry I felt good. It was a lovely sense of freedom, just talking, singing and being myself. I was booked to play Musselburgh, just outside Edinburgh, for the same price as The Humblebums, which was a nice ego boost. It was the headliner's spot – thirty minutes at the end of the first half and again at the end of the second in a show with other folkie people, just as I had done with The Humblebums.

Without Gerry, I could be more experimental onstage. I could be funny about diverse subjects – my life and schooldays, the shipyards, politics, sex . . . just getting carried away riffing. It was very refreshing for me. I knew I was different from everybody else, which really pleased me. I tried all kinds of nonsense; I would end my shows with: 'I'm William F. B. Connolly the Third. Here's some parting advice for you: "Lie on your back and you won't squash your nose."'

In order to survive on my own, I had to summon the nerve to stick my neck out and try things. On the way to the Musselburgh gig, I was listening to the news on the car radio. I heard about a guy who stowed away in the wheel compartment of a plane in North Africa and flew to Edinburgh, but when the wheels came down, he fell into the street. It was a sad, dreadful death but I ended up connecting it to the song 'Please Help Me, I'm Falling'. I tried some very edgy stuff, just trying to gauge my audience. In Hull once I told a very dark joke about Hitler and nobody laughed. Total silence. It wasn't an anti-Semitic joke, but just mentioning Hitler onstage shocked people to their core.

I just laughed nervously myself, then got on with the rest of the show. It was awful. I had to learn, and to learn I had to take risks.

I decided I much preferred being onstage by myself. It was the right way to create my own comedy because I didn't have to tailor what I was doing to fit Gerry. My earliest shows as a solo performer were basically folk music performances, but even so I'd been inspired by my folk heroes Hamish Imlach and Matt McGinn, who were funny without telling jokes. They sang songs and told the truth about real things like trade unionism. They inspired me to cast myself as the fall guy – to tell stories where I was with a woman and made an arse of myself. Comedians hadn't done that much before; they had rarely broken the rules of variety theatre.

———

I had enjoyed variety theatre from when I was a boy. I used to accompany my Aunt Margaret to the Alhambra Theatre in Waterloo Street (it was demolished in the seventies) and sometimes to the Empire Theatre in Sauchiehall Street. Margaret was mad about the French crooner Jean Sablon and a tenor called David Whitfield. I would sit there waiting for the comedians to come on, but those I saw had very limited subject matter. They told jokes about mothers-in-law, football, betting on horses, and people from Pakistan. I think they were stuck in a set format that didn't give them much room to experiment. They were only ever on for eight minutes at a time – mostly warming up for singers. People called them 'front-of-cloth comedians', not 'stand-up' comedians, because they told jokes in front of the main curtains while the scenery was being changed behind.

Some of them were extremely good and very successful, like Jimmy Logan, Lex McLean and Johnny Beattie. The successful comedians could headline at places like the Pavilion Theatre, doing twenty- or thirty-minute sets. Big shots. Even though I admired them, I didn't want to be like them. I didn't want to play in variety theatre, and I was lucky that I could approach the whole thing from a different angle and avoid the comedy establishment path. But in order to eventually do whole evenings by myself, I knew I had to take risks, and follow my own rules – and I felt vindicated when I could fill the town hall and the old guard couldn't.

But playing a concert that lasted a whole evening wasn't easy. I didn't have a director to help me organise what I was doing onstage – it never even occurred to me to seek help with that. And I had to find the right venues. At that time in Glasgow stage artists – whether they were musicians, magicians or comedians – had several options for performing live. If they were quite popular but not big enough to do a whole evening by themselves, they would do one eight-minute or one twenty-minute set in a show with bigger people headlining. If they became very good, they might even be given two twenty-minute sets in a single show, or perhaps even thirty minutes at the end of each half – which was 'headlining'. The next step – rare for comedians and only for extremely popular artists – was doing a full evening solo concert, which would be two forty-five-minute halves with an interval in the middle. Full-length concerts could be performed at venues like the City Hall in Glasgow, Edinburgh University, Glasgow University – or even the Apollo, where later on I broke the record by doing fifteen sold-out shows in a row.

Most people never transitioned to the solo gig, either because they couldn't sell enough tickets or because the idea was too daunting. I had the audience, and it didn't scare me at all. I enjoyed being a big shot. I didn't have to worry about preparing 'material' as other performers did, because I just went onstage and made it up as I went along. I'd sing my favourite Appalachian folk songs, and in between, I'd be funny about anything that took my fancy.

But in order to get to that solo concert stage I needed an experienced manager to book the halls, negotiate my fee and make sure I could get a cup of tea before I went on. My first manager was Dougie – a big Glaswegian dreamer and former taxidermist – who managed me for about two years. During that time, he tried to get me to clean up my act and wear more conventional clothes, which missed the point of me completely. After him I was with an agent called Arthur Argo, a wonderful student of folk music who had performed in America in the sixties. I benefited from his credibility in the folk scene. At that point I was still doing two thirty-minute sections, headlining at hotels and folk clubs – good folk circuit places where I'd previously played with The Humblebums.

I figured out a basic format: I would come on and play songs, then be funny and lead into a large piece I developed that attracted a lot of attention called 'The Last Supper' that was based on the biblical account of the final meal Jesus had with his apostles. The piece started as a two-line joke. My biker pal Mick Quinn's brother Tam came up to me one day outside the Scotia Bar. He said, 'Did you hear about the apostles? They were all sitting eating Chinese takeaway. Jesus came in and said, "Where did you get that?" and they said, "Oh, Judas bought it – he seems to have come into some money."' That was the basic joke. I just went onstage and expanded it massively, as I tend to do, so it ended up about thirty minutes long. I set it in Glasgow and padded it with all kinds of topical remarks and religious innuendo.

Some people thought it was shocking to be funny about such a subject, but before I did 'The Last Supper' there was a whole school of comedy based on the Bible. Newcastle comedians had a great tradition of it. They made it local – told it with their accent and set it in Newcastle. What they did was old-fashioned, but it was very, very good. I just took my turn. I suppose I was the first to really mess with it. Anyway, people loved it, and my audiences were growing because of it. But some Christians were writing to the papers, saying it was 'beyond the pale' – and evangelists were going apeshit. My father joined in with the people who disapproved, and complained that it was sacrilegious, anti-Christian and anti-Catholic. I didn't think so. In fact, I was surprised about all the fuss. 'The Last Supper' started like this:

———

There was a girl in Glasgow who worked in a printing works. And made a terrible misprint one day. In the Bible. And because of her misprint, people to this day think that the Last Supper was in Galilee. When in actual fact it was in Gallowgate. In Glasgow. The way the Last Supper actually happened was in a small tavern known as the Saracen's Head Inn. All the apostles were in there. Drinking wine and tearing lumps off the Mother's Pride. Singin' and shoutin' and bawlin': '*We are the Christians! – oh oh – Intae these Romans!* Give us another glass of that wine!'

A bit later, The Big Yin (Jesus) talks about what's going to happen right after dinner:

The Big Yin says, 'See *you*, Judas – you're getting on ma tits!' He says, 'All right, all right, all right . . . So here's ma prophecy: see right into this boozer today – you might've noticed there was a wee chicken standing ootside the door. See, before it goes cock-a-doodle-do three times, Ah'm for the off! One of youse gonnae shop me!'

And they say, 'Wait a minute—'

'No, no, one of youse is gonnae shop me, and two of them big Roman police are gonnae wheich me right oot of here – right intae the jail! And Ah'm gonnae do a one-night lie-in, me with a good dress on, too, and Ah'm gonnae get up in the mornin' an' say to myself, "First offence – Ah'm only on probation, nae further." But a big Roman's gonnae come into ma cell and say, "Probatium? My Arsium!"'

———

I thought Jesus would have had a good laugh if he'd seen it. And I'd always thought the Church was powerful enough to weather a bit of fun, but they acted as though it was on tenterhooks and might collapse at the first attack. From my point of view, it wasn't an attack at all – I did that piece strictly because it was funny. I was simply connecting the story of Jesus with Glasgow culture – and where was the harm in that? To be funny about something few people have been funny before is a great feeling – when it works. And it did.

I expanded it more and more. I never wrote it down, so it was fresh every time I did it. I discovered that, if I forgot bits of it, I could just make up more funny elements on the spot and it would be even better. It became this huge, unwieldy impro- vised thing that my audiences were crazy about. I was becoming famous for it. People were coming to my show because of it. They were actually screaming with laughter.

I was being regularly attacked by one particular evangelist called Pastor Jack Glass. One night I was on my way to a charity dinner in Glasgow, all bow-tied up, and as I came out of the limo Jack Glass hurled a bag of coins at me. 'Judas! Thirty pieces of silver!' The coins hit me hard, then went all over the pavement. It was quite a shock. We got into a shouting match, and for years after that Jack Glass and his followers would hang around outside my shows and try to hit me with coins. Sometimes he would offer me three nails and say, 'Crucify Christ again!' Once when Jack Glass was haranguing me, a woman walked past. Being a brave wee Glaswegian, she gave him his marching orders: 'Hey, Glass! Away and work!' He followed me around for years. I didn't enjoy his physical attacks, but his protests probably increased my ticket sales. Long after 'The Last Supper' was no longer in my act I just let him protest away merrily.

—

After I'd been performing 'The Last Supper' for a year or two I decided to stop doing it. It was becoming boring for me. I felt my audience was just killing time till I got to it. People had actually started saying the words along with me – and coming backstage with pictures of their children doing it at home . . .

But after dropping 'The Last Supper' there was a bit of a hole in my show. It felt weird. I never planned anything to take its place – I decided I just had to be brave and improvise in a different direction. So, I just talked about whatever came to mind, and the audience seemed to be happy – well, they never got a choice. But I did realise I had to try to shape the whole show so it was funny the whole way through. That was easier said than done.

————

I knew audiences liked it when I talked about things they could relate to – Chic Murray had taught me that. And Pete Seeger taught me how important it was to be accurate. His live Glasgow concert was brilliant and changed my life, but even so he made a mistake. The nickname for Edinburgh used to be 'Auld Reekie', meaning 'old smelly', because of the sewage running down the street in earlier times. Someone must have misinformed Pete Seeger, because he said to the Glasgow audience: 'It's great to be in Auld Reekie!' The audience groaned. '*Oooogghhh!*' I learned then how important it was to know your audience very, very well. I started going for walks before every show in a new town – just getting to know what people there saw every day – and then I would refer to it onstage that night. I didn't plan to talk about anything specific. I just soaked up the place, then that night something would come into my head to talk about. I would use the same language local people used, and I found this went down well with every audience.

————

While trying to work my way up to consistently playing solo shows, I was still playing smaller gigs on the folk circuit. Those folkie audiences liked the funny guys like Alex Campbell, Hamish Imlach, Matt McGinn, and some Englishmen – Mike Harding and Jasper Carrott – but I knew I was different. I had thought maybe some folk audiences would be disappointed that I wasn't doing traditional folk music, but they seemed to love it. In a way, the traditional folk scene was bizarre. All those people in pubs singing about tragic mining disasters – it was supposed to be a good night out! I bought a lovely badge in San Francisco: 'If I had a hammer there'd be no more folk-singers.' I didn't really feel like that about folk singers – I was still one myself – but I did write some parodies of the traditional style of folk song. I'd say, 'This should satisfy all your folk music desires for the evening.' Then I sang about twelve well-known, clichéd folk songs, all jammed together:

The tailor sat cross-legged on the bench
With an eye on the needle and another on a wench
Oh pretty girl will you marry me?
Oh no I love a sailor and he's far away at sea.

One day I said to Danny: 'How many folk singers does it take to change a lightbulb?'

'I dunno. How many?'

'Two – one to change the bulb and one to sing about how much he misses the old one.'

A little while later, Danny was at a folk convention in America, and he went up to Pete Seeger. 'Hey, Pete, how many folk singers does it take to change a lightbulb?'

Pete looked at him in mock-horror and said, '*Change??*'

———

As I became more and more successful, I wondered what my father thought about it all. A little later I met a guy who had worked in a factory with my father – it was either Rolls-Royce or Remington Rand, I can't remember which. He told me that visitors were often taken up to my father's work bench and told that I was his boy. I thought, 'God, my father would hate that.' Then again, maybe he was secretly proud of me, or of the fact that I was becoming known. Beyond his disapproval of 'The Last Supper', I don't think he liked what I did. He came to a gig once in Helensburgh, a seaside town outside Glasgow. It was quite a rough night with hecklers, but I won. Afterwards I gave him a lift home. He complained that I was cruel to the hecklers. 'It was unnecessary,' he said. I tried to explain: 'You have to nail them, to be able to continue your show.' He said, 'Aye, but you were too rough with them. It wasn't nice.' He took their side. After a while I came to the conclusion that, although I would quite like to have his approval, I could get on just fine without it.

———

Hecklers can be great in my show, but they can also be irritating. When I first performed on my own after splitting with Gerry, I did some student gigs, and they were exceptionally rowdy. It was good fun, but it was getting nowhere. It was a strain, and it was hampering my creativity. So I said to Alec Scott, my agent at the time, 'I've had enough. No more student gigs. Don't take them from now on.'

About six months later he said, 'I've got a gig for you – Glasgow University.'

'NO!'

He said, 'It's a hundred pounds.' My previous fee was seventy. He said, 'Once you go up there, you're not coming back down.'

So I said, 'Okay. I'll do it. But any trouble I'm off.'

He said, 'Yeah, okay. The slightest trouble, get off.'

So, I walked onstage. I said, 'Hello. Good evening.' A guy in the audience shouted, 'Get off!' And I said 'Certainly' and walked off. I wasn't paid, but it felt good. I knew I had to protect my integrity.

Another time I was trying to entertain people in Dundee, and I was doing a hillbilly banjo song about a rabbit stuck in a log. It's full of suspense. 'Got a rabbit in a log and I ain't got my dog' – *a-ruccu-rucca-rucca-tong-tong* . . . And this prick in the audience shouts out: 'Needle of Death!' He had this very irritating, flat, nasal voice: 'Needle of Death!'

I said, 'I'm sorry?'

'Sing "Needle of Death"!'

I said, '"Needle of Death"? That's a song about heroin addiction!' I said, 'Have you noticed this is a banjo? Banjos don't do heroin addiction. But you'll like *this* song, it's about a chicken: "There's a chicken on the limb and I've got my eye on him . . ."'

But he kept calling out: 'Needle of Death!'

I said, 'I told you I don't *know* the fucking thing! Don't ask again!' So I started playing again: *Dunk-a-lunka-dunk-dunk-dunk-dunk—*

'Needle of Death!'

I stopped. Took off my banjo. Pointed at him: 'Stay where you are.' I stepped down from the stage and went up the aisle asking people, 'Was it *you*?'

'No.'

'Was it *you*?'

'No.'

'Who did you say? The fat prick with the moustache? Thanks.'

So, I hit him. *Boof!* I gave him the Order of the Fat Lip. It was the biggest mistake I ever made. He was the treasurer. I didn't get a penny.

LEARN TO SPEAK BABY

—

I LIKE BABIES. The only babies I've known have been my own, but they were brilliant. I don't know why I'm so drawn to the wee things, but I am. I've startled a lot of people by staring into prams. Talking to strange babies in elevators. They're just delightful creatures, even when they're crying. Any love you give them they give you right back.

I like to talk to babies before they can speak actual words. I'll ask them questions. After Iris and I had our first baby I would have important discussions with him like: 'What do you think of this Vietnam situation?' Then Jamie would answer me in gobbledygook and go on and on. Then I'd say, 'That's so interesting. Do you really think so? What about Ho Chi Minh?' And he'd go off again. I once spoke to Paul McCartney about it, and he told me he speaks fluent baby. I believe him. His children seem extremely happy. I only wish he had met Jamie then – he could have translated for me.

Jamie was a very creative baby. He followed in his mother's footsteps by showing early talent in interior design. Iris, Jamie and I moved out of Danny Kyle's house and into a house in Parkhead. We decided to paint the living room pale blue. It took us most of the day, so we left the paint roller in its dish on the floor and went to bed. Wee Jamie got up early and toddled around the place in his wee onesie. When we got up, there were blue footprints the whole way along the hall and into the living room. He had added blue accents to the sideboard, the fridge and the coffee table, and he had finished the job by painting the entire TV blue. Iris was horrified, but I just pointed to the cat. 'Eh, Jamie, you missed a bit.'

I like to play babies like an instrument. If you gently hold the feet in one hand, then put their hands above their head, their body is all stretched out and rippled. They look like musical instruments. I used to go *Brrrring!* Play them like an autoharp. They always loved it. *Brrrring Brrrring Prrrring!* Play a song.

———

I created a musical show at one point because I wanted to do something to appeal to a broader audience. In 1972 I'd done a show called *Connolly's Glasgow Flourish* at the Cottage Theatre in Cumbernauld. It was a failed attempt to string my act together as a prepared cohesive solo show with a beginning, a middle and an end. I'd wanted to try this because when I came offstage after my gigs, I would feel there was something missing. But it was a disaster. It lasted one night, and afterwards I didn't want to try it again. Maybe I wasn't courageous enough – and maybe I was just approaching the thing from the wrong angle. I had written some of it, and improvised other bits, but the audience didn't like it as much as my old stuff in shorter sets, or when I just spontaneously invented things in front of them. For a while, I put aside the idea of creating a set show and just went on the road again doing what I normally did – singing songs with my banjo and autoharp, with funny bits in between. But I was frustrated. I wanted to do the whole evening and play to people who were just there to see me.

So I came up with this musical show with the poet and playwright Tom Buchan. It was for a short-lived festival called Clydefair. Tom was a friend of my manager Dougie, who had said, 'Can you come and work with Billy?'

It was a good collaboration, and we ran the show at the King's Theatre in Glasgow. The papers hated it, but the crowd loved it, and we went on to perform it at the Edinburgh Fringe and in London at the Young Vic Theatre. The piece was called *The Great Northern Welly Boot Show*, about workers taking over a welly boot factory. It was a parody of current events – the Clyde was in an uproar at the time because a workers' union had taken over one of the shipyards. I played a character called 'Big Jimmy Little John' – a spoof on Jimmy Reid the union leader. Tom wrote the script, I composed the songs, and John Byrne designed the costumes and scenery. John dressed me in silver overalls and boots with wings on them and he designed about a dozen, wonderful, themed welly boots – the Nurse Grant Surgical Welly, the Reggae Welly and the Dixie Flyer, which was a cowboy boot with a wheel for a heel. John Byrne is a genius, an astounding artist and playwright. I love him. He also designed brilliant album covers for The Humblebums.

———

In 1972 I made my first solo comedy album, *Billy Connolly Live!*, with Transatlantic Records, recorded at City Hall, Glasgow, where I told stories and sang daft songs with a band. This may have seemed to others like a giant leap for me, but I took it in my stride. There were very few things I found daunting then. I was young, and I could see the way forward. I had learned from Gerry to be very single-minded. A year or so later I recorded a live double album, *Solo Concert*, at the Tudor Hotel in Airdrie. It included 'The Last Supper' and did well in the charts. I continued marching merrily forward, and pretty soon I was playing full evenings by myself all over Scotland and England, with a show that was mainly comedy, with one-third music.

Structuring my full-length solo performances to include both music and comedy seemed the right way for me to go. I did a Scottish and English tour where my set was a park bench and a fountain with a parrot on it. My guitar, banjo and autoharp would be set by the bench, and every now and then I'd go over and sit there playing a song. Then I'd stand up and go back to talking again. The show was two hours long – started at eight and finished at ten. It was a normal show length but, looking back, that seems really short compared to the three-and-a-half-hour shows I ended up doing.

I once did a concert that lasted over four hours. It was in Dunedin, New Zealand, and it was my longest stage show ever. I suddenly looked at my watch and realised it was eleven thirty. 'Jesus!' I said, 'Look at that! It's almost been four hours . . . I better stop—'

'*Noooooohhhhh!!*'

'Well,' I said, 'I've actually always wanted to come offstage on a different day from when I went on . . . d'you fancy??'

'*Yeeeaaahhhh!!!!*'

I finished the show at one minute past midnight.

———

Even in the early days I probably could have managed to talk for at least a whole two hours – but I didn't want to. I didn't want to abandon folk music because it had been so kind to me. I felt immensely loyal to the banjo and could never think of giving it up – it was my pal. Years later, when I was doing huge arenas without any songs, I still took my banjo to the gig. People thought I was daft, but that instrument had taken me a long way and I couldn't bear to be parted from it. At one point I was going onstage with the banjo, but I'd end up just talking without playing. A bit later I'd just leave the banjo at the side of the stage. Finally, one night in Australia, I arrived at the gig and looked in the boot of the car, but my banjo wasn't there – so I just went on without it. It was a real milestone to realise I could do the whole show without relying on the banjo. Even so, I felt a pang of guilt. My love of the instrument has been almost lifelong. Even now, with my left hand affected by Parkinson's disease, it still gives me a lot of pleasure.

———

In the early to mid-seventies, I performed in some new venues such as at the Traverse Theatre during the Edinburgh Fringe Festival. I had previously been barred from the Traverse – once for being a drunken nuisance, and another time for putting my willy in a gin and tonic. The willy trick was to impress my friends. I would position it in my glass with a twist of lemon nicely arranged, then go over and talk to someone, who would hopefully be oblivious. My pals would be watching from a few yards away and it was a great laugh. Eventually somebody shopped me, and I got kicked out by the management. I didn't care. Most of the world was going mad around me – solo concerts, Great Northern Welly Boot Show, King's Theatre – it was all nuts. Like rock 'n' roll. I was beginning to think the rules didn't apply to me. And when Alec Naughton had the idea of arranging one's willy on a plate of salad during Festival buffets ('Go talk to the Mayor's wife!'), I thought that was a great trick too . . .

———

Babies play tricks on you. They pretend to be dead. We used to have one of those intercom walkie-talkie things where you could hear them from another room. We'd listen to them and be convinced they were sleeping. But, just when we had relaxed, they'd pretend to be dead, so we'd have to run in to save them – only to find them breathing contentedly.

I used to take pride in changing babies quickly. People go on about babies being smelly, but it's a doddle. It's your own child. Your own smell. You made it. It's a joy to release the baby of this burden. It's dead easy now. It used to be difficult, when it was the big towelling nappies you had to fold properly then fasten with a big pin. You were always scared that you'd impale the wee thing.

Toddlers are great too. They're the craziest people. They change their clothes six times a day, and they ask you the nicest questions. I was going down Buchanan Street in Glasgow with Cara on my shoulders when she was two or three. I was going to the House of Fraser to buy some Christmas presents. The street was full of people. They kept coming up and saying, 'Hello, Billy! Merry Christmas.'

'All the best, Big Yin!'

And after about the fortieth one Cara leaned over my head.

Her face was upside down. She said, 'Do you know everybody?' I thought it was a brilliant question. I said, 'Yes. Yes, I do.'

My Irish promoter Pat's three-year-old daughter woke him up at two in the morning. He said, 'What is it?' And she said, 'What'll we sing now?'

———

I can't remember how I met Frank Lynch but, as my manager at some point after Arthur, he was remarkably helpful to me. He tried to get me to give up the folk scene and go for the big theatres like the Pavilion Theatre and the King's Theatre. No one in my field was doing the arenas, but he could see the future. At first, I fought him tooth and nail. I wanted to stay with the smaller folk scene, but eventually I gave in and played solo concerts in the big variety theatre venues. He was dead right. In 1974 I sold out the Pavilion Theatre.

Frank also helped me develop my stage appearance. I had begun to dream up show clothes that would startle and amuse my audience, and Frank knew people who made things. He found craftspeople to make my welly boots, my tights and leotard, and my giant boots like half-peeled bananas – they were all great ideas, but if it had been left up to me, they would have remained ideas. Frank made them happen, and those costumes became really popular. People went crazy for my 'banana boots'. They were designed by John Byrne, and Frank commissioned Edmond Smith from a design group called Artifactory to make them. My tights were designed by a London designer, Alan Jeffries, who stuck a picture of my face on the bum. Alan also made the 'scissors suit' I dreamed up, with big red handles and silver blades down my legs. I also had beautiful velvet suits with the hoods of the jackets going right down to my knees at the back, and a target on my knee. I had wanted to be in the glam rock business – and, overwhelmingly, it worked. I was being noticed by people in other fields. I was invited to do great, starry gigs like hosting the *Melody Maker* annual awards. I was giving prizes to Led Zeppelin. People were saying I was hot as a pistol.

I had already started travelling overseas; Dougie arranged for me to play some gigs in Canada. Nothing big at first – I played a few halls – but it was good for me, and it grew. At first, I was mainly playing for the Scottish expat audience, doing 'The Last Supper'. They'd never seen anything quite like it and it went down a storm. My promoter brought in some journalists to see a show I did in a big pub lounge. It was sweaty and stuffed to the limits, and I tore it to bits. They wrote very positive reviews, which meant that the next time I played Canada – eighteen months later – I could play larger gigs like the Massey Hall in Toronto.

During that second Canadian tour I was on a talk show in Toronto – *Elwood Glover's Luncheon Date*. I wore huge platform shoes in olive-green leather with three green lizard-skin soles about four or five inches high. The talk-show host made a big fuss of them. At one point he said, 'You remind me of George Carlin.' I said, 'I've never heard of him.' The audience burst out laughing. They thought I was being funny. I said, 'Genuinely – I don't know the guy.' Afterwards I went out and bought Carlin's albums. I could see why they would say I was similar to him, but I disagreed. I felt perfectly content that my work was unique, and that I couldn't really be compared to anyone else. I just carried on with what I was doing.

Although I was now a family man, I knew that touring would always be part of my life. I didn't feel torn whenever I had to leave the family for long periods. I knew from very early that was the way it was going to be. You live a bit like a soldier or merchant seaman. You go off and do your thing, then you come home. I believed it was my duty as a father to provide things. I'd bring presents for the kids. I wasn't very good at it, and they soon got wise – sussed the airport presents, like the teddy bear dressed in a leather jacket. Once I unwittingly got them the same presents twice, so after that I had to try harder. I needed to show them I'd thought about them during the tour, not only on the way home. Next time I was in Vancouver I bought a native Canadian doll dressed in beaded rawhide clothes for Cara, and I got Jamie wee black cowboy boots with floral designs on them. At least I was trying.

My painful and complex relationship with my own father, as well as with my mother and aunts, made me even more determined to be close to and protective of my own children. Because a baby has no means of defence at all. It relies a hundred per cent on you. When it screams that's the only noise it can make to get what it needs, whether it's hungry or teething or whatever. It's trying to communicate with you. It's just come out from being an aquatic creature, and it's now an air-breathing creature, and it's not sure what to do. It no longer has the warmth of the womb, its legs and arms are adrift, and it's going, 'Help! Help!' You have to just love it. That's the only answer. Some people make a separate room for it and let it cry until it stops – until it's lost the will to try to appeal to you. I think that's an intensely cruel thing. Let it be. Let it climb all over you and feel that you're always there to save it, because it thinks it's in danger. Afraid of dying. Just let it be. Sometimes I'd push Daisy away from me just to watch her roll towards me again – a heat-seeking missile.

Babies should be constantly touched and reassured. There's no need to tiptoe across a room. If you want a quiet baby, crash around the room like a well-digger. Throw stuff about, make noises. It'll get used to the noises and just lie there. It knows the noises are you. You're its defender, so it relaxes completely.

I remember the best advice I got was from Pamela. She had to go out and I was to watch our daughter Daisy. I said, 'I can't stop her crying and I'm dying to see the snooker on television.' And she said, 'Surrender.' So, I did. I put the telly off, and Daisy stopped crying. Then, when she was asleep, I put the telly back on and she woke up but realised she was being cuddled – and she settled for that, snooker and all. You *have* to surrender to them. You can't make a deal with a baby, because for them it's life and death. It sounds ridiculous, but all it has to fear is death.

———

In 1975 I signed with Polydor Records. Frank represented a rock band called Slik with Midge Ure, and when Phil Coulter – a well-known record producer and songwriter – was coming to produce a record for them, Frank asked him to produce a single for me as well. Phil was lukewarm about this idea – after all, he was a big shot. Elvis Presley had recorded one of his songs. But once Phil had become helpless with laughter during my first session – fallen over the sound desk and destroyed the take – he knew he was on to something. A couple of guys in Nashville had come up with the song, a parody of Tammy Wynette's '*D.I.V.O.R.C.E.*' I changed the words a bit and it went to number one, which meant that I got to appear on *Top of the Pops*. I was

A one-man
ovation.

At a ceremony receiving an award for
record sales of *The Secret Policeman's Ball*.
Spot John Cleese, Peter Cook and Rowan
Atkinson. Maybe Anna Ford?

Look at the state of me!

Our wedding in Fiji with the whole family.

With my pal Michael Caine on the set of *Water* in St Lucia. I stole his umbrella.

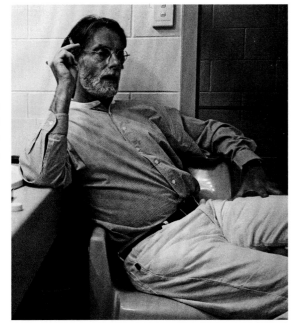

Steve Brown, my late manager, who made a huge difference to my life.

Living dangerously in Australia: bestriding the Opera House, 1995.

With an Aboriginal didgeridoo musician, Australia, 1995.

Taking the insanity test in NZ – naked bungee jumping.

On my purple trike during my *World Tour of Australia* – fun fun fun!

Proof that I know Dame Judi Dench. On the set of *Mrs Brown*, 1997.

On the set of *Boondock Saints*, 1999. It's not every day you get to kill Willem Dafoe.

On the set of *What We Did on Our Holiday*. It was all fun and games 'til I tried to get out of that deck chair…

Being threatened by Sean Connery. I had made fun of him from the stage: 'You've done well for a guy with a speech impediment'.

Spending time in a charity concert with one of the nicest men in the world – George Harrison.

Congratulating Robin Williams on surviving the hill race at the Lonach Games 2000 – while my badger nibbled his willie.

Showing off my hairy nether region to Fiona Kennedy.

David Attenborough is always good for a laugh! On *Parky* with him and Michael Caine, 2007.

Me under the mural of me by John Byrne (the artist known as Patrick) – one of three recent Glasgow murals of me by three different artists.

Posing with my wifey on Sixth Avenue in New York City… I led the Tartan Parade that day. Wonderful!

Drawing in my studio at home in the Florida Keys.

Unicorn with birthday loaf.

The day I discovered that having a gold banjo doesn't make you a better player.

thrilled. It shut a lot of people up. I called up my brother Michael and said, 'See? I told you!' But the truth was, two years earlier when I boasted to him that I'd be on *Top of the Pops* one day, I was just bullshitting. I never expected to be Numero Uno, up there with 10cc and Slade, in a purple polka dot suit.

At that time, when I was finally getting the level of fame I'd always dreamed about, people around me must have thought I was on top of the world. The kind of attention I was getting was a great ego boost, but there was another side to it. There was always this voice inside me that said I didn't deserve it, that I was worthless, that I'd soon be 'found out' and everything I had achieved would disappear. Sooner or later, I'd be unknown and penniless, and no one would care about me any more. For my entire life as a famous guy I have struggled with that voice. It has never let me be at peace with my success.

I made another single with Phil Coulter: 'In the Brownies', a novelty record based on the Village People hit 'In the Navy'. In my video I played all of the members of the Village People – as Brownies. I wore a Brownie uniform from the waist down, and my top half was a Hells Angel motorcyclist, a cowboy, a fireman and a sailor. It wasn't easy to find a Brownie dress to fit me. The people in charge of the uniforms were suspicious. 'What do you want it for?'

'It's for my little sister. We're remarkably similar in size . . .'

———

By the time my daughter Cara arrived we were living in Hyndland. Then a bit later I bought a beautiful house in Redlands Road in the West End of Glasgow, but people were looking through the windows. So, we moved to Drymen in the countryside. We had two Labradors with a litter of puppies, four Persian cats and two donkeys. Three acres of woodland with a river running through it seemed to be a perfect family setting. Wee Cara was a calm baby, just like Jamie. They used to sleep until nine or ten in the morning. We even had to wake them up on Christmas Day. I called Cara 'the sleepy dumpling'.

All our babies loved being washed and dried. I used to do a thing called 'Rub a Dub'. You get them out of the bath and kneel them on the floor on a bathmat and throw a big towel over them, then rub-a-dub their bodies. So, they're in this cave being rub-a-dubbed. But one day you go up to rub-a-dub them and you find that the bathroom is locked. The game has changed. You don't have it any more – they've grown up. You feel like crying because the baby has gone away. But it turns out lovely. Our babies have grown into very touchy people. They still kiss me goodnight now in their thirties and forties. Jamie's over fifty and he still kisses me goodnight. And it's a joy.

19

IF YOU CAN LIE ON THE FLOOR
WITHOUT HOLDING ON,
YOU'RE NOT DRUNK

——

I HAVEN'T VOMITED for a long time. I don't miss it. I knew a lot about vomiting when I used to drink. Drinkers can vomit without losing a step. They can walk along the street going: *bluuuurp!* 2, 3, 4, 5, 6, 7, 8, *bluuuuurp!* 2, 3, 4, 5, 6, 7, 8. I used to do great African singing when I was vomiting. *Weyhooh! Yehoooh!* I'll tell you what, though. How come every time you're sick there's diced carrots in it? Because I've never eaten diced carrots in my life! You can have lamb madras, a few bevvies, and *Huughhie!!!* Diced carrots. *Raaaalff!!!* More diced carrots! Every time! My personal theory is that there's a pervert somewhere, with pockets full of diced carrots, following drunk guys.

———

I've been vomited on by three women in my life. I know what you're thinking – 'First time: accident, second time: coincidence, third time: *your* fault, Billy' – and that's pretty much the case. I already told you about the first time – outside the dance hall in Glasgow. A few years later I met a hippyish girl at a gig in Edinburgh. She was American, and a bit naive. I told her that you could change your star sign in Scotland, and she believed me. She asked me what sign I was. I said, 'I'm Sagittarius. I used to be Gemini, but I changed it at the post office. Cost a fiver, and I've been much happier ever since.'

She said, 'Wow! You want to go to a party?'

I said, 'Certainly.'

There were a lot of people sitting around in silence, just listening to records and smoking marijuana. I thought it was boring. They were getting upset with me because I was fluttering round with the record player. I made a cylinder with holes in it and put a lightbulb inside it like a disco ball so it would spin around on the turntable and create light patterns around the room.

Eventually the girl said, 'Come on. Let's go next door.' She had an enormous army sleeping bag and invited me to join her inside it. I thought, 'Oh yeah!' The two of us got into the bag. Suddenly she started shuddering. I said, 'Are you okay?' She said, '*Urrrrgghh*', shuddering again. I said, 'What's wrong?' We were in the dark because I had tied the neck of the sleeping bag tight. Then she shuddered again. Violently. 'Jesus! Something wrong with you?' '*Uurrggg Brroghhh!*' She vomited on me. I said, 'Oh fuck!' I shot to the bottom of the sleeping bag, trying to get the vomit off me. But she vomited again. And again. Now it was like a wave, and I was swimming in it. I paddled up to the top of the bag to try to get us out, but the hole was all covered in sick and I couldn't loosen the knot. She just kept on vomiting. We were both flailing around in this Scotch broth. Well, it was apples – she was vomiting apples. Eventually I managed to break the knot and shot out of the top. As I was coming out, completely covered in sick, a guy wearing a cowboy hat walked into the room. I was yowling: 'Help! Heeeelp!!' But he stayed well away.

'Jesus Christ!' he said, calling to people in the next room: 'There's a giant maggot in here and it's giving birth!'

The third time a woman vomited on me was when I was doing a ninety-night tour. We were in the town of Newton Stewart in south-west Scotland, and my crew held a party in my room. I had passed out after my show – which may have been due to an interesting wee cigarette my roadie gave me; it was so strong I had to smoke it in bed. Once I was out for the count, the crew brought all their groupies upstairs to my suite – and invited half the town up there as well. It must have been like Gomorrah in my room. A Hieronymus Bosch painting. When I woke up in the morning, the place was wrecked, and I didn't know what had happened. 'Oh, *shit!*' I thought: 'I must have got up during the night and wrecked the place!' So, I put everything more or less back in order again and hoped the hotel wouldn't find out. Then I smelled something awful. 'Aw – I've been *sick*! Aw, it's in my hair ... Wait a minute! Spaghetti Hoops??? I don't eat *Spaghetti Hoops*!!! What the fuck was goin' on there???'

I found out later that during the party a girl had come over to look at me in the bed: 'Is that him?'

One of the roadies said, 'Aye, that's him.'

'I've never seen him in real life before! I've only seen him on TV! I'll tell you—' *Bleuuuuuuuuuuaaaaaaaaggghhh!* She vomited on my head. I didn't wake up, but mayhem followed – a rush out of my room, people panicking ... and that was the end of the midnight parties.

———

I always admired people who could take drugs and still function. I'm usually like an Egyptian mummy. 'Heeeelp me!' Drugs were never my thing. I could never handle them. In the early days of the folk scene, I mainly drank beer. I limited myself to nine pints at a time. Sometimes I had more than that, but nine was my usual. I wasn't exactly a connoisseur. I could never be bothered with real ale and all that. People talked about good beer and bad beer, but as far as I was concerned there was no such thing. There was only beer.

Once I became a solo artist and began to tour with roadies, I started drinking spirits. My roadies and I named whole tours after different drinks. There was the 'gin tour', the 'vodka tour' and the 'whisky tour'. As soon as I came offstage, I would be handed a lit cigarette and an extra-large glass of alcohol, and the evening would start right then and there.

————

Jamie Wark was my first roadie. I met him in the Scotia Bar when I was in The Humblebums with Tam. I was chatting to him one night, and I said, 'I'm stuck for getting to Fife.' He said, 'I'll take you for petrol money.' That was the start of a long and riotous assembly. He was honest and brave. He would wake me up in the morning with a cup of tea and protective equipment. He had to prod me awake with a sweeping brush because I would lash out and become very violent. Fortunately, Jamie managed to be fleet of foot. He'd do the Muhammad Ali shuffle. I don't really know why I was violent as I was waking up. Hung over, probably . . . although it might have been an early sign of Parkinson's disease. Recently, I was diagnosed with sleep behaviour disorder because, apparently, I have raging battles during the night. I yell and swear and thrash about – and have done so for years. I rarely remember the fights, although I did once wake up in horror after dreaming I'd murdered Paul McCartney and buried him at the traffic lights in Glasgow Cross. But during my early tours, Jamie would have to poke me with the brush and say, 'Get ready. You're going to America!' After I calmed down, I'd realise I'd have been out getting pissed the night before and hadn't packed. He'd throw my stuff in a suitcase and push me out the door. I was a mess.

Jamie was with me for many years. Knew where the bodies were buried. He could tell you some stories. Stuff I can't remember because I was legless. He always looked after me. Except . . . a stage hypnotist in New Zealand once put him in a trance and he became really aggressive towards me. At the time, I didn't know he'd been hypnotised so I was mystified because he was normally very helpful. I asked him to help me with something and he glared at me: 'What's your problem?'

I said, 'I don't have a problem – I just need a new banjo string.'

He said, 'Get it yourself.' It was impressive.

———

In a recent TV interview, Paul McCartney called me 'the first rock 'n' roll comedian'. Nice of him, considering I'd done away with the man. I suppose I did look more like a rock 'n' roll guy. I would perform like a rock star, in rock star venues, but for audiences the question never arose about whether I was a rocker or a comedian. I was just a Billy Connolly. But in those days I did think of myself as being part of the rock 'n' roll scene, and behaved accordingly. Bad behaviour, crazy behaviour, out-of-control antics – even dangerous stunts – were just expected of rock 'n' rollers and their touring bands. Rod Stewart's crew was legendary. Famous nutters. Once when they were performing in New Zealand a guy from the local promoter's team took them all to dinner, and in the middle of the meal one of them grabbed his toupee and flambéed it.

Rod and I once hitch-hiked up the M4 together. We were going to a football match in Scotland – Rod had invited me, and his uncle had picked us up in London and was driving us to Heathrow. But his van broke down somewhere around Slough, so we jumped out and tried to thumb a lift. Within seconds, a guy in a red Mini screeched to a halt and picked us up. He would soon regret his kindness, because just outside the airport there was a traffic jam, and Rod and I persuaded him to whizz us through on the hard shoulder. Unsurprisingly, police officers pulled him over just short of our terminal. We jumped out and scarpered to catch our plane, leaving the poor guy to fend for himself. He called a radio station and told his story, though, and was a bit of a celebrity for a while.

———

I'd always been drawn to the wildness of rock 'n' roll. I learned about it when I was at a school camp in Aberdeen. We were 'camping' in dormitories at a school in a little town called Torry, and they took us to see *Rock, Rock, Rock!* – a black and white movie starring Chuck Berry. It was brilliant. Berry blew everybody away with his 'duck walk'. I could hardly believe what I was seeing. We had a record player at the camp, and the teachers brought Chuck Berry's single 'School Days'. We played it non-stop. Berry was a staggering musician – the best rock guitarist in the world in his time. You couldn't keep your feet still. I also loved Gene Vincent, who looked like a Teddy boy and sang 'Bee-Bop-a-Lula'. Fats Domino wasn't so rebellious – just a fat jolly guy

– but he used to end his show by pushing the piano off the stage with his stomach, singing: '*I wanna walk you home*'. When Bill Haley's film *Rock Around the Clock* came out, there was mayhem in Glasgow theatres. We were dancing in the aisles, yelling: '*See You Later, Alligator!*' Meanwhile, our parents were still singing along to '*I'm a pink toothbrush, you're a blue toothbrush*' . . .

Both Little Richard and Chuck Berry claimed to have invented rock 'n' roll, but I thought Little Richard had the best voice, and wrote the best songs. He would stand on the piano and demand that his audience tell him that they love him. Wonderful. He even claimed to have invented the colour purple.

Chuck Berry punched Keith Richards once. It was captured during the making of a documentary. When Keith was alone in a room, he decided to lift Chuck's guitar out of its case, but Chuck walked in and caught him. The very thought of punching Keith Richards! It's like punching the Pope. Such people became my idols, and the more outrageous they were, the more I loved them.

When my manager Frank leased and renovated the Apollo – a music venue with 3,500 capacity in Renfield Street in Glasgow – I could watch the rock bands' rehearsals – bands like Status Quo, Fleetwood Mac and Lynyrd Skynyrd. It was thrilling, and a real education. When I was in The Humblebums, our sound check consisted of each of us reciting one short ditty into our microphone:

I wanted apple dumpling,
And do you know what came?
Rice pudding, rice pudding
Wasn't that a shame?

I was astounded by the skill of some of the internationally known rock bands. When I saw The Who, Pete Townshend suddenly did this windmill thing with his arm – hitting his guitar strings on the way down – while simultaneously jumping in the air with a scissors kick. I was so captivated by it that tears began rolling down my cheeks. It was almost unbearably exciting; Mick Jagger's dancing had the same effect on me.

In the sixties and seventies, rock bands were all trying to outdo each other with their antics – often acts of vandalism. John Bonham from Led Zeppelin phoned me once. He was in a hotel room in Seattle where the rooms had been built over the water. He told me there was a covered hole in the middle of the room through which you could fish. I said, 'That's nice, Bonzo. D'you like to fish?' He said, 'No . . . but I've broken up all the furniture and pushed it through the hole.'

He phoned another time and said he had hired a pool table. Once it arrived, he'd broken it up into tiny pieces that could fit into a matchbox. He had stacked these pieces together like a mountain of splinters and was waiting for the guy who rented him the table to come and pick it up.

Keith Moon had the same hobby. I heard he once threw dynamite into a hotel toilet. Blew it up. Then he went down to reception and said, 'Sorry, but I've had a bit of an accident in the bathroom.' 'Don't you worry, Mr Moon – there's no need to be embarrassed. We'll take care of it.' They went upstairs with mops . . . and found the place in bits.

I believe another time Keith went to Pete Townshend's room and glued all the furniture to the ceiling. I ran into Keith the night before I flew to Australia to start another tour. We were in a club called Morton's in Berkeley Square in London, with the actor John Hurt. Keith wasn't drinking that night – he told me he'd stopped. He said, 'I'm taking brandy suppositories instead.' I left Morton's at 1 a.m. and caught an early flight. By the time I arrived in Australia the newspapers all said Keith Moon was dead.

I met Led Zeppelin in L.A. at the Hyatt House – known in band circles as 'the Riot House'. That hotel was legendary for rock 'n' roll insanity. Behind the reception desk there was a photo of an unknown crazy-looking guy staring at the lens, with the caption: *'Be nice to him – he's probably sold a million'.*

Led Zeppelin band members had bought motorbikes for riding up and down the hotel corridors. I remember one night when they had a party in one of the rooms. They changed the guests every fifteen minutes, and there was a queue outside. A guy stood at the door with a box of glass vials containing amyl nitrate. He'd break one with his thumb and offer it to each guest to inhale as they went in. I remember kneeling on the floor with my head in the fridge. Good times.

———

I had known Elton's guitarist Davey Johnstone since he was fifteen. When I met him, he was a talented schoolboy with long blond hair, playing fantastic banjo in the folk clubs. Always laughing. Davey's still the same – finds everything funny. At the beginning of his career, he did a session playing the mandolin for one of Elton's albums, and afterwards Elton said, 'That was great – do you play guitar?' Davey said 'Yes' and ran out and bought one. Soon after, Davey joined Elton's band as his guitarist. One night I went to see Elton at the Apollo in Glasgow. We had a great laugh afterwards with Elton and his crew – and his manager John Reid. That night, someone – maybe it was Davey

– said, 'Why not get Billy for the American tour?' John said, 'Good idea.'

John Reid drove a Rolls-Royce. I had met him years before in Paisley when he worked in a fashion shop called Stylecraft. Then he disappeared to London and became massively successful, managing Elton John. His mother had lived on a housing estate in Paisley, and John used to drive up to see her in his Rolls-Royce. I knew a folk singer called Helen Gilderson who lived with her granny in the same estate. She told me her granny said: 'That John Reid . . . I think he's a motor mechanic. They let him bring cars home.'

At first, I thought opening for Elton was a great idea – but then I got nervous, because I'd never played such huge arenas or opened for anybody before. I was right to be concerned. Opening for rock 'n' roll stars is a mistake, because their audiences are not interested in anybody else. The roadies just stick you on with a microphone – no lights. 'That'll do you.' Then they use you to fiddle with the lights and sound. People are wandering into the auditorium as you're doing your thing. I wasn't on the marquee or the ticket or the T-shirt, so the first thing they knew of me was: 'Ladies and Gentlemen, please welcome Elton – *(Hrrrraaaaayyyyy!!!)* – John's friend – *(Ooooooohhhhh!!)* BILLY CONNOLLY!!! . . .' I'd be booed ON.

Elton's 1976 Bicentennial Tour was ten weeks long. I had some good nights, like Madison Square Garden – but they were very few. There'd usually be a pocket of about twenty people at the front going, 'Fuck Off! Fuck Off!' In Washington DC someone threw a brass smoking pipe and it hit me between the eyes. I fell to the ground and had to come offstage.

Elton is loved by other stars. Some great people came to see Elton. Elvis turned up in DC but didn't stay for the show. I tried to see him, but his entourage had encircled him, so I didn't even glimpse the hem of his garment. I told people I'd seen him, though. I did see Elizabeth Taylor – who looked beautiful. Big hair. And Alice Cooper – he spoke to me backstage. Asked me where I got my banana boots; I think he was jealous.

I felt comforted when I read a *Rolling Stone* article in which one of my heroes, Tom Waits, described opening for another band as 'a nightly exercise in terror', but I still hadn't learned my lesson. After Elton's tour I also opened for Elvis Costello, the Manhattan Transfer and Dr Hook & the Medicine Show. At least those artists played smaller venues, so I learned to be comfortable playing crowds several thousand strong. And they were listening audiences, so I had some very good nights. But with those artists I was playing almost every town in northern America, without really making a name for myself. I knew things would have to change – and they did. Within a few years I was returning to play those same large American venues – alone, and in front of my own audience.

EMBRACE THE NON SEQUITUR

———

I'VE BEEN WRITING this book by dictation, recording my thoughts into something called 'Otter' on my phone. I thought it would be simple. I thought it would automatically type everything up for me, but it turns out 'Otter' has never heard a Glasgow accent in its fucking life and has no idea how to transcribe it, so I had to get my daughters to slave away deciphering the whole thing. This kind of problem plagues Scottish people when they are talking into their TV remotes, in voice-activated elevators, and when trying to use automated phone systems. It's extremely irritating. Will someone please tell Otter this is an accent, not a fucking speech impediment?

Early on in my career, I knew I could become well known nationally – even internationally – but many people thought that was unlikely with my Glaswegian accent. Despite the way I talked, I was offered some national talk shows like *The Russell Harty Show*. I didn't want them. I thought, 'If I'm gonna do a talk show I'm going to do the best.' So, I said 'No' to them all for ages. Then it happened; Michael Parkinson was advised by Jimmy Reid that I'd be a great guest on his show. A taxi driver in Glasgow had also told Mike: 'You've got to get Billy Connolly,' and even gave him a copy of my album *Billy Connolly Live.* So, I got the call.

I didn't prepare what I was going to say on the show. In the car on the way to the studio my manager Frank Lynch was far more nervous than I. He said, 'What are you going to talk about, Billy?' I said, 'I dunno. Let's just see how it goes.' That was my usual approach for anything. Frank looked alarmed. He said, 'Well, whatever you do, don't tell that joke about the wife and the bicycle.' Big mistake. If someone tells me not to say something, it remains trapped in my mind until the pressure becomes too much, and I just have to let it out. So halfway through the interview, in front of the live audience, I thought, 'Fuck it!' and just blurted it out. I said, 'I hope I can get away with this. It's a beauty:

'This man, he says, "How's the wife?"'

'The other one says, "Ah, she's dead."'

'He says, "Wha?"'

'The other one says, "Dead. In the ground. I murdered her. Pffft. I'll show you if you want."'

'He says, "Aye, yeah, show me."'

'So, they go up to his tenement building, through the close – that's the entrance to the tenement . . .'

At this point I glanced sideways at Michael. He still seemed interested, so I continued.

'. . . And sure enough there's a big mound of earth. With a bum sticking out of it. He says, "Is that her?"'

'"Aye."'

'He says, "Why did you leave her bum sticking out?"'

'He says, "I need somewhere to park ma bike!"'

———

I imagine Frank was shitting himself, but he shouldn't have worried. The place was in an uproar. I was relieved that Mike wasn't afraid of that joke. Other TV hosts might have been scared that it would rock the boat, but he just laughed. The whole show worked well – in fact, the next day the whole country seemed to be talking about it. When I arrived back in Glasgow, people in the airport started applauding. Seeing someone being funny in their accent on the top BBC talk show really meant something to them. I ended up doing the *Parkinson* show about fifteen times over the years. I think I held the record. It was incredibly good for me, and I'm grateful to Mike. Being on his show even once did anyone's image and career the world of good. It made me think, 'Well, maybe I am quite good.'

Mike Parkinson knew exactly how to handle comedians. Many talk show hosts think that, when they have comedians as guests, they should try to lead them into 'material'– set up some funny bits in advance. Their producers call you and say, 'Tell us what you want to say, and we'll prompt you.' That's shite. You could do that with a ten-year-old. I never agreed to do what Americans call 'a pre-interview'. As long as the host can think on their feet it will always work well. They should leave us alone and trust us to be funny. Comedians are dying to be funny, and we'll deliver if you don't make it awkward for us.

The style of the chat show has appealed to me from the beginning. I have dreadful nerves before I go onstage for a live show, but I didn't have that anxiety before going on a chat show, even though there might be millions of people watching. I could always trust that Mike would plunge into a different subject if the interview was sliding a bit. Anyway, when you have a repu-tation for being wild, you can just look at the audience and they start to laugh. You gaze at them with a little threat in your eyes, and they think, 'Oh, this is gonna be good.' They will always rise to the fly. You mention your childhood, that you and your friend were competing to see who could pee the highest against a wall, and the audience will fall about. It reminds them of their own childhood.

You can do things in a chat show that you wouldn't do in a live show – gossip about people, mention that you either like or dislike politicians, film stars or sports figures. You can talk casually – about how much you admired Spike Milligan, for example. You couldn't do that in a live show. It would be weird.

The talk show is an underrated form of entertainment. But it's been ambushed by boring people who think they're funny. I think they've spoiled it. Johnny Carson's early shows are colossally good. I remember seeing Richard Pryor with Bette Davis and it was brilliant. If anybody had said to you: 'We'll have Bette Davis and Richard Pryor on together' there are people who would have said, 'Oh that won't work – they're so unalike.' Such people can always find something in common, whether it's their attitude to kissing on film or whatever. I always liked being on with David Attenborough. I could jump in and be funny, but I could also comment about something more serious and show my appreciation of his subject.

––––

I've always tried to wear Windswept and Interesting clothing on chat shows. And shoes – your shoes are always visible. If you look startling, the host will always have something to comment on. They like that. Once, when I went on *The Jay Leno Show* in Los Angeles, I wore a black wobbly Japanese suit and black open-toed shoes with silver buckles. Jay took in the whole thing, including my black toenail polish, and said, 'What are you – some kind of punk pilgrim?' For another appearance I wore my 'Irish Tiger' suit – a furry, green animal-print number. That earned me the title 'Tommy the Tiger's gay uncle'.

I went on a talk show in Canada with a famous host called Peter Gzowski. People there called him 'Captain Canada', but I called him 'Knife and Forksky'. On that occasion I wore my tights with a portrait of my face on my bum, with hair hanging down, so I could wave my hair by shaking my backside. That's where I met Robin Williams, who became my dear pal. Robin had his own views about my outfits: 'He does wear a lot of unusual clothes for a heterosexual, and I'm using the word "heterosexual" very loosely. The voice, the look, and clothes that even a drag queen would go "Oh, puhhlease . . . !"'

On one of my *Parkinson* appearances, I wore a jacket decorated by John Byrne. I'd run into John one day in Glasgow, when – for some reason – I was wearing a white suit. I'd had a ballpoint pen in the breast pocket, but it leaked, and ink had seeped through the cloth. I said to John, 'Look at this fucking mess.' And he said, 'Give it to me.' When he returned the jacket, the ink stain had been turned into a swallow's tail, and it was entirely covered in fabulous images – a rabbit, a dog, roses, hearts and a big baby in Victorian dress with a banjo. Brilliant.

My favourite *Parkinson* show was the one with Sting. We played 'Blue Christmas' together – guitar and banjo. And I liked being on with Lauren Bacall. She laughed easily – and I remember Angie Dickinson did too. She was on camera when I was talking about opening for Elton John in America and said that the audience made me feel *as welcome as a fart in a spacesuit*. Angie just lost it.

———

Whenever I think of something like that, I need to say the line right away. If it happens to you, give it air. Your first thought is to keep it for a better time, but you're much better to blurt it out, no matter where you are. People will remember it, and they'll tell other people. It's happened to me lots of times and I'm eternally grateful. I'll create some of these lines onstage when I'm in the middle of telling stories I've heard from others. I'll throw them in, then elongate and embellish them, get distracted and talk about something else in the middle, until they turn into very long pieces with only the bare bones of the original story.

I liked to adapt stories about life in Glasgow. Peter McDougall told me he was in a pub in Greenock and a fireman came in and stood next to him at the bar. He put a cardboard box in front of him and ordered a drink. Then he said to the guy on the other side of him: 'I'm going for a piss. Could you keep an eye on my doo?' ('Doo' is a Scottish word for pigeon.) The guy said, 'Sure.' The box was closed, though, and the guy was curious . . . he wondered if there was really a doo in there or not, so he couldn't resist opening the box. The pigeon shot out and started flying around the pub. Then it landed on one of the highest rafters. Everyone was trying to get it down. They were all making pigeon noises: *Wrrrwwwrr!! Wrrrwwwrr!!* – as if that was going to help. The fireman comes out of the toilet, furious. 'What did you do with my doo?'

'I just got curious and opened the box, and it flew out.'

The fireman says, 'Get me a ladder!'

Someone got him a ladder and they put it up to the rafter. He was halfway up the ladder – and had nearly caught the pigeon

– when the idiot who'd let it out decided to grab a cloth and take a mighty swipe at it. The bird took off in fright, and flew away to the other side of the pub. The fireman says to the barman: 'Do us a favour? Phone for two ambulances. One for the doo – and one for this bastard!'

That story eventually became a long, meandering piece that worked very well onstage. But when I went on chat shows, I didn't have the luxury of being able to tell a long story. I had to come up with very short stories and lines – and I mostly just threw out whatever came into my mind. As I said before, I'm a wee bit distractible. I imagine you already know that about me, especially if you saw any of my stage shows. Some people think it's a fault that I forget where I'm going and deviate to other subjects without warning, but I enjoy it immensely. It's like riding along on a wave. You don't know where you're going, but your path is laden with gems and rose petals of funny stuff that makes people scream and clap. They recognise that you're on a precarious trip. You can call it 'an inability to concentrate' if you like, but I'll have it any day over somebody who's got 'an act'. Sometimes I'll see comedians who are good, but they've written everything down first. You can always tell written material because it's in 'Aren't I the clever one?' language.

When I'm onstage, or when I'm having a conversation or trying to write, I get this thing in the side of my head saying, 'Me! Me! Talk about ME! I'M funnier than this!' It's like standing in a playground beside a roundabout, wanting to get on. That's what my ideas are doing at the side of my head – waiting to get on the roundabout. I can't ignore them. They threaten me: 'Talk about me NOW or I'll go away!' I just have to leave what I was saying before and go onto the new thing. If I don't talk about it right away, I forget it, and that makes me upset. Sometimes it does come back into my mind – but not 'til next April.

People do seem to recognise my jumbled weaving of stories as an art or skill, and if I ever manage to get back to the previous subject, a wonderful laugh erupts. But it's really just something I can't help. When I was a boy, my father subscribed to a monthly American pulp fiction magazine called *Argosy*, and I would borrow it. It contained short stories in various literary genres such as crime, war stories and adventure, but each story was interrupted by an advertisement. You'd get halfway through a story and it would say, '*Continued on page 32*'. You were supposed to thumb through the magazine until you found the next bit of the story, but I could never be bothered. I'd just keep reading through the magazine from page one to the end – so all the stories would be mixed together. I really liked the wee jolt I got when I turned the page and there I was – back at the continuation of an earlier story I'd almost forgotten about. I sometimes think that magazine may have affected my brain. Perhaps it irrevocably altered my thinking style, because my concerts took on a similar pattern.

––––

When I went on American chat shows I occasionally got to meet my heroes, like Mötley Crüe – we compared notes on piercings because the drummer and I had both been pierced by Cliff Cadaver in L.A. But most often, I didn't get to meet the other guests because we were on at different times. I met more of my heroes at live concerts, like John Prine, whom I met when we both headlined in Cambridge. I met Bob Dylan at a festival in London. I was backstage, watching Eric Clapton from the wings.

A familiar guy came wandering in and said, 'Hello!' like he knew me. I said, 'Hello' back, thinking, 'Jesus! Bob Dylan knows me!' Then I thought he might have mistaken me for someone else because I couldn't remember meeting him before. At the end of his set Eric Clapton came offstage and started talking to both of us. I tried not to speak too much because I thought if Bob heard my accent, he'd realise he didn't know me. Eric had a big patch of sweat under his arm. Dylan pointed to it and said, 'What's that?' Eric said, 'You wouldn't know, man.'

Next time I met Bob Dylan was on the David Letterman show in New York. I said to David, 'I was watching TV last night in the hotel and you said, "Tomorrow night my guests are Billy Connolly and Bob Dylan." In that order.' I said, 'Thanks for putting me in the same sentence as Bob Dylan.' A couple of years later Bob Dylan did an online radio show and he attributed a saying to me. It wasn't my line, but it's good: *'Before you can know somebody you have to walk a mile in his shoes. But by then he's a mile away and you've got his shoes so who gives a fuck?'*

21

IF YOUR HEART STOPS, APPLY VINEGAR

—

AFTER MY FIRST appearance on *Parkinson* there was a dramatic increase in the size of my live audiences. I sold out the Pavilion Theatre in Glasgow for two weeks, and people in other countries started becoming aware of me – especially in Australia, New Zealand and Canada. I started touring overseas, usually performing ninety nights in a row in each country.

Australia is one of my favourite places in the world. I love it. It has genuine optimism. The people are nice. It's an attractive place, with good-looking towns. There's a lovely devil-may-care attitude. They don't mind getting into trouble. They're not stiff-arsed people, they're fun-loving rebellious folks. I felt very comfortable in their company. I even married an Aussie – well, Pamela was born in New Zealand, which is a nice thing as well, but she grew up in Sydney.

Sydney's a brilliant city. One of the highlights of my Australian tours was walking over the Sydney Harbour Bridge in my cowboy boots with a film crew in a helicopter above me capturing it all for my *World Tour of Australia* TV show. I also climbed to the top of the Sydney Opera House and sat astride it like I was riding on a giant white sailboat. I have had a great time playing the Opera House over the years; I broke the record there, for fifty sold-out shows. And Sydney audiences remember the night my concert was so long the car park closed and nobody could drive home.

I was always starving after my show. Within walking distance of the Opera House was Harry's Café de Wheels, a food truck that sold delicious pies sitting in pea soup – pie floaters. Australian pies are the best. Adelaide had a brilliant pie floater truck just outside the Festival Theatre – I used to nip there after the show. It was so close I could take the pie back to eat in my dressing room. When I was doing my *World Tour of Australia*, we filmed that food truck in Adelaide. There was a queue outside it, and when the episode was shown on TV in Scotland, a woman recognised her son in the queue. She hadn't been in touch with him for years. I got my Australian promoter to help her find him. They put a picture in the paper, and mother and son found each other again. I like when those things happen.

———

The best reunion was when I was playing at a university in San Diego. A man came up and said, 'Hello, Billy. Did you ever know a man called Jimmy Logan?'

I said, 'I know two Jimmy Logans. One was a comedian and the other one's a welder.'

He said, 'It's the welder I'm talking about. He's my brother.'

I said, 'Oh great! I knew Jimmy well. We often went to the dancing together.'

He said, 'Oh, I know that. He wrote to me and told me. You were his first Catholic friend. We used to give him pelters about it.'

They were all Rangers-supporting Protestants, while I was a Celtic-supporting Catholic.

He said, 'I've lost touch with Jimmy.'

I said, 'I thought he went off to be a football player in Bloemfontein? What became of him?'

He said, 'I think he fell on hard times with the drinking . . .'

I said, 'Well, I'm going to South Africa. I'll look for him.'

He looked at me doubtfully. I explained: 'A lot of Scottish people come to see me – they might know his whereabouts.'

So, while I was touring South Africa, I'd go out in the morning to meet homeless people, some of whom were Scottish. Finally, in Johannesburg, one of them said, 'Oh I know Jimmy! He's in Durban.'

When we got to Durban, I went out on the prowl again. There was a guy standing in a park with a toilet roll in his hand. I said, 'Are you Scottish?' – not because of the toilet paper, but I'd heard him shouting to somebody.

He said, 'Aye, who wants to know?'

I said, 'I'm looking for a guy called Jimmy Logan.'

He said, 'What for?'

I said, 'His brother wants to be in touch again.'

He said, 'That's him', and pointed to the ground. There was Jimmy, lying in a flowerbed.

I went up and said 'Jimmy Logan?'

He said, 'Billy Connolly. Ya bastard. What are you doing here?'

I said, 'I'm looking for you.'

He said, 'You cannae find me. I'm a hobo.'

I said, 'I was talking to your brother in San Diego. He's worried about you.' Then we spoke about the dancing. He was always a big star at the dance halls – dead flashy.

Jimmy seemed to be in an awful state. I went to my merchandise guy and borrowed some cash. Then I went to see Jimmy's pal Willie Waddel – a second-hand car dealer. I'd learned that Jimmy went there most days for cups of tea and company. I gave the money to Willie. 'See that Jimmy gets it. But don't give it to him all at once!'

'Nae problem, Billy.'

I met Jimmy the following day. He'd got some of the money, and he was plastered, but he'd got in touch with his brother. He said, 'Can I come to your gig?' So, I said to my promoter, 'I've got some friends coming tonight. They're a little rough around the edges.'

'No problem, I'll sort them out.' He set up a little circle of beer crates with food and drink just outside the big 3,000-seater tent I was playing in – and Jimmy and his cronies sat there and had a whale of a time. They shouted at me all night. 'Yer rubbish! Get arffff!'

———

I rode around the Australian continent and New Zealand on a trike for my *World Tour of Australia* and *World Tour of New Zealand*. I'd had a long-term fascination with trikes. I'd seen them in magazines, and they fitted into my motorcycling fantasies – a cross between a motorcycle and a hot rod. I liked the idea of posing around on one, so I picked up a purple Harley trike in Australia, had brilliant adventures on it, then shipped it back to Britain after the tour.

I wish I could ride a trike again, but a few years ago I nearly killed myself on one. I was filming an American tour on a trike with a Ford engine, travelling the whole of the famous Route 66 highway, from Chicago to L.A. At a point where Route 66 changes, you have to come off the freeway and do a sort of U-turn back onto a new road. I drove under a bridge to do the U-turn, but for some reason I tried to drive up a mound of earth and the bike tumbled on top of me. Broke my ribs. They had to medevac me to the hospital. I was lying in the helicopter and the paramedic said, 'On a scale of one to ten, what's your pain level?'

I said, 'About two.'

He looked at me in disbelief. 'C'mon. You've got two broken ribs. You can talk to me about it.'

I said, 'No – it's about two.'

He said, 'Billy, you can tell me. I've got the whole candy store here!'

I said, 'I'm still a two.'

It was a huge mistake, because at that point I wasn't moving. I was strapped down. When I had to change position, it was much more painful. Getting in and out of bed was like being assaulted by professionals.

You can damage yourself any place in the world, but Australia is special; they have a lot of unique things that can hurt you. Not so much New Zealand. When you see those guys doing the Maori haka – like the All Blacks do before a rugby match – you always think New Zealanders will bite your face off, but, in reality, the worst that will happen to you in New Zealand is you could scrape your toe on one of those wee ferns. Australia is much scarier. The sun there, for example – Scottish people can't take it. The hotels are full of British people with no skin. We really don't know how to *do* it, do we? We don't know how to sunbathe. Especially Scottish and Irish people. We should never be in hot places. Our skin just falls off. You see these people in the morning: 'Don't *touch* me! Don't fuckin' TOUCH me!' Whole families with no skin, all of them screaming, 'DON'T TOUCH ME!' Honeymoon couples: 'DON'T TOUCH ME!' Children on their fourth nose of the week! There's a wee pile of Nivea cream where their noses used to be!

I went into a shop to get some sunscreen because I'm a pale-blue Scottish person. It takes me a week to get white. The suntan oils and creams in Australia usually have SPF factors from fifteen up to sixty. I said, 'I need a ninety-six.'

The woman in the shop said, 'Ninety-six? Christ – how about a shed?'

I said, 'Fuck it, never mind. I'll just wear my boiler suit and balaclava.'

As for the wildlife in Australia – I really don't know how Pamela survived to adulthood. There are so many scary creatures sneaking about the place, just waiting to pounce. I went into a corner shop in Palm Beach once, to buy my favourite sweeties – Minties. Australia has delicious sweeties. There was a jar, like a honey jar, on the counter, and in it was the nastiest-looking spider I've ever seen in my life. It was in liquid, and had been dead for years, but it was still terrifying – shiny, with giant fangs and a pointy willy between its second set of legs. I said to the woman serving me, 'What's *that*?!!'

She said, 'Oh, that's the famous funnel-web spider.'

I said, 'Oh yeah? Where do they live? Miles away, I suppose, way out in the bush?'

'Oh no,' she said. 'These killer funnel-webs are local. Their venom's deadly. Watch out you don't get bitten. We caught this one in a garden across the street.'

I said, 'I'm staying here – right *near* those fuckers!'

Then she said this thing that thousands of people have said to me in my life, and they were all lying. She said, 'Don't worry. It won't bother you if you don't annoy it.' Who the hell annoys these bastards? Is anybody that bored that they get up in the morning and go: 'Aw, I'm so bored! I think I'll go and annoy that funnel-web spider!' The woman failed to tell me what annoys it. Probably breathing and stuff.

———

My own breathing annoys other people. I've got sleep apnoea. I used to say I 'suffered' from it. But I don't. *I've* just 'got' it. My *wife* suffered from it. It's a snoring disease. I'd breathe normally at first, then pretty soon I'd be snoring heavily – then suddenly I'd stop breathing. Anyone in the vicinity would think I'd died. Then suddenly I'd snort into life again: *Cccchhhhhhrrraggggghhhh!* Pamela's jumping up in the air. I took some convincing about this. You never believe you've got sleep apnoea because you're not awake. In the mornings, she'd say, 'You were a *nightmare* last night!'

'Nonsense!'

Eventually, I gave in and went to a sleep specialist. The guy had a big telly in his surgery. He put cameras up my nose, and we looked at the inside of my nose and down my throat on the telly. 'Aye, fine, very good, yeah . . .' Then he told me that at my age, when you lie on your back, everything around your nose and throat sort of collapses. All the fleshy bits settle on top of each other. I had already tried putting a big pile of pillows to stop me rolling from my side onto my back, but it was a waste of time – I just pushed them away in my sleep. Then the specialist said, 'One of my patients had a breakthrough.' He said, 'You get a T-shirt with a pocket on it and wear it backwards. And you put a tennis ball in the pocket.' So, when you try to roll over you feel the ball sticking into your back – 'Ow!' So you move back onto your side again. Well, that worked quite well. I was actually waking up feeling okay. But the tennis ball was too soft, so I got an apple. During the night it would get warm, and I'd eat it in the morning – perfect!

A bit later I went on tour in Australia. I said to my manager, Steve, 'I've forgotten my T-shirt and my ball.' He's looking at me like I'm mentally ill. So I explained it to him, and I went off into the town to get replacements. There was one of those stores that sell everything – bags and things and plastic spades and stuff. I saw a football and I thought, 'Well . . . if an *apple* works, a football would be amazing – I'd never roll over on top of *that*.' So, I got myself a football, and I bought a plastic backpack. At night, I was completely naked with a backpack on. When Steve heard about that, he says, 'I want to see you when you're going to bed!'

I said, 'Fuck off!'

The next day I was sitting having breakfast with Steve, and the waitress said to me, 'You look a bit tired.'

Steve said, 'No wonder – he's been *hiking* all night!'

———

Once I went for a walk in a town in north Queensland before my gig. There was a big notice board saying *'Beware!'* So, I was being as ware as possible. *'Beware – Stingers!'* Stingers? I didn't know what they were. I don't know if they burrowed holes in the ground, dropped out of trees or arrived in taxis. I thought

I'd better read on: *'Stingers are box jellyfish'.* My God, I thought, these fuckers are gift-wrapped – what kind of country is this? It said, *'If the heart stops, douse the wound liberally with vinegar.'* Back in Scotland we prefer to treat a heart stoppage with CPR and major surgery.

On the same tour I was watching the Australian news and they said, 'Don't go among the rock pools today, as we've seen the unwelcome return of the blue-ringed octopus.' They put up a picture of it. This wee killer's got bright-blue rings on its legs, and it's going 'Fuck off!' If he stings you, you don't even make it to the phone. You're looking for a stinger to take the edge off the pain. I'm warning you. Australia is a dangerous place! Australians must be the bravest buggers on the face of the earth. Imminent danger every fucking day.

———

When my kids were small, we'd all go to Australia – my wife and I and the children – get a place by the beach, and have two or three weeks of family holiday time before I started my Australian tour. Then they'd fly home, and I'd go to work. It was a nice arrangement. We were there once, and my plan was to swim and get fit for my tour. So, I started to swim in the sea, and it was wonderful. I was getting stronger and a bit braver every day. I don't really like swimming, and I've never been good at it. Pamela tried to encourage me. She said, 'I was watching you yesterday, you're getting better all the time, aren't you?' I said, 'Oh, yeah, I'm doing okay. But d'you know what gets on my nerves? Those bloody car alarms! Every day when I'm swimming in the ocean I hear car alarms. Again and again!' Pamela looked at me with that look that women give you that says, 'Why have I put up with you for so long?' But all she said was: 'Billy – that's the shark alarm.' It took a while for this to sink in. Because after the alarm went off, people were still swimming. I suppose they work on the basis that sharks only eat one person at a time. If I'd known, I'd be headed for the shore like a Polaris missile, throwing children behind me, screaming, 'Get out of the fucking water!' They'd be saying: 'What's with the blue prick?'

Something similar happened to me when I was snorkelling in Barbados. I was a bit nervous because I'd just seen *Jaws* for the first time – you know that movie about a shark that plays the cello? It put me off being in the sea. Every time I put my head underwater, I heard, *'dun dun dun dun dun dun dun dun . . .'*

'What the hell? There's some bugger playing a cello here!' I kept telling myself: 'Conquer it, Billy, conquer it!'

In Barbados you don't need to go far out to see incredible things. I was just enjoying myself looking at all the wee fish when something told me to look behind me. I turned round, and my heart stopped. Not five feet behind me was a black fin. I thought, 'Oh fuck. Shaaaaark!!!!' I took off like a motorboat, thrashing the water to a foam. I was streaking through the water like a torpedo. I turned round again to see if it was gaining on me . . . and that's when I realised – it was my own flipper.

We don't belong in the sea. We've no business being there. The things that live in there don't like us! They sting and nip us. I've even been *burned* by fire coral in the Bahamas. Some of these creatures like to eat us, or they have arms that stick to us and drown us. When are we going to take the hint? We are not welcome in there! Underwater stones are covered in slippery stuff, so you fall and hurt your arse. And it's wet and uncomfortable in there! Our species spent thousands of years getting out of the sea, and the first thing we do when we go on holiday is run back in! People go diving, and when they get down there, they see a hole and go, 'Wonder what's in there?' and they stick their hand in. No wonder something bites them: 'Ow, bastard bit me!' they say. That's not a bastard, that's his *house*! How would *you* like it if you were eating your Sunday dinner, and a big hairy arm came in your window? You'd jab it with a fork, right? 'Fuck off!'

———

I was filming on an island in the far north of Australia. Aboriginal Australian women were catching mud crabs, and they were incredibly good at it. Once we finished, we were making our way along the beach, headed back to our boat. Some of our crew, who'd been taking a wee dip to cool off, came running out of the water shouting, 'Shark!! SHAAARRRKKK!!!' The women immediately dropped what they were carrying except for their spears and ran *into* the water yelling, 'DINNER!!!'

There's been a change in the way I see sharks. I don't really mind them now. It always surprised the hell out of me that when you're next to sharks underwater, you're not frightened by them. You can stand outside the water and see the sharks and be quite frightened. Then you dive in and go down beside them so you're in the same world as them, and you're not frightened any more. Then when you come out, you're frightened again. It's beyond me. They're the most beautiful creatures but they've got weird eyes. Sleekit. Deadly eyes that have gazed upon awfulness.

Most sharks are not our predators, and we're not their food. But people say, 'They *might* bite you – but it would be a case of mistaken identity.' Mistaken? Do I LOOK like a walrus? Maybe so. But you have to be resigned. If a pan-aggressive shark turns on you, it turns on you. The game's up. There's absolutely nothing you can do about it. Your tea's out – as they say in Glasgow.

I learned to scuba-dive in Fiji, and it was wonderful. I had a few mishaps at the beginning, like dropping my weight belt and forgetting to check my gauges. I had to be rescued a couple of times, but I finally got to be like Jacques Cousteau, swishing around the coral, gliding around the seagrass, watching all the strange wee creatures down there, just going about their business. It was weird though, because being under the sea is like swimming through a giant sex act. Everything down there looks like a giant penis or vagina – sea cucumbers, eels, anemones, clam shells . . . Cousteau never brought that up in his TV shows.

I started to feel comfortable being in the sea. I didn't mind coming across a giant, open-jawed barracuda or a big green eel with ferocious teeth – after a while I realised they didn't really want to bother with me. Eventually, once I got the hang of diving, I started messing around, doing skits at thirty or forty feet. My favourite underwater trick is to get my buoyancy bang on and stand still vertically. Just stand there looking bored when people swim past. Nod to them as if you're waiting at a bus stop. Look at your watch. You get the most extraordinary looks from people.

I remember going to a shark cave in the South Pacific. Pamela, my daughter Scarlett, a dive guide and I all went to a cave where sharks go to rest. Enormous buggers. I don't know exactly what they were doing in there. Some people say they sleep. If they find a place where the current flows through, they can lie still with their gills working and relax. The guide said sharks have 'hospitals' where, if they're injured or ill, they can go to recuperate. Some of these ones were pregnant. I was upside down, pulling on the entrance of the cave to get my head in, peering at these monsters. Nine or ten feet long. They could have eaten me in one bite. It was the most extraordinary feeling, and I loved it. I felt part of everything. I think that's the loveliest thing about scuba-diving. Or parachuting. You feel part of the system. You know what birds see. You know what fish see. You know what the world looks like from their point of view. It's good to reach a point in your life where you spiritually meet the rest of the animal world.

———

New Zealand's a kind of spiritual place. You're surrounded by nature a lot of the time and it's wonderful. Puts your mind in a peaceful place. I was in the middle of a tour in Christchurch in New Zealand about twenty years ago, and I needed to escape from the street, so I went into my room and started to meditate. It felt so good I did it for about two hours. Then I left the room, and as I was walking up the road, I suddenly thought of a Glaswegian guy I hadn't thought of in years. I was just wondering how he was doing when I turned the corner – and there he was! This kind of thing started happening more and more; I would think of people, and they would show up.

After the tour was over I was flying into Glasgow, looking down over Partick, where I was brought up. I looked roughly near the street where a particular school friend lived, and I was reminded that his parents had changed their religion, so he'd had to leave the Catholic school and go to a Protestant school. I thought, 'Wonder how he's getting on?' I got off the plane, and he was standing right there, first in the queue.

My next tour was around the UK. I was going down to play the Scottish Border towns, the stronghold of rugby union, so I decided to take a little detour to visit Samye Ling, the Tibetan Buddhist Monastery and Tibetan Centre that's in the region. I went to visit the abbot, Choje Lama Yeshe Losal Rinpoche.

'I knew you were coming,' he said.

'I'm glad,' I said. 'I wanted to see you. I'm kind of disturbed about something.'

He said, 'Sit down.'

I told him: 'I think about people I haven't seen for twenty years and they walk right into my life.'

He said, 'What's disturbing you about it?'

I said, 'Well, nothing really, it's just unusual.'

He said, 'Well, don't let it disturb you. Nobody knows what it is. You're exercising your brain, your consciousness. It's coming to life in various forms and showing you things it's never shown you before. My advice to you is just enjoy it.'

I was so relieved. It was brilliant advice. You'd never get that kind of counsel from a Catholic priest or a Presbyterian. They would say you'd done something terrible to bring this upon yourself and your only recourse was to hang weights from your private parts.

The theatres I played in New Zealand were great and the audiences there can take being teased. I would always kid them that their country was discovered by Scotsmen, who bypassed the warmer north island and settled around Dunedin because it pished with rain all the time. I said, 'The two explorers who discovered New Zealand were "Donald Dreich" and "Angus Dreary".' 'Dreich' is a Scottish word meaning 'bleak and dismal'. New Zealand gets even more dreich as you go south, but I played a great gig on Stewart Island, which is way down off the southern coast. I had the best fish and chips I'd ever tasted there. Black cod. I ate roasted mutton bird there too. Delicious. We had half the population inside the Stewart Island hall, so we put speakers outside to accommodate the other half.

I went to a Maori tattooist in Auckland. I said to him, 'Do you think you could do something around the tattoo I've already got?' I just fancied tarting up my 'sailor' heart with Pamela's birthday on it. He tattooed my family history on my upper left arm – all my girls and Jamie. It's beautiful work. It has all kinds of symbols – mountains and farms, with jagged bits that are supposed to be our protectors. After he finished, he drew a traditional Maori *moko* or face tattoo on my forehead with ink. I think the people there know Pamela has Maori heritage. Her great-great-great-grandmother was a Maori woman. I should probably call the place by its Maori name, Aotearoa.

The last time I was in Christchurch was just after the big earthquake. Understandably, it was looking hellish. When I went for my usual walks, I was always getting lost because all my points of reference had fallen down. But there was no stopping the people there in Christchurch – I saw some great restoration. They had erected a whole shopping centre made of shipping containers that was nothing short of brilliant. It had different levels accessed by stairs, and all beautifully lit and heated.

I'd love to get back to Aotearoa and go fishing again near Hamilton. I had three weeks off in the middle of filming *The Hobbit*, so I got to spend that time at a fishing lodge. The whole country is trout heaven. It has some of the best fishing in the world. They imported brown and rainbow trout that thrived there. Big buggers. Ten to twelve-pounders.

Canada is another place where you can travel for days and not see a soul. I did a TV series travelling all the way from Nova Scotia to Vancouver. It has breathtakingly beautiful rivers, waterfalls, forests and mountains – and there's no bugger there. At one point we were flying close to Alaska – the American border – and the forest there went on and on and on. We had a guide with us – a ranger wearing one of those Mountie-style hats. I said to him: 'You know, looking down there, it's suddenly dawned on me what "lost" means.' He said, 'Oh yeah . . . if you're lost down there, you're really lost.' He said, 'It either takes two hours or twenty years to find you.'

I played the Canadian cities for many years. Wonderful audiences. After some of my shows, I met people I'd known in Scotland – like Mattie, my old babysitter. Ian Meikle came to see me too – he used to live through the wall from me in Stewartville Street and was as nice as I remembered. I met loads of guys who'd been to my school. They'd show up with school photos and say, 'Are you in this?' I was onstage in Hamilton, Ontario, talking about Rosie MacDonald and what a bitch she was, and I happened to mention Peter Langhan, a fellow classmate. The following day I got to Toronto, and there he was – standing on the pavement when I arrived at the theatre. He was going to the show that night. I meant to mention him onstage, but it just didn't happen.

Sometimes I intend to do or say something when I go on, but I forget. I get waylaid by other subjects. I've never yet managed to wish anyone happy birthday; I've gone on perfectly happy to do it, but *ppfff!* it evaporated. Not to mention the time I left my good pal Ralph McTell standing behind the curtain waiting to come on. It was at the Albert Hall, no less. I'd invited him to play along during one of my songs, but it completely slipped my mind. At the end I said, 'Cheerio!' to the audience and went off through the curtains – and there was Ralph, standing there with his guitar. 'Oh, fuck, I'm sorry!' He took it extremely well. He still laughs about it today.

The stage is a strange place. Weird things happen when you're up there. I've even gone on with the flu and come off without it. I once had to leave the stage at the Sydney Opera House and go for a pee. The show was going really well, but I was in dire straits. I explained to the audience: 'Look, I'm not well at the moment and one of the symptoms is, I need to pee. Back in a jiffy!' I shot off and peed into a bucket in the wings. When I returned, the audience cheered.

————

My extensive overseas touring was wonderful for my career. On every one of my tours, my audiences were growing. I had exceptional promoters, like Kevin Ritchie and Harley Medcalf in Australia, and Ian Magan in New Zealand. However, none of this helped my home life with Iris. Pamela once explained I had a 're-entry problem'. After all the adrenaline, excitement, high living, star treatment and the appreciation shown by my audiences, it was hard to switch back to being a father and husband when I came home. I'd be exhausted, lying on my own bed, wondering how I could dial room service. I don't think I was the only performer with that problem. In fact, I defy anyone to go comfortably from 'Would you like another of the large ones, Sir Billy?' to 'Feed the dog, and take out the fucking trash.'

MISBEHAVE IN PUBLIC . . .
BUT BE ENTERTAINING WITH IT

—

CHIC MURRAY ONCE told me he was lying in the street and a woman said to him, 'Did you fall?' He said, 'No, I'm trying to break a bar of chocolate in my back pocket.' When I was a boy, the street was our entertainment centre. It was a healthy thing; you went outside, met other people and played and fought and sang and laughed and misbehaved. I miss that. Television changed it, so we no longer have that kind of contact. I still like talking with strangers in the street. Having a laugh.

One night after a show in Australia I went out on the town with Michael Parkinson and got sloshed. I was directing cars on a busy street in Sydney's Kings Cross, and dancing like Fred Astaire in the middle of all the traffic. People in their cars were joining in, honking their horns and shouting their approval. 'Whooooaaa! Good on ya, Billy!' I think Mike coaxed me back to safety.

———

I got up to a lot of antics when I was drunk, but I can't remember most of them. Other people have told me stories. I do remember being stuck in a public phone booth in London, somewhere near Primrose Hill. I'd been out for the night with Peter McDougall, and I went into a phone box to call a taxi. But I couldn't get one. Maybe they didn't want to pick up someone as incoherent as I was. When I tried to exit the phone booth, I couldn't find the way out. In desperation I called Pete Brown, my manager at the time, and woke him up. 'How can I get out of here?'

He said, 'Where are you?'

'I'm stuck in a phone box.'

'Yes, but *where* are you?' he asked again.

'I've no idea.'

So, Pete got out of bed and traipsed around all the places I normally went until he found me. All my managers have been very long-suffering. I wasn't exactly a responsible person once I'd had a bevvy.

Back in Drymen, my home life was going awfully wrong. I wasn't getting on with Iris, and she was obviously very unhappy. She drank at home in a secretive manner – in contrast to my habit, which was public, loud and expansive. Once she locked me out of the house because I was drunk and disorderly. I hung around outside causing a disturbance, so she called the police. They took me to the police station, gave me a bed in a cell overnight, then let me go with a warning.

My career was taking off, but I had to be away from home a great deal so I wasn't much help to Iris, who was in a terrible state. And so was I. I didn't know what to do. I was scared. I could see a big black cloud coming towards us, but I was afraid of facing it, so I stayed away from home even more. I still feel very guilty about abandoning Iris. If I'd had the chance to do it again, I would have stayed home more instead of going to the pub. We were both drunks. Neither of us was happy. It's amazing how you can kind of know something but don't entirely admit it to yourself. I talked to Iris about it a couple of times, but she'd get angry. I wish to God I'd known more, had an idea how to help her then but I didn't even know how to help myself. None of it was fair on the kids – I think they missed out. I was never there, which must have been very hard on Iris. She hadn't signed up for that. When we met, she didn't know living with me would be the way it was, and I didn't know how to be a good family man. I had never learned that.

It was around this time, when I was staying in London doing various shows and avoiding Drymen, that I met Pamela Stephenson. I wanted to be recognised as a good comedian in England and I knew it would take London to do that. I'd already made my name on *Parkinson*, but I wanted people in the south of England to see me working live on the stage. Out of the blue, John Lloyd and Sean Hardie, the producers of the BBC2 topical comedy show *Not the Nine O'Clock News*, invited me to come on the show and do some sketches. The show was extremely popular nationwide, and I fancied being a part of it. There were four comedians in the show – Rowan Atkinson, Mel Smith, Griff Rhys Jones and Pamela Stephenson – and I thought they were excellent.

I went to meet the *Not the Nine O'Clock News* team in the hall where they rehearsed. The first thing I saw was Pamela flying past the door on a trolley. I watched the way they were all working together to create sketches. It was a very impressive way of working – completely different from mine. I'd never seen comedians developing material in a group before. Led by John Lloyd, they had writers who would come up with a basic sketch, but then they would improvise and change it until it was right. I did two scenes with Pamela and I thought she was very good. Very professional. She made me laugh uncontrollably with her impersonation of Janet Street-Porter.

––––

I didn't see her for a year after that show, but then she turned up to see me in Brighton when she was filming for *Not the Nine O'Clock News*. I was in the middle of my *Big Wee Tour of Britain* – a tour of sixty-nine shows. I was exhausted – and totally distraught about my life generally. By then Iris and I had split, although my stuff was still sitting in Drymen. Pamela perched on the handbasin in my dressing room, and I told her some of my problems. She let me know her marriage was over too. Then we went to the bar in my hotel, and I got stuck into the bevvies.

My roadie Jamie Wark had never thought anything about barging into my hotel room in the morning to pack my instruments when I was with a woman. And after quite a few years on the road, I wasn't too bothered either. But the next morning, Pamela was appalled. I could see she was a bit shocked by the way I behaved generally. In a different way, she was wild too, but mainly in her comedy. She was brave and unconventional – a sexy, bold Australian.

We kept seeing each other secretly when we had time, but we were both very busy, and we were terrified people would find out. We knew it would be big tabloid news. After my tour was over, I stayed in London and got to know her a bit more, but I think I was too much for her. She said my drinking was a big problem, and that sometimes I changed personality and became nasty when I was drunk. That was news to me. I never remembered the night before. She was worried that I was on a self-destructive path. She disappeared to Bali for a few months, and I assumed it was over. I learned later she had gone away to try to forget about me because she could no longer take the way I behaved. She took books about alcoholism and addiction with her and studied them.

Pamela brought me a black seaweed bracelet from Bali. She seemed a bit distant, but she hung around, chatting about her trip, then brought up my drinking. Most people on the receiving end of a *'You're drinking too much'* conversation become defensive, and I was no exception. But Pamela seemed to be ready for that. She said she cared about me, but I was damaging myself and she couldn't be part of that. I knew in my soul she was right. No one had ever confronted me about it before; everyone else in my life just enabled it because I was 'Billy Connolly the wild man'. Pamela made me see the seriousness of it, and that I'd have to change. Although she didn't actually say it, it became clear she would leave for good if I didn't. Being a person with a terrible fear of being abandoned, I panicked. I didn't want her to leave, and I could see a chance for happiness with her if she stayed. I promised to try to stop drinking, even though I doubted I'd succeed.

―――

It was very difficult for Pamela and me to be together without massive attention from the British tabloids. We thought we could be relaxed abroad, so we went to Morocco to try to have a quiet romantic break – but people recognised us, and the word got out. The whole thing became very messy. Iris read about it in the papers, which was terribly unfair. Journalists even approached my kids. It was awful, and we had no idea how to handle it. We needed help, but it was difficult to get good advice or trust anyone.

Eventually, we moved in together. Pamela was busier than me, doing movies and TV shows, so I started to cook. We were living in a house near Walton Street in London, and there was a great kitchen there, so I spent my days learning how to make nice food. There was so much chaos in my life, it helped me feel calm. I was gaining some control over drinking – although it wasn't easy, and I lost the battle a few times.

After we were publicly 'together', we sometimes went out to restaurants like Langan's and clubs like Tramp and Legends, but we always attracted too much attention and it ended up being a mistake. Around this time John Cleese invited both of us to appear in a second edition of *The Secret Policeman's Ball*, which was a charity show for Amnesty International. It was good to be around the Pythons and some of my rock 'n' roll heroes like Eric Clapton. When we left Drury Lane after the show the paparazzi were out in force. Pamela walked out with Eric Clapton, but even so the photographers were crazed. I gave them a warning: 'You better grease up that camera 'cos it's going up your arse!' I got in a fight with one of them and ended up smashing his camera. I liked the noise it made when the bulb exploded, but the guy took me to court, and I had to pay for it.

I've had quite a few run-ins with paparazzi. After a while, I realised it was a waste of time fighting them; while you were hitting one, his mates would be taking pictures of you. One time a guy came up to me in Walton Street on my way back home from the grocery store. He leapt out of someone's garden. 'Billy, I'm from—' Before he could finish his sentence, I hit him with my loaf of French bread. We still ate it.

When Pamela became pregnant with Daisy, we both realised it was time to get serious about a lot of things. We moved into a more private house in Fulham. Pamela had begun to spend time with Cara and Jamie. I was disturbed about how their lives were going in Scotland, especially when I learned Jamie had not been attending school. I went to court to seek custody of the children. Soon after Daisy arrived, we were a sizeable family. Pamela found schools for Jamie and Cara, and we began living regular, settled lives. Amy and Scarlett were born two years apart, so by 1988 I was a father of five.

Iris and I were divorced in 1985, and she went to live in Spain. Soon after Daisy was born, I stopped drinking completely for one year. But after that year, I tried drinking again, to see what would happen. It was a big mistake. In fact, some of my subsequent antics were so extreme they could have had tragic consequences. I was filming the movie *Water* in St Lucia in the Caribbean. One night I had a jolly evening with Michael Caine and some of the other cast and crew. By the time we left the restaurant I was steaming. We had to ride back to our hotel in a local bus that took a precarious route on a terrible road beside a steep ravine. For some reason, I thought it would be a wheeze to cover the driver's eyes while he was driving. To prevent us from careening off the edge of the cliff, Michael Caine had to intervene. He talked to me about it the following morning, and I decided to quit drinking again.

Back in London, Pamela arranged a fortieth birthday party for me at our place. There were people I knew there – like Elton – and some I didn't. A hilarious Pakistani Elvis impersonator called Elvis Patel entertained us, and a man came out of my birthday cake dressed as the Pope. He was a Welshman called Mr Meredith who had woken up one day and found out he had a whole new career because he looked like the Holy Father. There was also a guy who did an act about how to stop a nuclear bomb using Wonder Bread, and a magician who ate his brains out of his head. It was a brilliant party and I loved it.

Straight after the guests left, I had to drive to Cornwall to film more scenes for *Water* the next day. On the way, I fell asleep at the wheel. I left the motorway and shot into a field in Weston-super-Mare, crashing my sparkly green convertible Volkswagen Beetle. I had a nasty concussion. I remember thinking, 'Oh God – don't let me die in John Cleese's home town.' But at least I hadn't been drinking. That could have been the end of me.

———

At the end of 1985, I stopped drinking for good. Pamela had always avoided giving me an ultimatum, because she knew it would have to be my decision – but while she supported me in my struggle with alcohol, she had made her position perfectly clear. She took Daisy to New York when she became a cast member of *Saturday Night Live*, and I was worried she wouldn't come back. So, I decided to quit while it was still my idea.

I had my first drink in a pub in Troon in 1960 and my last drink twenty-five years later on 30 December 1985. Just the other day the American chat show host Conan O'Brien sent me a bottle of tequila with some crisps and an invitation to watch some new comedians online. But it's been thirty-five years since I had an alcoholic beverage. I'm not sure what would happen if I tried. I think I'll just stick with my Snapple.

BEWARE THE INDOMITABLE JOBBIE

I HAD A period of about three years when I was scared of flying. I had thought the more you fly, the less horrible it would become, but that's not true. It just got worse. Logically, I should only be afraid of crashing when the plane is between the ground and twenty feet. There's no point worrying about it once you get above maiming height. If the plane hits the ground at speed, you won't feel a thing. It's always minor injuries that really hurt. Like someone kneeling on your balls.

I've had to fly a lot of miles on aeroplanes. But being strapped down while someone talks to me like I'm mentally ill is not my favourite thing. The flight crew are all nice and civilised when you come on: 'Oh hello, Sir Billy, can I get you one of the large ones?' As soon as the plane takes off, they start behaving like they're doing children's TV, talking to you in this singy-songy voice: 'This is your safety belt' – they're smiling at you like it's a cute wee duckie or something. We're not idiots! 'This bit goes into this bit . . .'

All that shit about 'in the highly unlikely event of a loss of cabin pressure, oxygen masks will fall down as if by magic, and you'll be able to breathe, and it'll all be jolly, and if you secure your safety belt you'll be very, very safe with your nice seat belt on . . .' When were you ever watching TV and the newscaster said, 'Today, a jumbo jet smacked into a mountain in Peru, but luckily, all the passengers were wearing safety belts'? No! You're sitting there with your life jacket on, heading upside down towards the Atlantic Ocean. Are you thinking: 'I'm all right – I've observed all of the safety procedures'?

If they were to tell you the truth, they'd have to say, 'Ladies and gentlemen, in the highly unlikely event of loss of power on all four engines, then, in all probability, we'll be going towards the ground like a fucking dart. You won't be screaming – you'll be trying to get the seat in front of you out of your mouth.'

In any case, I find travelling on aeroplanes difficult now because of my Parkinson's. It's hard to get out of my seat. But standing up was hard even before I had Parkinson's. The thing you need most of all is your legs, and you've buggered them by sitting down for so long. There should be more handles on aeroplane walls, like the ones you get in the bath.

Aeroplane toilets are made to frighten you. There's no safety belt – you're just sitting there hanging on to the sink: 'Please, please, don't crash! I don't want to be found with my trousers around my ankles!' And you can never find the button to flush. Flushing is very important. It wheeks everything away and down into the ocean. They always do it over the sea. It's called 'organic redistribution'. They don't do it over towns, for very obvious reasons – there could be a guy there directing the traffic, and one minute he's waving people on and the next minute – *splat!* – a jobbie hits him on the side of the face. If you do a jobbie on an aeroplane it crashes down into the sea: *thuuumsshh!* It bobs around there on the surface, and along comes a fishie: *swimmetty-swim,* 'Jesus, I'm starving!' Then it spots the jobbie:

'Ahoy there!' *Munchetty-crunchetty*. Happy fishie. Then along comes a fisherman, spots the fishie: 'A-ha!' Catches the fishie, into the boat – *rowitty-home*. Up to the market, he sells the fishie. You come along, you buy the fishie. *Munchetty-crunchetty*. Then you go in an aeroplane. Into the toilet, do a wee jobbie, close the lid – *weech!* And that's organic redistribution.

Aeroplane toilets have a very, very proficient flush. That pressure could suck your arse out of the plane if you were still sitting there. That's important, because otherwise it would be like the toilets on trains. For years I talked to audiences about the terrible problem of the indomitable jobbie. I would describe it a bit like this:

'You go into a train lavvy, and there it is: "Oh, for crying out loud!" There's a wee beige jobbie. You flush and flush with all your might, then *doo-de-doo-de-doodle-a-doo*: it's back. Sometimes it actually goes under the bend and hides. You think it's gone, but just as you start taking your trousers off: *Bing!* It's back! There's no way you're going to bare your bum above somebody else's wee beige jobbie. You try battering it to death with paper towels. "*Go awaaaaaaayyyy!!!*" You're *stuck* in there with this bloody thing! Finally, you have to leave because people are knocking on the door. You walk out, hiding your face: "Er, by the way, *that's* not mine!"'

———

I travelled a lot in the eighties. I went to Mozambique twice to do documentaries for Comic Relief. The people of Mozambique were suffering from starvation and terror attacks, so the UK sent a comedian. Pamela was pregnant for the third time and begged me not to go because she'd heard they were shooting down passenger planes there. But I went, and it was hellish. I visited hospitals where the conditions were dire. While I was being filmed speaking to one patient on his bed, a goat wandered into the ward, had a pee and walked out again. I met people who'd suffered unspeakable traumas, and I went home from Mozambique a changed guy. But that kind of experience changes you in a way that is of no use to anyone. You just come to the conclusion that people can be awful bastards, given half a chance. I was glad to try to help, but I felt the problem was too big for a banjo-playing comedian to do anything about.

We were flown around the country by a Christian organisation. They have those small propeller planes – the Buddy Holly jobs. I hate them. Personally, I prefer sitting up at the front in a jumbo jet, being spoon-fed caviar. Is that so wrong? Those single-engine pieces of shit can be seriously on the hairy side, especially in the stormy seasons. They have a habit of suddenly going silent before making a noise again: 'Eeeeeeeee . . . . . . (NOTHING). Eeeeeeeee'. *'Don't fucking do that again!'* My least favourite is when they very briefly shut off and you feel this lurch downwards. That's what's known as the Atheism Test.

The pilot would arrive wearing shorts, T-shirt and flip flops. He'd gather us in a circle. 'Before we take off let's say a little prayer.' They would kneel down. 'Lord, please take care of us . . . lead us in your Way . . .' I'd just bow my head, thinking, 'For fuck's sake just put the Bible down and concentrate on the manual. Try to miss the trees at the end of the runway.' Frankly, I would have preferred him in lace-up shoes and a shirt with epaulettes. I used to talk about it onstage: 'I want a see-through pocket so I can see your pack of Rothmans shining through. Sleeves rolled up, hairy arms, stainless steel Rolex – and a moustache if you can manage it . . .' Then I'd do all the noises of the plane taking off.

From the air the jungle looks like broccoli. One time, the pilot said, 'Fasten your seatbelts, and just be careful. We sometimes have bandits shooting up at us.' I was thinking, 'How can I be careful? Jesus – I might get shot in the head.' Then I thought, 'Wait a minute, if there's bandits down there and I'm in a sitting position up here I'm not going to get shot in the head. I'm going to get shot up the arse.'

———

By the second half of the eighties I felt I was in a great position in my career. I did a show for ITV in London – *An Audience With . . .*, in which I performed in front of a live celebrity audience. When I talked about incontinence knickers, I could see some of my heroes sliding off their seats. It was fun. I began my *World Tour* series, including performing six nights at the Royal Albert Hall that ended up as the *Billy and Albert* video. It was a great time for me. I was happy in my home life as well as my work, and things were pretty much tickety-boo.

Once I was settled with Pamela and the children I started cycling again, and for the first time in years I felt healthy. I took part in the London to Brighton charity bike ride with fifty thousand other cyclists. Elton John was one of my generous sponsors – a hundred pounds a mile! I also did a London-to-Glasgow charity ride. It was a return to something that had always calmed and pleased me. I used to cycle up to Richmond Park regularly, just for pleasure.

———

My first bicycle had been a purple Royal Hudson. My father gave it to me for Christmas when I was around eleven. It was shaped like a racing bike, with drop handlebars. Having that bike meant that I was finally able to join my pals on camping trips to the countryside. I had that Royal Hudson for years. It was a good old friend. When I was around fourteen, I was given a Flying Scot, made by Rattray's of Scotland. I had always wanted a Flying Scot. It was all tarted up as a sports tourer with mud-guards and other features. I kept it covered at home on the verandah; you had to stay ahead of the rust. Good cyclists try to keep their bikes immaculate. You don't want to look like a scruff.

There are some old art deco public toilets in a place called Anniesland Cross in the west of Glasgow. When I was around sixteen, I used to meet other cyclists from all over Glasgow there on Tuesdays and Thursdays. We called ourselves 'The Bunch'. We'd take off and cycle to Loch Lomond and back – about twenty-five miles. It was conducted like a race, with a Peloton. You took your turn at the front and got scored on the hills. If you were first up the hill, you'd be the 'prime' at the top of the hill. I never joined a cycle club – I've always been wary of joining anything – but I liked being out with The Bunch. There were about forty of us, all in cycling jerseys and shorts, although it wasn't a uniform. My mother's brother Uncle Hughie gave me his cycling jersey – with the name 'The Glenmarnock Wheelers' on it.

I had my Flying Scot for three or four years. When I became an apprentice in the shipyards, I cycled to work on it. All the workers left their bikes inside the shipyard. We didn't lock them – there was no need. Sometimes when I was seventeen or eighteen I took the ferry over to Gourock, then cycled the thirty miles back home. Cycling was an escape.

There's a lovely thing – I hope it still happens – a 'drum-up'.

You take a tin with tea in one end and sugar in the other, and you leave it in the wall on the shores of Loch Lomond. There's space between the bricks, so you shove your tea in there, then have a 'drum-up' – you set a fire, fill your can with water from the loch and make a cup of tea. Afterwards, you leave your tea and sugar in the wall for other guys who might not have any. It's such a good thing. As you're cycling along you can smell the tea and the wood burning so you know that's the 'drum-up' spot.

Even though my family and I were settled in London, we visited Scotland as often as possible. We'd always drop in on my sister, 'Auntie Flo', with her husband Ian and their children – and she would always lay out a lavish afternoon tea, with all those sugary Scottish treats – Snowballs (chocolate-covered marshmallow balls), Tunnock's Teacakes, chocolate Bourbons and millionaire's shortbread.

We made the effort to see my Grandfather MacLean too – my mother's father – who lived by himself in Eastwood. I think he lived on biscuits. He was the only British person to have scurvy in the twentieth century. When I first took Pamela to meet him, he was ninety-six and the grumpiest man alive. He couldn't be bothered with anyone. You'd go up to see him and he'd immediately say, 'You'll have had your tea?' Then he'd fling you out. The record for the shortest stay in his house was seven minutes. I took Pamela to meet him, and I said, 'You'll love my granddad, but check your watch before you go in.'

'Why?'

'Just check it and see. Seven minutes is the record.'

'What do you mean?'

'Wait and see.'

So, we went in, and he was very nice. 'Hello, son! And this must be the lovely Pamela! Hello, darlin', how're you doing? You must have a cup of tea – sit on the couch there.' He disappeared and we heard a lot of banging and crashing going on in the kitchen. He was shouting and bawling, '*Who left this here??*' Remember, he lived alone. In no time at all, he appeared again – no teapot, no tray, no cups, no biscuits. He came over to me and said, 'Well, I'm sure you're a very busy man . . .' and we were back out on the street! I said to Pamela, 'Look! Five and a half minutes! We broke the record!'

————

I introduced Pamela to my father when he came down to London. We had dinner in a restaurant. Pamela did her best to be nice to him, but by then she was aware of Mona's treatment of me and was angry that he had not prevented her from terrorising me. At that point she didn't know the full story. Then one day my sister sent for me. She said, 'Dad's had a stroke.' He had collapsed at home. Florence found him lying in his hallway. He was taken into hospital and he couldn't speak properly. I dutifully flew up to Glasgow to see him. He was lying there, paralysed down his right side. His tongue was paralysed as well, and so was his eye. My sister had brought a priest, but my father was swearing non-stop. 'Faah-fuh-fuck!' He couldn't say anything else. 'Faah-fuh-fuck!' 'Faah-fuh-fuck!' It was constant.

The priest took off. I was trying to make conversation, but I didn't know what to talk about. So stupidly I blurted out the first thing that came to mind. I said, 'You're lucky you're in here – it's raining outside.' Florence shot me a look that said, 'You idiot.' But what I said actually helped my father's medical progress. For the first time since his stroke, he managed to put TWO words together: 'Faah-fuh-fuck . . . Ooooffff!!!'

After that first stroke, my father got better and was back to normal, but then he had another – and another. It was cruel. After his eighth stroke we knew he was dying. I went to say goodbye to him, and I was in a terrible state. I had never told anybody about his abuse, but as Pamela and I sat in the car park of the hospital I felt so tormented I just blurted it out.

I hadn't thought about it for years, and I had thought it no longer bothered me. But at that point when he was dying, it bothered me terribly. All my sadness and shame and fury came pouring out. As we sat in the car Pamela listened to me silently. She was obviously shocked, and deeply upset on my behalf. We were both crying, and I couldn't even bring myself to go to his hospital room to say goodbye.

At some later point, Pamela asked me: 'What was your father thinking? Do you think he was just ignorant, lacked impulse control, or truly evil? Maybe he was perpetrating something on you that had been done to him . . .'

I said, 'I think maybe he was homosexual – which of course doesn't make him an abuser. I think he had experiences in the air force that he couldn't come to terms with.'

'Yeah,' Pamela said, 'if that's true, then that's one thing, you know, being gay at a time when it wasn't accepted, where you had to be very closeted . . . but it's a whole other thing to perpetrate sexual abuse on your child, whether you're gay or straight.'

Even now, if I dwell on it, it really gets me down. I have it tucked away the way you can tuck away a death in the family. But I'm finally at one with it. It happened, and there's nothing I can do about that. I had help – books by John Bradshaw about healing and shame and forgiveness, and I went to therapy. The most memorable was the 'empty chair' exercise, where you sit opposite an empty chair and imagine the person who assaulted you is seated there. You ask them questions, imagine the answers, and try to forgive them for it. Even if the person is dead, you can still forgive them. Once I did that, I was able to more or less move on.

———

My mother died not too long after my dad. I had told myself I never held any grudge about what she did – leaving me and Florence when we were just wee kids. I reasoned that there was a war on. The Germans were dropping bombs in the Clyde. My father was in India, and she was eighteen. War will do strange things to you. But when it came to it, I couldn't say goodbye.

I heard through my cousin Neil that my mother was gravely ill with motor neurone disease. I had a strong urge to go to see her. I drove to Dunoon and arrived at three in the afternoon – I saw the time on the town clock – but then I felt overwhelmed with conflicting feelings and indecision. What would be the point of seeing her? What would I say to her? Would she even want to see me? Maybe her family wouldn't like my showing up . . . In the end I just couldn't face seeing her, so I turned round and went right back to Glasgow. Later, I was told that at that exact time, three o'clock, she'd said to her daughter Mary: 'Billy's here.'

She died that weekend, in the hospital in Greenock across the River Clyde. The funeral was in Dunoon and her son gave me the first tag. The rope you hold as the coffin is lowered into the grave relates to your importance in the family. He said to me: 'You're the number one son.'

24

SWEAR LIKE A GLASWEGIAN

—

ALMOST EVERYBODY SWEARS. I bet the Pope swears. Only he's dead sneaky – he swears in Latin. George Square in Glasgow is the place to hear swearing. That's where you see swearing experts. You'll see a wee man at the George Square bus stop, walking with one leg because the other one's dead, staggering around in a circle and wondering why he's knackered and not getting anywhere. He manages to wobble his way along and find another drunk. So, he sits down and talks to him. Well, they don't really *talk* to each other; they sit and swear at each other for a wee while. To make it really convenient they drop all the other words and just swear: 'Yuhfuckin'bastardfuckin' fuckin'bastardyuh.' And the other guy's so drunk he sounds as if he's drowning: 'Ack-Ack-*gasp*-Huuh-*gasp*-mmmm-mmmm . . . Ack-Ack-*gasp*-Acker-Haaa . . .' And the first one's still going: 'Yuhfuckin'bastardfuckin'fuckin'bastard . . .' It's usually a short conversation, because pretty soon the drunkest one will decide that it's time to be sick.

I've never tried to control my swearing. People have criticised me for it: 'Oh, he swears too much,' but I care not a jot. I like it. Swearing is very natural for me – and for most Glaswegians

– and we're very, very good at it. If you're going to take up swearing, you have to learn how to do it properly, and make it sound like it's normal conversation with a normal meaning. For example, *cunt* is not a word I usually use, especially in America, because it frightens people on that side of the Atlantic. It's weird, because they don't seem to mind 'motherfucker'. Being a Glaswegian I'm used to it. You can use 'cunt' casually, in all sorts of circumstances. Like, when you're trying to remember a film star's name, people will say, 'You mean Dustin Hoffman?' and you say, 'No, no, not him. Some other cunt.' In Glasgow I actually heard somebody say, 'Hey, who's that cunt with the Pope?'

Glasgow swearing is extremely sophisticated. It's a highly developed art. There are *grades* of cuntishness. For example, you don't need to be a *complete* cunt: 'What do you think of the new prime minister?' 'Oh, seems a bit of a cunt to me.' Close your eyes and think of someone you know who's a *right* cunt. Got it? Now think of a *complete* cunt. You see? There's a scale.

By the mid-eighties, I'd already performed in quite a few cities in the USA but I still had the sense many Americans didn't really know me. I was very drawn to the country. I admired many American performers and liked the way the show business industry was structured. I badly wanted to make it over there.

———

The first time a sizeable American audience got to see me was for a Whoopi Goldberg special on HBO. I got on well with Whoopi. She's incredibly bright as well as funny, and I owe her a lot. She introduced me to her audience in Brooklyn – in fact, she pushed me to do the bulk of her show – and I had a great time. I said, 'You people appreciate violence the same as we Glaswegians do, and you know how to swear properly.' After that, HBO gave me my own special, *Billy Connolly in Performance*. And from there I was asked to take over the leading role in the American TV sitcom *Head of the Class* from Howard Hesseman. At that point I knew I would be in Los Angeles for quite some time and Pamela put her foot down. 'You're not commuting to L.A. Let's move there and start the children in American schools.' She was right. After *Head of the Class* I was given my own sitcom called *Billy*, in which I played a guy who'd married an American woman for a green card. Pretty soon I had a green card myself – legally.

I already had a pretty good sense that Los Angeles was a great place for me, but when I heard there was a 24-hour drive-through taxidermist there, I thought, 'I really need that in my life. I might need to stuff a dead cat at three in the morning. That's the town I want to live in!' The place is nuts. I was driving on the freeway and I saw a sign that said, '*To the Braille School*'. Who the fuck was that for?

Once I was fully based in the USA, we bought a house in the Hollywood Hills. It wasn't easy to go house-hunting with Pamela. She couldn't see the things *I* liked about the house, she just saw . . . *potential*. We found an artist's house – he was an Italian painter who used enormous canvases, so all the rooms were gigantic – we both liked that. But as soon as she saw the wee, fifties kitchen with rusty appliances, Pamela said the words that made my blood run cold: 'We'll have to renovate.' Oh, for fuck's sake. I *liked* the wee tiny cupboards and the brown flowery tiles. And I liked the weird trees outside that the artist had painted red. All of a sudden, guys in overalls arrived and started knocking down walls.

'Who are *you*? Get out of my house! What are you doing to the wall?'

'Oh, this wall has to come down because if the kitchen's going to go there, this has to be a supporting wall, this has to do that, and the roof has to . . .'

'What the FUCK are you talking about?'

When you buy a house in California there are no safety guar-antees. You find one you like: 'How many million is that?'

'It's on the fault line, you know, for earthquakes.'

'Sure, but wrap it up! I'll fucking take it right now!'

The house we bought was right on the San Andreas Fault. If there was the slightest rumble, we'd all be watching the telly at the bottom of the valley. But no one cared.

I was in an earthquake once. It was the weirdest feeling – like an elevator going down quickly, with a jolt at the bottom. It's like your liver has just passed your Adam's apple. I was watching TV when it happened.

Wee jolt.

I thought, 'Fuck . . . what was that?'

I let it go, but then it happened again an hour later.

Bigger jolt, five seconds long. There was a reporter – Connie Chung – on the news. Her studio shook, and she jumped: 'What was that?' she said.

And – out loud – I said fearfully, 'I dunno!'

Pamela settled our three school-age children into L.A. life. After my own school experiences, it was refreshing to see how Americans approached school lessons – no rote learning, belit-tling or battering of children. No shoving of religion down their throats, no humiliating kids who wear glasses. Boys and girls could be educated together, so they learned to socialise, and they actually allowed students to question the teacher – a complete novelty for me.

At that time, they had a lottery system for green cards. Pamela applied successfully, so as a result we all became American residents. To make things easier, before we formally settled in the USA Pamela insisted we be legally married. Our wedding took place in Fiji in December 1989. I was very nervous about it. We gathered some friends on a sea-snake-ridden tropical island in the middle of hurricane season and got married in knee-deep water. It was mad. I wore a cotton kilt. It was really a sarong printed to look like a kilt. But we did have pipers marching along the beach in full Scottish regalia. We had a Fijian church choir singing the theme from *The Archers*. They wanted to rehearse it first. 'What are the words please?' they said. And we said, '*Dum de dum de diddle dumb, dum de dum de daaah daaah.*' They sang it instead of 'Here Comes the Bride' as Pamela was walking down the beach towards me. It was perfect. Like a dream. Especially when Ringo Starr came charging out yelling that there were snakes in his hut.

———

Once we were settled in Los Angeles, I was able to focus on making a proper name for myself there. My American TV shows were moderate successes, but I'm especially proud of how well I did in the movies. I made fifty films. I wasn't exactly a matinee idol, but I had fun playing all sorts of characters – criminals, a florist, a pirate, a tennis player, a priest, a gravedigger, a dog, an auctioneer, a scalper, a professor, a cavalry sergeant, an antiques shopkeeper, a doctor, a squirrel, a fisherman, an angel, several kings, a queen's lover, an opera singer and a zombie . . . There's a few more too.

People don't much recognise me from my movies, because I usually look like a different guy. I was filming a documentary in West Virginia a few years ago, and I was at an addiction rehab centre. The people receiving treatment there were really nice guys who'd obviously been through a hell of a time. They listened dutifully as I rattled on about my own struggles with drinking. Then the woman in charge said, 'I guess this must be a big change from making movies.' I said, 'Sure is.' They were all looking at me as if to say, 'I've never seen you in a movie.' I told them I had just finished *The Hobbit* and they were suitably impressed. But when I mentioned I was in *The Boondock Saints*, the room changed. One of the guys – a big, bearded fellow – said, 'You weren't in *The Boondock Saints* . . . ?' When I said, 'Sure. I was the father, Il Duce,' he came rushing across the room and grabbed me. Gave me a hug. Next, they were all up to shake my hand.

The Boondock Saints is a very violent movie. Some people criticised it for that, but I have violent tendencies myself. Not so much in recent years, but early on I found there were quite a few people who needed a smack in the mouth, and I tended to oblige. If someone deserves it and you leave it out, he'll behave worse and worse. A healthy smack in the mouth does a power of good.

——

When I was young, I could be very violent if provoked. There was an Indian restaurant I used to go to – Mr Huk in Glasgow. I was having dinner there with some friends late at night. Two guys came in and started throwing their weight around. One of them said something racist to a waiter. I got up, climbed onto my table and ran across the other tables to theirs. I dived on them, grabbed them and pulled them out onto the street. The racist guys got what they deserved – and from then on, my dinners there were free.

And I remember going up Union Street in Glasgow with Iris. I was wearing a black policeman's cape down to my knees and a black floppy hat with a snakeskin band. Four guys were standing by the entrance to Glasgow Central Station and, as we walked by, they started making a fool of me, calling me 'Batman' and all that. When I reached the side street where there's another entrance to the station, I said to Iris: 'Hold my banjo.' I darted in the side door, through the station and downstairs to where they were standing against a wall, and battered the four of them. My hat and cape stayed on. People were cheering. Iris was still up at the corner watching my banjo.

I was young then, so it wasn't hard to take on four people if I really needed to. I'd hit one first and quickly work my way along the line. After the second one the other two would have made off. Surprise is everything. I don't have a special technique, but if – out of nowhere – you've got a madman in a cape lunging at you, hitting back isn't your first idea. *Running* is.

———

I'm not really a violent person at heart. I just learned to fight wherever fights happened. It's a cultural thing. Over the years people have gone on and on about 'Glasgow fighting', because the town doesn't take shit from anybody. We've gained a reputation for violence. There's a medical scale called the Glasgow

Coma Scale for people who've injured their heads. Over the years, so many people have turned up at accident and emergency rooms after Friday-night fights in Glasgow that doctors and researchers had enough study subjects to devise this landmark head-injury measure.

When you're a little boy in Glasgow you learn – wrongly – that, just because you come from Glasgow, you can fight. That's not true. Plenty of country boys can pack a heavy wallop. Pamela hates it when I talk like this, but I like to remind her that I'm also a very cultured person. I now have four honorary doctorates plus a knighthood – not bad for a punch-happy comedian. A tabloid newspaper once described me as 'punch-prone'. I took great exception to it. I said, 'I'm not punch-prone. I punch people. A puncher, not a punchee . . .'

———

The movie *Mrs Brown* got people excited about my acting. They said, 'I didn't know you could act so well . . .' blah blah blah. It was the first time I did straight acting in a main role in a major film. It was a brilliant movie to take part in – made for very little money and elevated by word of mouth. Of course, the fact that Dame Judi Dench played Queen Victoria did it no harm at all. She's more than a brilliant actor; she's a gambler. She used to mess with me. She'd say, 'When do you think we'll be finished tonight?'

I would say, 'Oh, seven.'

She'd say, 'Eleven!'

I'd say, 'Never!'

She'd say, 'I'll bet you fifty pounds.'

I'd say, 'Okay.'

I would have to give her fifty pounds because she invariably won. Then she'd buy me something at the fishing shop. Salmon flies. She's dead sneaky. A lovely person who can change a room when she walks in, but she doesn't have the 'la-di-da' aura. She just oozes elegance and greatness.

I like the culture of movie-making. People complain about all the waiting around, but I always liked having time to play my banjo. I like the way you can become a team of people working so closely together in a big bubble. And it's always nice to be fancied by a fellow actor; when I was making *The Last Samurai*, Tom Cruise's horse fell in love with me. She would amble over and rub her head on my chest, which made my uniform all white, so I'd have to have it cleaned. She was a lovely beast.

One of the best things about movie-making is that you often have to learn new skills and get to be trained by experts. For *The Last Samurai* I had to learn how to safely ride a horse down a hill with a straight back and how to shoot a rifle while I was riding. I also had to learn how to sword-fight – which took me ages. I was given a very complicated fencing routine – well, it was complicated for me. Tom Cruise arrived, and the fencing trainer said, 'Billy, could you show Tom the routine?' I said, 'Sure' . . . *chhh chhh chhh chhh* . . . I showed him just once and he could immediately do the whole thing. Clever guy.

Quite a few of the movies I did required new training for me. When I played the King of the Dwarves, Dáin II Ironfoot, in *The Hobbit*, I had to learn to ride a pig. Well, I actually rode on a barrel, which became a pig through animation. I also had to fight with a spear and an axe. Luckily, everything was done in small sections. We never did a full run of a scene – it was too complicated. I'd do a few moves – *'duff duff duff!'* – and they would say, 'Cut', then move the camera to a new position. I had to practise hard with that axe. I stood in a circle with the stuntman, and people came charging at me, so I'd have to fend them off. I had already been diagnosed with Parkinson's disease – I told them that before we started – so they were patient with me. I had very heavy clothing. It was like wearing a Volkswagen. I couldn't sit down in my costume, so I had a metal support that I could lean against. I had a vest that came down to my knees with hoses inside. I could plug into a tap, so water swirled around and cooled me down.

In *The Hobbit*, I had to learn to speak dwarf language – give orders and so on. It wasn't too difficult once you got the rhythm of it. Tolkien had invented the language (clever bugger) but he hadn't seen a movie coming, so he hadn't issued instructions for pronunciation. Luckily, there was a 'spoken word' expert on the set who knew Dwarf. She helped me from the side when I was struggling.

My biggest thrill during that shoot was that Stephen Fry and I were invited by the director Peter Jackson to see his aeroplane hangar full of World War One biplanes. He said, 'Which one would you like to go in?' I said, 'The Bristol Fighter.' I'd made a model of that one as a boy, but I'd never seen a real one. A pilot took me up in it. The plane carried huge yellow fake bombs that I could drop down into Peter's garden. It was brilliant.

There was a lot of merchandising for *The Hobbit*. I was a wee plastic toy in a breakfast cereal. It was lovely to think sleepy children all over the world would dig out a wee statue of me first thing in the morning. I was even in a McDonald's Happy Meal. I didn't tell anybody in Glasgow that I was in *The Hobbit* – no newspapers or anything. My opening line in the movie is:

'Let's kill the bastards!' When it was released in Glasgow, the place erupted.

———

I played the pirate Billy Bones in *Muppet Treasure Island*. People have a deep love of the Muppets. They think of them as people. Every drummer in the world knows Animal the Muppet drummer. It's a joyous thing. When I did the movie, I saw that the attitude of the actors towards the puppeteers was one of deep respect. Our main scenes were in a tavern. There were Muppets every-where. I'd be waiting between scenes and I'd look up and see a deer's head on the wall – and it would wink at me. The puppets watched me all the time, ready to communicate. I said, 'Could I please meet some of the others?' They said, 'Sure', and took me up to a room where the puppeteers were preparing. They said, 'I'm sorry but Miss Piggy won't come and meet you. She says you're not big enough.' Apparently, nobody has ever seen her naked. She changes behind a screen, has tantrums and throws the clothes over the top: 'I can't wear this!' After the movie was finished, I got a letter from Miss Piggy written in pink felt-tip. '*Dearest Billy*'. It was a crawling letter . . . '*I'm bringing out a book of my celebrity friends' recipes. Would you kindly add a recipe to my book?*' I wrote back: '*No. You're not big enough.*'

I played the only character who has ever died in a Muppet movie; I got the 'Black Spot' from Blind Pew. I've died in a lot of movies. I rather like dying, but my children don't like to watch. I wanted them to see *What We Did on Our Holiday*, but they wouldn't go because I die in it. Beautiful movie. I taught the child actors a song, and in the film we all sing it on the way to the beach.

Mother can I go out to swim?
Yes my darling daughter
Watch the boys don't see your bum
Keep it well under the water.

I played a zombie in the Canadian-made comedy movie *Fido*. It was great being a character who was so disguised, and whose voice could barely be recognised as mine. I learned zombie walking, and practised my zombie growls – '*Uuuuggghhh!!*' The make-up process took about an hour. I had a bolt in my neck, and they put big ravioli on my cheeks covered with pancake make-up, so I had high cheekbones.

I loved being in movies and I loved living in L.A. I used to enjoy talking with the guys in a cigar shop called The Big Easy. The craic was much more important than the tobacco. I met all kinds of people. It was like going to a pub, but without getting drunk. I used to smoke cigarettes, but I stopped many years ago. Everybody smoked when I was a boy. After Mass, men would gather along the building opposite the church with their backs to the wall, watching everybody coming out. They would smoke and talk about football. When you're a boy you always long to be there with the men. I remember the priest scolding them. 'When you leave this church on a Sunday, I'm amazed the church isn't blackened at the front with all that smoke. You can't wait to light a cigarette! It's as if it's a relief to be out of the church!'

The people I met in L.A. cigar stores were writers, actors, set designers, caterers. They were a jolly crowd. I spent a lot of time there. My kids had the number: 'Can you tell my dad it's dinner-time?' I carried on smoking cigars when we moved to the East Coast. In the New York cigar shops I met stock exchange people, retired guys, songwriters, musicians and internet people. Quite a few of them had been drinkers and had given it all up. We talked about everything imaginable. Since I stopped smoking cigars, I've missed that. It was nice to be in their company without getting special attention, just being one of the guys.

25

STRIP AS MANY WILLOWS
AS YOU CAN

———

I DIDN'T HAVE any idea how long I was going to be in America. I was pursuing work in the film industry, and for that I needed to be in California. I've lived in America for many years now. There's always been a big part of me that wanted to live in Scotland, but for several career and family reasons that just wasn't feasible. However, we bought a place called Candacraig in the Highlands that we used to visit whenever we could. I had always wanted to experience the best Scotland had to offer, and I decided that at that time in my life, it was time to damn well grab it. It was the kind of Scottish experience normally reserved for clan leaders and royalty. I knew I'd be considered an upstart, but there was nothing new about that. Umpteen bedrooms, enormous dining room, great hall, library, billiard room, extensive land with a walled garden and its own loch . . . Fuck 'em.

We held house parties at Candacraig that were like gloriously extravagant summer camps for comedians. Our family would gather, and many of my American-based pals would show up. I'd take them round the countryside and to the local Highland Games. It was a great laugh. Pamela would set up treasure hunts and we'd eat dinner and enjoy Scottish country dancing in kilts with lots of lovely local people – the whole place alive and thumping with Strip the Willow, the Gay Gordons and the Dashing White Sergeant.

At that time, I became very friendly with the kilt. I decided I liked to wear my mother's tartan – MacLean of Duart – especially the pale-pink weathered version, but I also like the pale-green, hunting version of my father's MacDonald of the Isles tartan. I started really enjoying all the paraphernalia of the male Highland dress – the hose, shoes, sgian dubh, sporran, kilt pins and brooches . . . all of it, even plaids. Only trouble was, you can't throw it on in five minutes; getting kilted up takes me a fucking decade.

———

When I was a boy, we didn't see kilts much, except on people in pipe bands and the army. Apart from them there was a definite type of person who wore a kilt – a stuffy type of person. We used to shout at them in the street: 'Kilty kilty cold bum!' Many people wear them now for weddings, but it wasn't like that when I was a boy. Well, certainly not in Glasgow.

The Highland dress keeps being reinvented. It didn't take long for the Scottish boys to fall for the jabot instead of the bow tie. You can cut a fine dash in that. Sean Connery wore it, and you can't go wrong if big Sean wore it. I think a huge change for the better has come over tartan. There was a stuffiness to it that I'm glad is disappearing. The people who are designing the new stuff don't pay any attention to the pseudo-heritage stuff. It's given rise to great new designs and a more casual attitude, with some guys even wearing leather and tweed kilts now. Beforehand, people would say, 'You're not allowed to wear such and such a tartan.' Load of crap. They seemed to make up those rules as they went along.

Sitting down in a kilt is a bit uncomfortable. I'm sensitive to wool, and it's rough on my bum. It can chafe. It's okay having the sporran banging into your willy, though. If you get a good rhythm going, your kilt swings at the right pace. It just gives your willy a wee dunt. Reminds you it's there. No bad thing. I know this because I was invited to lead the Tartan Parade along Sixth Avenue in New York City a couple of years ago, with thousands of Scottish people and Scottophiles lining the route. I was nervous that I wouldn't be up to it, but I managed to stride out the whole way, keeping ahead of all the great pipe bands and other groups. A Scottish kilt-maker called Howie Nicholsby had made me a fantastic kilt for the occasion. He's at the head of the movement to make the kilt a Windswept and Interesting alternative to trousers all over the world; I love that.

_____

When people first visit the Scottish Highlands, they tend to fall in love with the place. It certainly happened to me, years ago. Our guests would stumble out of their car in crumpled clothing, bleary-eyed and parched from a transatlantic flight and a long drive. They would take in the lofty stone seat of Wallaces, Andersons – and later of Roddicks – nestled in a majestic landscape of green and purple hills, with a silver trickle of the River Don running through it all. The sky seems higher in Aberdeenshire, and although there's a scant two or three weeks of fantastic summer weather per year, well, we always hoped our friends' arrival would coincide with that. Once a bagpiper in an ostrich-feather bonnet had piped our American pals into the house, they'd know for sure they weren't in Kansas any more. Miraculously, they'd entered a kind of living fantasy, a real-life *Brigadoon.*

The next ten days or so would be a riotous festival of hilariousness during picnics, hill walks, afternoon teas, dinners and ceilidhs, with funny people all trying to spar with each other. On a certain date in August, we'd get up early and dress in Highland gear in time to greet the Lonach Marchers – a 200-strong band of fiercely proud people who parade around the neighbourhood in their bands and clans before the annual Lonach Highland Games. They would arrive at Candacraig around nine in the morning. We'd welcome them with a dram each, and then they'd be on their way to the next stopping point, leaving us all moist of eye after witnessing such a moving display of the power and richness of the Highland culture.

———

When I turned sixty, Pamela organised an extraordinary birthday party weekend for me at Candacraig. It was a pretty enormous affair, attended by a couple of hundred people including family, neighbours, comedians, movie stars, musicians, artists, authors and other friends from all over the world. It was the most ridiculously frivolous way to spend a lot of money, but Pamela insisted I deserved it. It was nuts. She sent out invitations that read:

> *Doctor and Doctor Connolly*
> *Request the Pleasure of Your Company*
> *To Celebrate His Sexageniality*
> *And His*
> *Not Giving a Saggy-Arsed Fuck Thereof.*

Strip as many willows as you can

Pamela also organised the order of events:

Saturday, 17th August

6.30 P.M.:   HIGHLAND WELCOME. WEE BEVVIES ON THE LAWN. PIPE BAND.

8.00 P.M.:   DINNER AND SPECIAL ADDRESS TO THE HAGGIS.

10.00 P.M.: DANCE A WILD JIG.

MIDNIGHT: STOVIES AND CHAMPAGNE. BARE BUM CAVORTING.

Dress – Formal, Black-Tie Kilt or Windswept and Interesting.

Sunday, 18th August

12.00 NOON: CALEDONIAN BRUNCH. ADDRESS TO THE QUICHE.

AFTERNOON: FISHING, CABER-TOSSING, GORGE-WALKING, CYCLING, HIKING, ABSEILING, BANJO-PLAYING, OR SHOOTIN' THE BREEZE.
             (WARNING: ALL GOLFERS WILL BE FUCKED AND BURNED)

4.30 P.M.:   AFTERNOON TEA. ADDRESS TO THE SCONE. FALCONRY, ARCHERY, PUNTING, PONTIFICATING . . . OR A VICIOUS GAME OF CROQUET (GLASGOW RULES. FULL CONTACT).

7.00 P.M.:   BARBECUE, CAMPFIRE AND MUSIC. ADDRESS TO THE SAUSAGE. FIREWORKS.

11.00 P.M.: TALL TALES AND OUTRIGHT FABRICATIONS. ADDRESS TO THE NIGHTCAP.

Dress: Jeans, Breeks, or Rumpled Intensity.

It was brilliant. My only contribution was deciding who should address the haggis (it's a semi-serious tradition to have a dramatic recitation of the famous Robert Burns poem 'Address To A Haggis' before serving up the wee grey sausage). At our regular summer parties, the haggis had been brilliantly addressed by professional declaimers – and occasionally by clever friends such as Eric Idle and the actress Lizzie Bracco – but my birthday address took some consideration. I decided on Jimmy Reid, who gave a wonderful traditional reading, but he was unceremoniously eclipsed immediately afterwards by Robin Williams – who offered his unique 'Ode to the Haggis and Fiery Bums'.

———

Robin came to Candacraig every summer with his family. He was a fellow savant, another aficionado of the blurting-out of whatever comes to mind. We used to cycle from Strathdon to Ballater together, across an enormous, high-lying, treeless range of long hills like a bare, white moonscape. It was hard going. No jokes till we got there – just two guys freezing their bollocks off, battling through the heather hills.

But when our guests and I showed up at the Lonach Gathering – the Highland games in Strathdon – there'd be a wall of photographers facing us across the grounds. We were very torn about that. I suppose if you're sitting there with a gaggle of luminaries it would obviously attract interest, but I was always afraid it might kind of spoil the event. It was such a precious, local celebration of Highland culture – all the wee Scottish dancers tramping through the mud to get to the stage for their competitions, the children running their races, the big beefy caber-tossers, the tug o' war, and the marching pipe bands. The pibroch (traditional piping) competition was always the highlight for me, but generally it was a wonderfully low-tech affair; the judges used tennis shoes to mark the long jumps, and there would be an egg-and-spoon, sack, and three-legged races.

Occasionally, one of our group would bravely enter the hill race – an extremely challenging uphill run with natural obstacles threatening every step. Robin Williams took part in it each year. He was such a strong athlete, it's still hard to believe he's gone. I miss him terribly. And I sorely miss my best friend Danny Kyle, who died in 1998. And big Sean Connery . . . what a shame he's gone. I presented his BAFTA Lifetime Achievement to him. I said, 'You've done awfully well for a man with a speech defect . . . Congratulations, baldy. I wish I had your money!' My manager Steve Brown's death was a huge loss too, and I miss Florence every day of my life.

After the way I've lived, I consider myself very lucky to still be alive myself. I nearly died in the Highlands a few years ago. I was driving my bright-yellow Land Rover with a black 'om' sign on the bonnet. Just after I did a tour in it, I crashed it on an icy road and somersaulted into a field. Wrote it off. A local farmer witnessed the whole thing. He described my accident in lovely terms. He told people: 'Billy changed the shape of that Rover. Then he popped out the top of the window like a jack-in-the-box.'

Maybe I'm a bit accident-prone. Or maybe even a lot accident-prone. If you take the somersaulting yellow Land Rover and add the exploding Morris Minor, the Volkswagen Beetle crash in Weston-super-Mare, a red hot-rod I had that burst into flames, all the times I came off my motorbikes on corners trying to be an Isle of Man TT driver, the crash on my Shooting Star in which I hurt my elbows, a Golden Eagle Jeep accident I had in Scotland with Iris, the trike that fell on top of me when I miscalculated that U-turn while I was filming *Route 66* . . .

Yeah, I must be accident-prone. Most people would have had maybe one of those accidents in a lifetime. But they don't live the way I lived. If you come off the rails now and then it's just to be expected. There are two kinds of people. One group thinks motorbikes are exciting and the other thinks they're dangerous. I prefer the exciting crowd.

Last year I even fell off my bicycle. I overbalanced while mounting it and headbutted the gravel pavement. I had to get a couple of stitches in my eyebrow. Fuck. I wasn't even riding the damn thing, I was just trying to get on it, right outside my house. I had to be helped to my feet by the seafood delivery man. I miss riding my bicycle, but I guess those days are over. Pamela gave me an electric scooter for my birthday last year, but after she saw me trying to balance on it, it quietly disappeared . . .

I've told you before, I'm a lucky bugger. I survived a lot of shit – much of it brought on by myself. I probably shouldn't have escaped those years of the Wee Sui, my childhood, the shipyards, the twisted parachutes, exploding cars, motorbikes, all the drinking and not caring one jot what happened to me . . . but I did. Maybe what doesn't kill you fucks you up for life – but at least I'm still here. I'm fishing happily in Florida, and I'm not yet dead or broken. I once ran into the Geordie writer Ian La Frenais in Tramp nightclub in London. I was wearing my leather jodhpurs and a leather jacket. Pink socks and mules. I was sashaying towards him, and he said, 'You know what you look like?' I said, 'What?' He said, 'A welder who got away with it.'

26

**DON'T EAT ANYTHING
THAT COMES IN A BUCKET**

———

I'M DEAF. IT took me a while to accept it. I found all kinds of ways to avoid the truth – and the inevitable hearing aid. I tried to tell myself there was some foreign object in my ear. Some people mistakenly think they've gone deaf when, in fact, something's crawled in their ear and set up shop. My doctor told me a lot of people get creepy-crawlies trapped in their ears. He had someone with a gnat and a whole blowfly stuck in his ear; he was the Madame Tussauds of the insect world.

In my case, though, not one wee beastie had made its way past the forest of hair that, for reasons best known to itself, now flourishes and sprouts from my ears; I'm just plain deaf. After all those years in the shipyards without ear protection – plus all the rock 'n' roll concerts – I now have to wear hearing aids. I resisted them for a long time, but then a couple of years ago I was playing in Ireland and people thought I was forgetting what to say. They were writing about it in the papers. I wasn't forgetting a thing – I just couldn't hear the audience. It's terrible for a comedian if he can't hear the laughter. You can't *time* anything. Timing is an essential part of performing. A response to a funny line is a bit like a wave. The laughter might erupt suddenly, or it might arise slowly and build, but whatever the starting shape is, it will peak somewhere and then begin to die down. A comedian *must* be able to hear when that peak comes, and the exact moment on the fall when he should start talking again. It's an art form at which I got better and better over the years and eventually never had to think about. It's essential if you want to keep an audience laughing continually over a long period, which is what I like to do.

———

I guess my hearing slowly declined over many years. At that time when I was struggling in Ireland, I said to my manager Steve: 'I don't know what I'm doing wrong. I'm not going down as well as I normally do.' He said, 'What are you talking about? You're tearing them up!' But, realising I could no longer hear the audience's response, he sent away for a pair of those one-size-fits-all hearing aids. Enormous buggers. I didn't want to even try them, but once I did the difference was astounding. I realised what I'd been missing.

At that point we had moved to New York. Our three youngest children had finished school and disappeared to colleges in New York State, so we thought we'd move east too. After the tour in Ireland, I went home to New York, and Pamela got me to a hearing specialist for proper hearing aids. He did a few tests, and then he said, 'Do you want the ones that link to your phone and TV?' I had no idea such things even existed. They even did custom colours. 'I'll take a purple pair!' After they were fitted, the doctor held a piece of cardboard across his face. He said, 'What do you hear now?' I just burst out laughing. I could hear him perfectly. I found out I'd been lip-reading for years. With my new hearing aids, I could finally look away from people when they're talking to me. The first time I came home with them, I walked into the kitchen in our New York apartment. I said, 'What's that noise?' It was the floor creaking as I walked along. I'd never heard it before. Welcome home.

Nobody should be embarrassed about having hearing aids. The technology is impressive – the way they can connect with your devices by Bluetooth. Years earlier, I had come across men in Los Angeles who had older-style hearing aids that seemed to be extremely troublesome in restaurants and gatherings. You'd see Ronald Reagan trying to adjust his. David Hockney, the painter, had lived down the street from us in the Hollywood Hills. He had custom hearing aids – one red with yellow controls, and the other yellow with red controls. At a big starry party in Beverly Hills one night Pamela introduced David Hockney to Frank Sinatra, and they compared notes about deafness. That same night I was asked to say a few words at dinner. I hate performing in any place that's not a proper theatre, but I obliged and did a few minutes. After dinner, everyone started moving into the drawing room for coffee. Frank Sinatra's wife Barbara came up to me. She said, 'Oh Billy, Frank really enjoyed you!' I said, 'That's great, thanks very much.' She said, 'Wait a minute . . .' She turned to Frank, who was a short distance away, standing in a doorway of another room in which a live band was playing background music. Frank was focusing intently on the band. He was singing along – not with a microphone or anything, just crooning with it and snapping his fingers. He was really getting into it. *'That's why the lady is a tramp . . . She likes the coooool, fresh wind in her hair . . . Life without care . . .'* Anywhere else in the world this would have gotten everybody's attention, but there were so many huge stars around nobody was taking any notice. Barbara Sinatra persisted. 'Frank! Frank! FRANK!!'

'Life without care . . . She's broke . . . It's oke . . . Califor . . .'

'Frank! FRANK!!'

I'm going 'Oh fuck.'

He turned around and came stomping over. 'Whaaattt? WHHAATTT??'

She said, 'This is Billy.'

He said, 'Yeah?'

'I was just telling him you enjoyed him.'

He said, 'YEAH? Is that IT?'

She said, 'Yeah . . .'

He turned on his heel and went back to the band.

––––

We moved to New York in 2005. When the moving van arrived, I was looking forward to it. Manhattan just exudes life and humanity – the sheer numbers of people and the size of the place. It's a Windswept and Interesting *city*. I really enjoyed walking there – looking in the shop windows and picking up a bagel. New York bagels are sensational. Taste explosion. I just loved the street life. All the mad people. A woman on Madison Avenue accused me of killing Jesus. 'There he is!!! He killed Jesus!! That's him!!!' I was thinking, 'Nothing's changed since St Peter's . . . It's STILL my fault.' Mad people have become more difficult to spot, though. There used to be a lot of lovely crazies talking to the sky. But since the smartphone and Bluetooth were invented, everybody walks along talking to the air.

Sometimes New York was so crowded that every time we

came out of our apartment onto Fifth Avenue it was like entering a shopping mall on Black Friday. Shopping terrifies me. You've got those fuckers coming up behind you: 'Hello, can I help you?'

'No! *NO!*'

I hate those bastards. You pick up a tie and they race over with a pair of shoes. 'These will go with the tie!'

'FUCK OFF! Don't come back or I'll *hit* you!'

———

In some parts of the world, men and women have a different experience when they go shoe shopping. There's a lack of variety available for men, which always frustrates me. There'd be one wall for women that's a *blaze* of colour – pink, yellow, red, blue, green – with shoes made out of plastic, leather, cloth, hessian, hemp, velvet, suede, with thin straps, wide straps, no straps, slingbacks, stilettoes, boots, half-boots, wee tiny boots, leopardskin flap-over things, laces, Velcro, belt up the leg, tie under the sole . . . Then you'll go over to the men's section: brown and black. Lace-ups, slip-ons, boots – goodbye. 'Do you do that in a nine and a half?'

'No half sizes.'

I'll be going: 'For fuck's sake! They HATE men!' But New York is different. Shops there fully cater for the adventurous type of guy. I bought green velvet lace-ups there – my all-time favourites.

Shopkeepers shouldn't discriminate. They should offer equivalent variety for men and women. It would be worth it, because men are actually the best, the low-maintenance shoppers – since we don't know the price of anything: 'That's great, how much is it?'

'That's five hundred and twenty.'

'Oh, okay, then, there you are, thanks, bye.'

If that was a woman, she'd go: '*What*? Are you *serious*?'

———

It rains a lot in New York. I like that. If you're born in Scotland or Ireland, you have to like the rain, because it's there whether you want it to be or not. I mean, these two countries didn't get green by mistake. They have the kind of rain that can remove your tattoos. In New York, the rain gives you a bad hair day every day of your life – so that's something you don't have to worry about. You just get yourself a sexy raincoat and get on with it.

I had a campaign a while ago – it obviously didn't work very well – to make the TV weather people in Britain stop calling rainy weather 'bad weather'. If it rains every day, and they say it's 'bad' weather, you're going to be seriously pissed off most of your life. 'Sorry, ladies and gentlemen, it's going to be yet another crap day tomorrow.' That can seriously affect the national psyche. When people are setting off each day to earn their living – or, even worse, setting off for a nice leisurely day out with the family – they really don't need these characters telling them it's going to be shite out there. Anyway, there's no such thing as bad weather; only the wrong clothes.

I taught my children to like rain. They were brought up in Los Angeles where it only rains occasionally, but I taught them how to take their shoes and socks off, jump in puddles, and just experience it. To me rain feels natural, it feels normal, it feels right. In Scotland, they say, 'The graveyard's full of people who would love this weather.'

Rain has done me a huge favour. Changed my life. I was in

Montreal on tour a few years ago, and during the day I was bored watching the telly. I went out for a walk, but it was freezing. It was pishing down that frozen rain they get in Canada that really hurts your face. After a while it got even worse. I was being bombed by blocks of ice and I couldn't even see properly, so I started walking back to my hotel. There was a pet shop opposite, so I nipped in to warm up. I watched the tortoises and puppies until the owner started looking at me like I was a kitty-rustler. Next door was an art store. I went in for a look and – for some unknown reason – bought myself some felt-tip pens and a sketchbook, then went straight back to my room and started to draw.

In the past I had never been able to draw, but I started drawing blobby-type things I called 'islands'. I divided them up into different backgrounds and colours and became utterly engrossed in that. I stuck to that style, drawing different kinds of islands for about a week. When the tour was over and I arrived home in New York, I said to Pamela: 'I've been drawing these things . . . they're pretty crap but do you think they're getting better?' She said, 'They're definitely getting better.' So, I carried on.

Then I started to develop my drawings. I started drawing people who looked as though they lived in sleeping bags, doing various things like standing in a circle, kneeling, and standing up. I liked them. I stumbled on a way of drawing the background with random lines, and eventually I changed the lines from being the background to being across the people like bandages. 'Why are they wearing bandages?' people asked. I couldn't explain. And I couldn't draw eyes, so I drew the people with blindfolds . . . and it went from strength to strength.

———

When I was a boy, my sister used to take me and Michael to the Kelvingrove Art Gallery. There was a great painting there by Salvador Dali – *Christ of St John of the Cross* – that was way superior to the crude religious pictures I'd been exposed to at school. That school stuff had put me off art, but my appreciation for it was restored by the great paintings upstairs at Kelvingrove Art Gallery. We used to spend hours there. One of the best sights I ever saw at the gallery was not one of the exhibits. It was a fully kitted-out Teddy boy, leaning by a pillar in the foyer. This guy looked brilliant – long jacket, suede 'brothel creeper' shoes, drainpipe trousers. I never forgot him – in fact, I've been drawing him lately.

Over the years, I've become very friendly with a few artists – John Byrne, whom I've already mentioned (also known as 'Patrick'). I love some of the well-known Australian artists – Ken Done, Asher Bilu and Brett Whiteley. Brett died at fifty-three of a heart attack, which was a terrible loss. Apart from being a stunning painter, Brett was one of the wildest wee men I've ever met. He came to my show at the Sydney Opera House, then arrived backstage afterwards and asked a terrible question that lots of other people have asked: 'How do you remember all that stuff?'

I patiently explained there was no 'remembering' involved, that I pretty much made it up night after night.

He said, 'Fuck off. I don't believe you.'

I said, 'It's true! Everyone knows that.'

Then Brett says, 'Okay. I'm coming back tomorrow night to check it out.'

He did. The following night I did a completely different show, not even bringing up one subject I'd mentioned in the previous concert . . . which wasn't that easy at that late point in the tour.

Brett came back after that second concert and said, 'Okay, Billy. I guess you're right. That was incredible . . . I've never seen anything like it. But just to be sure, I'm coming back for the third time tomorrow night . . .'

'Fuck off,' I said.

Ken Done is a remarkable painter. I just love his work. Many years ago, he taught me something important about painting and drawing. I was staying at Pearl Beach in New South Wales. He said, 'What catches your eye outside there?' I said, 'Well, I get up in the morning and eat breakfast outside on the verandah.' He said, 'What's that like?' I said, 'Well, it's really peaceful, then all these really brightly coloured galahs swoop down and try to eat my toast . . .' Ken said, 'So, you could use the colour of the galahs, but it's more important to try to get onto the paper the *feeling* of them swooping down.'

On a good day now, I can get a feeling onto the paper. Andrew White, the director of publishing at Washington Green/Castle Fine Art, showed interest in my drawings, which was an extraordinary thing. He's promoted my artworks and mounted exhibitions for me. I took it as a great compliment. I'm not a very confident artist, though. I keep waiting for someone to say that it's rubbish. I don't do 'art speak', so I don't know how to describe them. They're just . . . thoughts. I sometimes drift off what I've been doing, and the thing ends up cartoonish, which I don't like – so I toss it.

I'm immensely proud of some of my best drawings, though. I did one that is a dachshund with wheels supporting its middle body . . . I had to sign some prints of that one the other day, and the more I did, the more I loved it. I'm really proud of the one called *Purgatory* – it's a man standing in the bow of a boat with a box on his head. He looks like he's a prisoner of the man at the tiller steering the boat who's wearing a black cowl. I drew something the day before yesterday that I'm quite pleased with. It's not finished, but it's quite exciting. It's a person on his own, just passing time, doing things people do when they're all alone . . . taking a little thread off their jeans, fiddling with a button. I'm creating sculptures as well, which is a delightful thing.

I can't quite handle it when I go to one of my exhibitions, though. I've met people who collect my stuff, which is a serious compliment, but I still can't get my head round it. Maybe you shouldn't dwell on that kind of thing. I find it extraordinarily wonderful that people want to buy my drawings. Biggest surprise of my life.

———

There are great people in New York. I had a wonderfully funny doctor – he always had a joke for me. He'd do my regular medical exam, and when it was time for the prostate examination he'd slap on his gloves. 'Billy . . . it's your favourite bit! Get yourself ready!' Then he'd hold up his gloved hand. 'Pick a finger!' I'd go, 'Ehhhh . . . I'll have the one with the signet ring. Don't tell me what it says, I'll read it inside . . .'

Next time I went in to see him I'd say, 'What, no flowers? Dinner and a movie?'

But as soon as I moved to New York, strange unwelcome things started happening to my body. Parkinson's disease, deafness, prostate cancer, sleep apnoea . . . I ask you, is that coincidence? Or is the place jinxed? In fact, once I turned fifty, every part of my wee body came under review. It was horrible. My doctor lost interest in my testicles and took a morbid interest in my arsehole. Because the chances of testicular cancer recede as you get older, and the chances of prostate cancer increase. Isn't life a bowl of cherries?

Parkinson's disease is named after James Parkinson, who studied it at the beginning of the nineteenth century. It used to be called Shaking Palsy, so I'm real glad *he* showed up. It affects the left side of me, mostly. It makes me walk stiffly, and my left hand behaves like it's got a mind of its own – shiggles about and creeps up my body. When I'm talking about something else, it thinks I won't notice, and starts climbing up. The strangest thing is, if I look at it, it dashes away guiltily. Bastard.

Being diagnosed with Parkinson's was weird. I was in L.A. doing Conan O'Brien's talk show. They put me up at a hotel called the Sportsman's Lodge. It was near the cigar store, so in the late afternoon I would walk there and back. I had done that on two consecutive days, and when I came back to the hotel on the third evening there was a little crowd of people in the lobby – young girls and some adults. I was walking through the lobby and a guy came up to me. He said, 'Excuse me . . .'

'Yeah?'

He said, 'I'm a big fan. I'm here with some dancers from Tasmania.'

'Oh, that's nice . . . blah de blah.'

Then he said, 'Listen, I'm a doctor, and I've noticed you walking in here and . . . er . . . your gait . . .' He said, 'You have the gait of a man with Parkinson's disease.'

That stopped me in my tracks. 'What??'

He said, 'I think you should check it out with your doctor.'

I went to my L.A. doctor and he did some tests, then said, 'You're fine.'

A bit later Pamela and some of my friends noticed my hand shaking. I also started to kind of freeze from time to time – I'd just stop moving, or I'd stop talking in the middle of a sentence. So, I went to see a Parkinson's specialist in New York. She diagnosed me with the disease and started treating me. It was a huge shock, and quite frightening. This thing wasn't going to go away. It was a big unwelcome aspect of my life that was going to have to be dealt with.

After a while, the symptoms came crashing in. I didn't have to look for them. It became very scary once I started having trouble getting out of chairs, because I thought I was going to be condemned to that for ever. It would be downhill all the way. Even though people said, 'You've got a very mild case – you're going to be okay,' I didn't believe them. I thought they were just being kind.

Eventually, the scariness diminished, and I was just accepting of it. You can't stay scared for ever. I used to wonder what people thought when they saw me in restaurants being helped out of my chair, but it really wasn't as bad as I imagined. There was no pain involved. There was just a sort of doom that came with it, but you soon get used to it. You just carry it around as another wee burden. All in all, it could have been a lot worse. I expected to shake a lot more than I do. Once I started being funny about it, everything seemed better. I'd quote Rick Shapiro, who said, 'Shaky is the new cool', and my theme song became Jerry Lee Lewis's 'Whole Lotta Shakin' Goin' On'.

———

Even the cancer could have been a lot worse. It could have been one of the big ones. People said, 'Prostate cancer? That's an easy one.' Ask Frank Zappa if that was 'an easy one'. He died of it. To tell the truth, I thought it was coming. Not through any symptoms – I just had the feeling that I might be next. When the cancer doctor did a biopsy and said, 'It's cancerous,' I thought 'Oh fuck.'

It's over now, anyway. I got the all-clear. I was lucky. They caught it very early. The doctor who did the operation said to me: 'First of all, you're not gonna die.' He did a little drawing on a piece of paper. Nerves and muscles. He said, 'We just do this . . . and we'll keep that there.' It was good. He ripped it out and now I pee like a racehorse. I went back to see the doctor about two months after my surgery, and he started to ask me very personal questions. He said, 'Can you still achieve erection?'

I said, 'Oh yes.' I'm thinking, 'Please don't ask me to show you!'

He said, 'We have various pills and potions, you know, and we have a little class for penile rehabilitation.'

I thought, 'I'm not sitting in a circle wanking with *strangers*!'

———

By the time we moved to New York I had already made some of my *World Tour of* . . . series. The first of these was my *World Tour of Scotland*, in which I drove all over the country in my yellow Land Rover – the one I eventually totalled in the Highlands. I performed nightly in theatres all over Scotland, and interviewed people in lovely Scottish places each day. The Tour started in the Isle of Arran, where I played some folk music with a few of my old friends like Geordie McGovern. In Glasgow I filmed in Dover Street, where I was born. They pulled our house down when I was in my twenties – which is a shame 'cos now where are they gonna put my wee plaque? I also pointed out the tenement in Stewartville Street where I first lived with my aunts. I filmed at Loch Lomond, where I jumped off the pier naked, and I toured around my favourite bits of Inverness, Wick, Edinburgh. When I got to Dundee, I climbed a tower to look over the River Tay. I was reciting the poem 'The Tay Bridge Disaster' by William McGonagall, about a tragedy that occurred in 1879. As I read the poem, snow started falling on me – heavy snow that quickly became a blizzard storm. It was very fitting:

So the train mov'd slowly along the Bridge of Tay,
Until it was about midway.
Then the central girders with a crash gave way,
And down went the train and passengers into the Tay!
The Storm Fiend did loudly bray,
Because ninety lives had been taken away

Next, I made the *World Tour of Australia* and *World Tour of New Zealand*, which made Pamela very jealous, because I saw far more of her native lands than she ever did. My *World Tour of New Zealand* combined performances from my *Too Old to Die Young* live shows with filming from Stewart Island at the extreme south of New Zealand to Ninety Mile Beach in the north, much of it on my custom-made purple trike. In Australia I covered a lot of ground too. I even got to Fraser Island, and sat playing my banjo at sunset on the largest sand island in the world. I'm not really into the main tourist sites; I prefer the weird – like in Melbourne I got to see some original 'anti-masturbation' gloves from the nineteenth century. Call me old-fashioned, but even with those monstrosities I think a chap could manage. And in Alice Springs, they have the weirdest boat race in the world. The river there has no water most of the time, so teams of people race in bottomless boats, running along the dry riverbed. They've even had to cancel the race some years, due to rainfall causing river flow; it's nuts.

My favourite animal in the world is the hairy-nosed wombat, and I got to visit one in Adelaide. They are the most extraordinary creatures, snuffling around like a big fat living haggis. One of the nicest things I ever did in New Zealand was releasing a kiwi into the wild. It had been raised in captivity since it was an egg. They had just cleared the terrain of mice and rats – things that were its predators – so it was safe to release it, and I got to let it go. It was a beautiful wee thing. I saw far less benign creatures in Australia. Off Darwin in the Northern Territory, I came across saltwater crocodiles. Oh fuck. If they can't get you while swimming, those bastards climb out of the water and go after you on land. It's like being chased by a hungry train.

———

I made some other TV series while I was based in New York – *Journey to the Edge of the World*, in which I travelled from the Atlantic Ocean to the Pacific Ocean by the fabled Northwest Passage, *Route 66*, in which I rode my trike the full length of the famous highway from Chicago to L.A., *Big Send Off*, which was all about the American style of death, funerals and memorials, and *Tracks Across America*, in which I travelled by Amtrak train in a giant circle all over the USA.

During the filming of *Big Send Off*, I started feeling ill. It was not long after my prostate surgery. I was in New Orleans, and I got quite sore in my groin department, so I went to the hospital. The guy said, 'I think we'll have to flood your bladder and take a look.' I said, 'Sure,' but I was panicking. 'If they're going to flood my bladder, they'll have to create a leak somewhere, so water pours in and out. Maybe they'll jab my willy with a fork and stick me outside in the rain?' But he put me on this big table, naked, and there was a very nice, very beautiful nurse, holding my penis. I was trying to send a message to my penis, 'Don't fucking MOVE!' The doctor shoved some kind of tube into my willy and started to flood it. I got an overwhelming desire to piss up in the air. I thought, 'Oh God, please don't pee over the lovely nurse!'

He said, 'This is the camera and the light.' Before I could yell, '*Whaaattt???*' he stuck it in.

He said, 'Would you like to watch this?'

I said, 'Sure.'

A big screen lit up on the wall. It was like a pink aquarium, with the seaweed swaying in the bottom. The doctor was pointing out areas of interest. He said, 'This is your sphincter.'

I said, 'What's it doing *there*?' I thought your sphincter was your bum-hole! But apparently, you've more than one sphincter. I kind of like my bum-hole. Because it's a circular muscle. It's very interesting the way it works, like a lens in a camera. And its function in life is to keep your arse closed – for obvious reasons. Otherwise, you'd drown in the bath, wouldn't you? That's why they invented soap on a rope. Well, the tour went on.

'This is this and this is that . . .' He was down among the seaweed, and he came upon a piece of white plastic and a piece of metal, both the same size. And together at the same time we said, 'What the fuck's *that*??' They'd been left in from the oper-ation and they'd gone adrift.

He said, 'Oh, we'll have to get *that* out of there.'

I said, 'I couldn't agree more.'

So, he sent in this other thing to try to catch hold of them remotely, and on about the fifth attempt he got both of them. 'Oh, y*aaaayyyy*!' Then he said, 'Now we'll have to remove them.' But during the tour I hadn't seen an emergency exit, so I said, 'Oh, God, you don't mean they have to go out the same way they came in?'

He said, 'Yes, I'm afraid so.' He said, 'Do me a favour, could you move' – it was the sneakiest thing I've ever had done to me – he said, 'Could you move the toe next to your big toe?'

I went, 'Yeah, I—' and he yanked it out: *scccwwwiiippppp!* 'Aaaaaggghhhhhh!!!!!!!!!!!!!!'

———

At least my heart's in good shape. Florence had a friend who lived in a place called Pollokshaws, which is kind of posh, and her next-door neighbour was a welder who was as rough as a badger. He was always swearing, and so was his wife. This friend met the wife in the street. 'How's Willy doing?'

She said, 'Oh, he's not well at all.'

'Oh really? What's wrong with him?'

This was the answer, verbatim: 'The doctor says his heart's fucked.'

I wanted to be a fly on the wall in the doctor's office. 'Well, Mr McBumferty, I've given you every possible examination. I've thumbed through every one of these copious volumes, and I've given you electrocardiograph tests. I've come to the conclusion, in the words of the great Hippocrates himself: your heart's fucked. But fear not, Willy, fear not. We shall amble, you and I, into Glasgow, to the Royal Infirmary, where I believe they have just taken possession of a brand-new Defuckulator.'

I have longevity in my family, I sometimes say to people: 'I don't think I've got long . . .' but there's no scientific reason for that. My grandfather lived 'til his late nineties. So, I could live another twenty years . . . if I look after myself. But I don't really *want* to look after myself. I don't *want* to exercise like a madman and eat lettuce all day. I want to sit in front of the telly and eat chocolate biscuits, okay?

My wife tries to get me to eat healthy food, but her efforts are in vain. I eat what I please. I'm well aware of the rules of nutrition. The way I see it, if I want to eat a bag of Licorice Allsorts for lunch and spend the afternoon battling explosive diarrhoea – that's my fucking prerogative. Yes, I should lose some weight. But I don't like the things you have to do to slim down. As they say in Scotland, 'You're a long time looking at the lid.' Pamela says, 'Billy, why don't you try the wholewheat bread instead of the white? It'll be much better for you.' No, it won't. I LIKE white bread and I fucking LOATHE wholewheat bread. If I stop eating white bread it might increase my life expectancy by one whole week . . . but it won't be a week when I'm young and shiny and shagging everything that moves. It'll be a week when I'm stuck in bed moaning and bawling and smelling of piss.

Anyway, I could never live without pizza. New York pizza is the best. They get it so right there. Especially at Joe's on Bleecker Street. But they do something I don't agree with – they sell pizza at the movies . . . and NO ice cream. Now call me old-fashioned but, to me, movies and ice cream are inextricably linked. I tried to buy some ice cream at a downtown cinema. 'Can I have some ice cream?'

The man said, 'We don't have any.'

I said, 'What? It's the *movies*! The movies with no *ice cream*? I can't watch a movie without Haagen-Dazs!!!'

He was completely unmoved: 'Oh, we don't have any in the building, sir.' Then he said brightly: 'We have pizza. Thin-crust pizza, thick-crust pizza, stuffed-crust pizza, deep-dish pizza . . .' And on and on came this big list of other shit, including hot dogs, hamburgers, cheeseburgers, nachos, tacos, waffles, barbecue flatbreads, pizza flatbreads, buffalo chicken flatbreads, 'Bavarian pretzels', chicken wings, chicken thighs, chicken breasts, chicken bites, chicken tenders, mozzarella sticks, fries, curly fries, mega fries and popcorn. And everything came in a bucket.

My advice to you, if you want to lose a bit of weight: Don't eat anything that comes in a bucket. Buckets are the kitchen utensils of the farmyard. There's nothing more discouraging than sitting waiting for your movie to come on, and somebody comes into the row with a great big armful of stuff. And a bucket of Coca-Cola to go with it. 'Excuse me . . .' It's raining popcorn and butter. 'Could I have more butter in my bucket, please?'

'Do you want the Large Bucket, sir, or the Family Trough? You could sit it between the four of you and tuck in hands-free . . .'

27

SAVE THE BABY CRIMPLES

———

I HATE SAND. Horrible stuff. It gets in every little crease in your body. And I've got *plenty* of little creases. It sticks to you. The mixture of sunscreen and sand on your skin is hideous. A well-oiled body plus sand turns you into a jelly donut. Sometimes, on the fancier beaches, there might be a shower, so at the end of the torture you can wash the sand off your shoulders, chest and back. But you can't get it off the parts of you that have the most creases, because there's children nearby. And they've all been taught about perverts. '*Daddy!* There's a man over there touching his willy!' You can't wash down there so you have to leave the sand in your crotch, and it sandpapers your scrotum all the way home. *Scrrrr-scrrr-scrrr-scrrr-scrrr.* Your willy's like a lobster with its throat cut! The beach would be a good idea if it wasn't so physically demanding.

———

I was happy in New York because there's no beach for miles, but after I got Parkinson's disease my wife decided we had to get out of the city so I could relax, be healthy, and go fishing.

Where did she move us to? The Florida Keys. It's one big fucking BEACH! I was condemned to live at the beach for the rest of my life.

Luckily, the place where we live isn't actually on a sandy beach. It's by the water, though – between the Atlantic Ocean and the Mexican Gulf, and as close to Cuba as you can get. When Pamela suggested we move here I pretty much thought it was a good idea. She's usually right about that kind of thing. I was finding New York hard going – the extremes of weather didn't suit me any more. I didn't want to slip on ice and end up face down in the snow without the ability to get up again, so I was starting to feel like a prisoner in my apartment.

I don't know Florida very well. I had read that Key Largo – and other islands of the Florida Keys – were great places to be, and quite different from the rest of Florida. Mainland Florida has a lot of retirement communities. It's a bit of a cliché to leave New York and spend your final years in the wealthy beach suburbs of Miami, but the Florida Keys are very different – more of an infamous hideout for crazy fuckers.

I had been on fishing trips to the Florida Keys in the past, and I liked what it stands for. I like the 'Conch' attitude. They don't care about the outside world. They see themselves as being independent from mainland America, although they're not. They got pissed off with a few things and just declared that henceforth they would be the 'Conch Republic'. They decided: 'Right. We think differently, we behave differently. You don't like it? Fuck off.'

A person who is born here is called a 'conch'. Everywhere else in the world they'd say it like 'consh', but here they say 'conk'. I became an honorary conch. That means I'm now aligned with the group of rebels who formed the Conch Republic. I was filming my *Ultimate World Tour*, all about South Florida, and one of the original conch guys was explaining their revolution. In the early eighties, the locals here were furious that federal border control agents set up a roadblock just past the mainland and started searching vehicles for contraband. So, they announced they were seceding from the rest of the USA and forming a 'micro nation' called the Conch Republic. They even got on a biplane and pelted the US Navy with bread rolls. That really appealed to me. I was laughing out loud. The guy who was explaining it said, 'You sound worthy of being a conch!' I was immediately inaugurated. There was no big ceremony involved, just a statement of fact. I now fly the Conch Republic flag at my home.

———

For more than a year from March 2020 I found myself locked down in Key West. It wasn't a strict lockdown because most people in the Keys couldn't give a fuck. But there are worse places to be quarantined. And we're well protected from other threats – the Conch Republic has its own petite army, navy and air force. The Conch navy is particularly impressive – around ten wee civilian boats, with an admiral and everything. They even have their own peculiar musical instrument. It's made from a giant seashell with a neck on it and is a bit like a ukulele. I tried playing an electric one and it was rather nice.

All kinds of pirates, vagabonds, scoundrels and nutters created the place, and that suits me just lovely. In the early nineteenth century, it wasn't just big-name pirates like Blackbeard who used hidey-holes in the Florida Keys to cause havoc for passing ships. Until there were proper lighthouses and marine markers around the coast, the locals had a vast wrecking and salvaging industry, and became very wealthy from it. There was a Cuban-style cigar factory here; in fact, there was a lot of contact with Cuba – including direct flights – until Castro came along. Then there was a mass influx of Cubans fleeing his regime.

———

Key West is known as a town for artists and writers. Ernest Hemingway, Tennessee Williams and Robert Frost lived here, and Judy Blume still does (she runs a bookshop downtown). Shel Silverstein, who wrote *The Giving Tree*, had a house here too. He wrote a great song called 'Freakin' at the Freaker's Ball' that I always meant to do onstage. The big tree that was at the front of his little house in the historic downtown area fell down in the last hurricane. See, that's what happens when you live in a hurricane belt. Your house blows away. I'd seen the black and white movie *Key Largo* with Humphrey Bogart and Lauren Bacall and I remembered that it was about a big storm, so just before we left New York I thought, 'Hurricanes go there. Maybe it's a silly place to move to.' On the other hand, places we'd lived in before didn't necessarily make much sense either. There always seems to be something – earthquakes, tornados, pollution . . . at least you know in advance when a hurricane's coming so you can prepare your place and get out.

We had a big one – Hurricane Irma – just after we moved here. When they announced it was on its way, it was looking pretty serious. Seemed like it could flatten the place. We were all ordered to evacuate and even the Coast Guard was leaving. I wanted to stick around and experience it like the conchs do. Those crazy buggers just put on life jackets and hide in the cupboard with a bottle of rum. Pamela made me leave. She said, 'I'm staying another day to board up the house. You and Daisy are leaving in a few hours.'

I said, 'No! I'm not going.'

She gave me THAT look. 'You're on the midday flight to Los Angeles.' And that was that.

———

I love the light here. It's kind of yellowy. Almost always sunny. Puts me in a positive mood. I've mainly lost my sense of guilt about being in the sun. Scottish people tend to see the sun appearing and frown. 'Och . . . we'll pay for this!' I've had to train myself to like it. The residents seem happy to be here, which is always a plus. It's a good thing about Australia too, and New Zealand. The people are glad to be there. And it makes such a difference.

There's something wonderful about living near the water, whether it's Loch Lomond or the Zambezi or the ocean. The tide comes, the tide goes out, the water's choppy, the water's calm . . . It's a constantly changing backdrop. The fishing here is extraordinary. The water is shallow, and it is very fertile. It encourages all sorts of fish to come and eat here. Huge fish. The breeds of fish I like to catch – tarpon and permit and bonefish – are difficult to catch and they are not sought out for eating, so they'll always be there. The people who catch them put them back. At a fishing place I stayed at in Mexico they gave out prizes – if you caught a permit or a tarpon or a bonefish, you got a silver badge to wear on your hat. I won it one day and wore it proudly at dinner. There were other guests there who weren't fishing – they were just there for a holiday. One of them, a big American guy, said, 'I don't know why you put the fish back. It seems stupid to me. You should eat them.'

The manager said, 'Do you take part in any sport?'

And the guy said, 'Yeah – tennis.'

And the manager said, 'When you finish the game, do you eat the ball?'

———

I like all the wildlife here in the Keys – all the feral chickens, the six-toed cats you see at Hemingway's house, and the enormous green and orange iguanas that most locals hate. I love the tiny indigenous deer, and the roosters. You forget how beautiful roosters are 'til you see their feathers glinting in the sunlight. You see them out strolling in the main street with their babies, and when the sun hits them, they're spectacular-looking creatures. We were in town the other day and a chicken was crossing the road with twelve or so baby chickadees. It was the most beautiful scene. People were slowing down to let it cross. There are harmless nurse sharks, barracuda, snowy ibis and huge pelicans. The manatees are a good reason for coming here. I just love them. Some bastard wrote 'Trump' on the back of one in 2020; luckily, it was written in algae, not scored into the flesh. Many of them have scars from running into propellers. They are endangered creatures. I think it's because they're so sociable. They like people and get too close.

Manatees seem familiar to me. The first time I went to Ballyconneely in west Connemara where my ancestors came from, I went into the local bar and ordered a drink. There was a man sleeping at a table in the corner, and the barman tried to wake him. 'Arthur! Arthur!' The guy looked up suspiciously.

'Arthur! Look who's here! – Billy Connolly!' Arthur stuck his head up and gave me a very old-fashioned look. 'Connolly?! . . . Yous came from the sea and yous'll fucking go back again.' In Irish mythology, the Conneelys were creatures a bit like seals that came ashore and shed their skin to become people. Such mythological creatures are called silkies. I really like the idea.

I'm all for being a silkie. I was thinking about it the other day when I was sitting on my deck in Florida and a big manatee came swimming up. I was thinking, 'That's my family!' It's probably just my imagination, but those manatees seem to know me. They come to see me all the time. I love them. Big peaceful vegetarians, sauntering about in the water and checking me out. They lie on their backs flapping their flippers and guzzle the fresh water that runs off our deck after it rains. They're the hippies of the sea. Make me feel great. '*Hoila Noila Noila*' – that's what you're supposed to sing to silkies. I think I'll try it with the manatees.

———

Some brilliant human crazies have gravitated to this place. In past years I used to come to the Florida Keys to fish with my son Jamie. We would stay on a small Key at the Sugarloaf Lodge and go fishing in the back country with a brilliant guide called Will Benson. The guy who owned Sugarloaf Lodge told me that the writer Hunter S. Thompson stayed there and held a fireworks display indoors in his room.

Lockdown here was peculiar. Just to go out in a car, drive through the town and back again was a big deal. I sat my dog on my knee and looked through the window. Complained about people who were not wearing masks. Sometimes we'd get a takeaway chicken sandwich from Popeyes – that was a big day out.

My dog Django is a delight – he's such a lovely character. Although he turned on me this morning. He'd taken my glasses and I was trying to get them back. He's a wee bugger. A while back he ate one of my hearing aids. It was awful to be kept away from Scotland, and from family, but you get to like where you are. Besides, we were dead thankful that we had the means to get our groceries delivered; outside on the street there would be lines of cars waiting for their turn at the local food bank.

During the Covid pandemic, someone asked me what I wanted to do when it was over. I said, 'I dunno. Maybe go for dinner at the Square Grouper restaurant.'

You know about 'square fish'? That's what they call packages of drugs that are found floating around in the ocean — most likely having been dumped by smugglers running from the authorities. They keep a careful eye on that kind of thing here. A few months ago, they found a shitload of marijuana – 150 pounds of it altogether – floating off the island chain and washed up on shore. Just after that a man fishing off Sugarloaf Key found seventy-four pounds of cocaine. The local newspaper ran a classic piece of journalism: '*The Keys sheriff's office came across some white stuff Christmas week. But it wasn't the usual kind of snow . . .*' I love the local papers.

———

During the Covid lockdown in 2020 I broke the world TV-watching record. I even returned to my old habit of shouting at the television. This had begun when I was around sixty: 'FUCK you ya WANKER! You think I ZIP UP AT THE BACK???!!!' I did this at the news, shows about current affairs, political interviews, anything like that – like they could *hear* me. 'RUBBISH!! LIAR! ANSWER THE QUESTION YA DIRTY BASTARD . . . ANSWER THE *QUESTION*!!!!!' But after a while, a change came over me. I realised that all the people I was shouting at had become such well-established wankers that it was no longer a surprise. After that epiphany I'd just nod and go, 'Aye, there you go again, ya lying bastard.' Anyway, if you shout at someone on the TV they're not going to turn round and try to whack you on the jaw. So, where's the fun in that?

But during lockdown, I lost that complacency and returned to active TV shouting – especially while watching 'ghost hunter' shows. I'm not a believer, but I find them riveting. The search for the 'entity' is always disappointing, but I live in hope. I keep waiting for a ghost to appear; I wish someone would come in the door with no head, or there would be a visitation by a 'Lady in White' or a 'Lady in Grey' – they always gave them names like that, to make them sound elegant. If they were just 'Woman in an Apron' or 'Guy in Baggy Shorts' nobody would give a fuck. In the American shows they have electronic equipment to track down ghosts, and instruments so they can ask the spirit a question: 'Did you murder somebody?' 'Whom did you murder?' The instrument goes '*bsjkqwldb*', and the presenter interprets the gibberish any way he pleases: 'Did you hear that? It said Alexander!' That's when I shout at the TV: 'NO IT FUCKING DIDN'T!!! IT SAID, '*BSDJQWLDB!!!*'

What would those shows do without somebody squealing, 'What was that?!!' The investigators always act as though they got a fright. They'll be in some big creepy mansion at night-time, in total darkness, with a night vision lens. And they'll go: 'What's that? Jesus! What was that???!!!' I want to smack them. You shouldn't be frightened if you're in there looking for a ghost. It's like going fishing and getting a fright when you catch one.

Those shows have been on TV for so many years now that if there was such a thing as a ghost it would have showed up by now. All that shite about energy. *'A certain energy'* . . .

Mind you, one evening in Ireland I was in my dressing room preparing to go onstage. I didn't have my watch, so I didn't know whether it was time to start or not. I always waited in my dressing room until someone came in to say, 'It's time.' Well, this night in Dublin I was bored in my room, so I went for a walk through the corridors of the theatre and ended up beside the stage. Normally I stood with my manager Steve, who would announce me: 'Ladies and gentlemen, please welcome Billy Connolly!' And then I'd walk on. Well, on this night, Steve wasn't there.

As I said, I don't believe in ghosts. I don't believe in the supernatural. I don't believe in any of that crap, but there was something strange in that theatre that night. Instead of Steve, there was a man sitting at a desk right beside the stage. He was a dapper wee guy, with short hair and a moustache. I said, 'How are you doing?'

He said, 'Fine. I don't always come in.'

I said, 'Oh, aye? Fair enough.' Then I said, 'How is it out there?' Meaning the auditorium. 'Is it full yet?'

And he said, 'It's fine.'

So I said, 'Great, I'll go on.' I went onstage to start my show, but the place was only about two-thirds full, and people were still pouring in. Not only that, but a fight had erupted to the left of the stage. About six rows up there was a man in the aisle, trying to hit a man five rows in. 'Ya fooking gobshite!' *Biff! Boof!* This guy was half man, half beetroot, covered in tweed clothes, with fists like hams. *Biff! Boff! Bash!* He was trying to beat seven colours of shit out of this poor innocent man, the bouncers were all up at the back of the theatre, going: '*I'm* not fuckin' going *there*, no way, I'll get my fuckin' face punched in. Jaysus! No way at all! Fuck it, *you* fuckin' go there!'

It seemed as though it was up to me. I went over and said, 'Hey, hey, HEY!! What's the story here, big man?' and the full story unfolded. It turned out that Mr Beetroot had bought tickets for my show, and he'd kept them in the glove compartment of his car. He'd been looking forward to the show for weeks . . . but then somebody stole his car. Luckily, he'd jotted down the seat numbers in a wee book. He thought, 'I know what I'll do – I'll get another ticket so I can go inside and batter the shit out of the gobshites who stole my car . . . because they'll be in my seats!' So this poor guy was sitting there with his wife, minding his own business, waiting for me to come on, and suddenly: BIFF! BOOF! 'Ya *bastard*!' As it turned out, the guy who was being set upon had bought the tickets in a pub – from the bastards who had actually stolen the other guy's car!

I sorted it out, but when I went backstage again the wee guy at the desk had gone. He was nowhere to be seen. I asked about him, and someone said, 'Oh, he doesn't actually exist. He's just one of the Gaiety Theatre Ghosts. There are several of them!' Apparently, the place is famous for all kinds of visitations, and dancing orbs of light, *blah blah blah*. I've got a simpler theory. I suspect he just fucked off home for his dinner.

———

Shouting at the TV isn't my only litmus test of ageing. Every now and then I used to test myself to see how long it took me to get out of a bean-bag chair. Once I turned sixty, it was game over. I'd be like an upturned turtle, flopping about – I could be lost in there for *days*! I'd have to wait until someone wandered into the room and found me. But these days bean-bag chairs are the least of my worries – ANY chair is a big challenge. I get trapped and can't get up. My physiotherapist taught me to rock back and forth to build momentum, but that's dangerous, because I fart more than when I was younger. I don't know why. I just do. And the most acute farting risk is when I'm getting up out of a chair. *Bbbbbbbbbrrrrrrrggggghhhhhh!!!* The rocking just accentuates it. I got myself a leather chair because I thought it would squeak by itself and cover the farting . . . but nothing covers these thunderclaps. *BBBBBRRRRRGGGGHHHHH!!!*

Maybe it's American food . . . but to be honest I fart just as much in Scotland. Maybe there's a scientific reason . . . like my stomach's getting bigger but my arsehole's getting smaller. According to my extensive knowledge of the science of physics, that could account for a monumental backlog. It's another reason why I don't want to get on aeroplanes any more. A kind stranger who hauled me out of my seat could be rewarded by Hurricane Hilda.

If God had wanted us to fart, he should've given us a bloody *chimney.* I was flying to Australia once and there was an empty seat beside me. We stopped at Singapore and a guy got on and sat beside me. After a while he said, 'Has it been a good flight so far?'

I said, 'Yes. Very good.'

He said, 'I've just come off a Cathay Pacific flight. It was extraordinarily good. You ever flown Cathay Pacific? The food is amazing. They served barbecue goose . . . I've never tasted anything like it.'

The conversation died away, and he went to sleep. We were flying along, and he started farting. Oh my God. He was in a funny position – bent over, with his bum pointing up towards me. He just kept doing the worst farts. *Ppppphhhhhhhhuuuuu uuuuggggggggggghhhhhhhhhhhhh!!!!!!!*

It was the longest one I ever heard. *Pppppppppphhhhhhhuuuu uuugggggggggggggghhhhhhhhhhhhh!!!!*

And people around were saying, 'Oh for goodness sake!!!' I turned round, and they were all looking at *me*. Since he was bent over, they couldn't see that it was him. One of the most embarrassing moments of my life.

———

I've told you a lot about myself. Embarrassing and otherwise. It's the first time I've done this. Other people have written about me – or for me – in the past but this time it's purely my words. I never wanted to write my own story before. I always thought it would seem too jumbled and thoroughly piss people off. I was afraid that, with me doing the telling, my story might not come out in the right order. I might forget things or get the dates wrong. But it's not really that important, is it? I personally couldn't give a fuck. I don't think dates are important. I've never remembered them, and I've no fucking idea what happened on such and such a day. If a police officer came up to me and said, 'Where were you on the second of November?' I wouldn't have the foggiest idea. I'd be doomed. I'd be straight to jail.

I've lived a great life, so thinking about the end of the story doesn't affect me at all. I just think, 'Well, this is the way it is.' I don't worry that I might not see the rest of my life, because I've already seen the rest of my life. I've only got the old bit left.

But it's a rather jolly old bit, I must say. At this point I'm really in no hurry to travel – although naturally I'd like to go to Scotland. I miss it terribly. I'd like to see my pals and go to a Celtic match. Despite having Parkinson's, I can still do lots of things. I can walk well. I can draw. I don't do live concerts any more, and movies would be hard . . . but I can write, and film TV shows . . . I consider myself a lucky man.

I've got my wee pal Django here. I've got no complaints whatsoever. I'm very fortunate. I've got shelter, food and my wifey and my girlies and my son and my grandchildren. I've got children I can be really proud of.

———

We got really lucky with our neighbours here in the Florida Keys. People who look out for you. That kind of neighbour is disappearing in the world generally. So many people have enemies as neighbours. I've always wanted to live in a really diverse, ordinary wee neighbourhood where I can be just an ordinary guy, and I've pretty much achieved it. I talk to people when I'm out with the dog – usually about politics. They all say different things. Some are pro this and that, and some are anti. Some are waiting for the civil war to begin, which is weird. You get the feeling they're looking forward to it.

———

I used to become engrossed in novels, but I don't read them so much now. I've read some of the heavy stuff; I discovered the Russian novelists when I was in my forties. I had previously thought they would be too intellectual for me. My favourite was

The Brothers Karamazov. I loved *Anna Karenina* too. It's a style of writing I really like – that particular rhythm and flow. I love the colour of that world – the gambling, the social life, the murder and mayhem. And I liked the fact that the characters were struggling in terrible circumstances – poverty unfairly laid upon them. Their royals were thieves, and the lower classes were shat upon.

I read Proust's *Remembrance of Things Past* and was absolutely astounded – it was such a ridiculous task to write your life story in seven volumes. At one point there's a sentence that's about ten pages long. You get out of breath when you're reading it – it's the weirdest feeling. I lived in Malta for a short while and I went through a period where I decided I would read everything that I should have read before. That's when I read all the Russian authors. We still have a place in Malta, in a lovely quiet village on Gozo. People have often looked at our library there and said, 'Jesus, you've got great stuff!' The Irish writer Dominic Behan once said to me: 'You're good, Connolly. And if you read in the next five years all the books you should have read in the last twenty, you'll make it.' I met him at a Dubliners concert in Govan in Glasgow. He was in the middle of a fight and I had to break it up. Great guy, great brain.

I've been rereading *The Tibetan Book of Living and Dying* by a Buddhist guru I met in Australia. I was with my daughter Amy and he gave us his book. He has the best handwriting: '*To Billy Connolly and Amy, warmest wishes – Sogyal Rinpoche.*' He marked off bits for me to read: 'In the middle of death and impermanence and reflection and change, bring the mind home.' He asked me if I meditated, and I said, 'Yeah – but not all the time . . . I go back and forth.' He asked, 'What meditation practice do you do?' I said, 'The Mindfulness of Breathing' and he gave me some tips. He advised me to meditate with my eyes open, which took me aback. And not to bother trying to eliminate intrusive thoughts. 'Just let them be,' he said.

I mostly read books about American history, like Howard Zinn's *A People's History of the United States*, and I read a lot about authoritarianism and fascism. I've been poring over biographies of American presidents and reading books that explain the political system so I can make better sense of current events. I try to balance my TV news watching between left and right views. What has been happening in America over the past few years has been mystifying but, instead of just getting furious, I've been trying to understand the reason why that orange prick got such a foothold. In this country there's a type of American of a certain age who's a real worry. They believe the country isn't as good as it was, and that the reason is immigration. Some of those bigots are downright nutters. I've been reading about the right-wing attitude. Eric Hoffer said people become more right-wing when they get older because they get a peculiar idea of what the world was like when they were younger. All those people who say 'We never locked our doors' would have you think that, in the thirties and forties, America and Britain were full of people who never locked their doors. But it's total bollocks. I think it comes of decay in your body. Your teeth aren't as good as they were, and your eyes aren't as sharp. You can't eat as well, and you can't run any more. And you credit this decay to the world's going wrong. You decide it's not your fault – it's the world that has changed. But the world's the same as it always was. And you *did* lock your door.

I remember a guy called Batchelor who lived near us in Partick when we were growing up. He went on holiday and forgot to shut the door. That was a great laugh for everyone because it was so unusual. We used to go and look at the open door. It was an ordinary working-class area, and nobody had anything that anyone would want to steal. You wouldn't have dreamed of stealing from his house. I always think of him when people say they never lock their doors.

———

There's a French bakery near where I live now. Over the years as I've bestrode the world like a giant colossus, I've learned from being in France there's nothing so nice as a fresh baguette covered in butter, with ham and good cheese. On the other hand, I can't often be arsed going out in the heat. An ordinary toasted sandwich with lashings of butter, Vegemite and two fried eggs 'over easy' usually does me just lovely. I feel a bit rotten, though. I've been eating too many chocolate biscuits and they've ganged up on me. Some of my clothes don't fit me any more. Despite the sand, it's nice to live somewhere that's tropical and warm all the time because I don't need to wear a lot of clothes. It's getting harder for me to dress myself, so I try to wear easy stuff now. Pamela doesn't seem so sure about my tropical look. She says, 'Is *that* what you're wearing?' Translated, it means: 'Where did you find that? I threw it out a month ago!'

———

Tropical clothing isn't a kick in the arse off what I've always been wearing – loud, gaudy colours. Mixing colours and patterns most tasteful people think should not sit side by side – I've always had a penchant for that kind of thing. I still want to look Windswept and Interesting, but I can't be arsed to put too much thought into it. I always wanted to dress like Mark Twain – to buy six identical suits and look the same every day and not have to make decisions. I've almost achieved it – I wear similar stuff most days. My footwear now is bare feet or sandals that show off the fabulous flowery tattoos on my feet. I miss wearing my cowboy boots, though. You can't find good jeans or get your shoes repaired here, but you can buy all the T-shirts you need – with terrible jokes on them.

Tropical clothing can be a bit on the awful side. I was in Sydney, Australia, and I saw a man in a pale blue crimplene safari suit. Now, that's enough to get you put in jail, as far as I'm concerned. Because I am into animal rights, and killing baby crimples is just a fucking disgrace. Have you any idea how many crimples it takes to make a safari suit? They hit them with big sticks! Every time a crimple dies, part of me dies too. The worst thing about that pale-blue Crimplene suit was – the jacket had short sleeves. He was in long trousers, but the jacket had short sleeves. *And he was wearing a long-sleeved shirt!* I followed him everywhere, just to marvel. It was the best thing I've seen since I saw a guy with platform shoes and a kilt! Oh God, it was brillo!

Hot weather is a great excuse to swish around in a panama hat. I put artificial flowers on mine, and I think it's a great look. I'm pretty much a floral boy. But the flowery stuff – feet tattoos, shirt and hat – is offset by my skull bracelet. I like Keith Richards's reason for wearing skulls – it's proof that human beings are the same under the skin. Did you hear he's quit smoking? Everyone's dying to see what will happen. Will he put on weight? That would be the ultimate – a fat Keith Richards. I love him. He's an extraordinary guy. He looks like a wild man, but I believe he lives the most sophisticated life.

There are a lot of tourists in the Florida Keys. People coming from colder places like Colorado and Minnesota to flop into pools with giant pink inflatable flamingos. I see them wandering around the touristy streets in their shorts and T-shirts, drinking margaritas out of pineapples. Some of those poor wee souls suffer from a terrible affliction – the Hungry Bum Syndrome. That's where your arse eats everything in its way: *Chomp-Chomp-Chomp!* You see this when they walk up the street with their Bermuda shorts way up their arse. That's Hungry Bum. *Chomp-Chomp-Chomp!* You take your clothes off and there's no fucking underwear there – your arse has eaten it. You have to retrieve it with a crochet needle.

Some ladies in a knitting circle kindly knitted me and Pamela matching woolly bathing suits, a kind of homage to my 'Pale Blue Scottish Person' routine. The suits are in frames on our wall. When I venture in the sea these days – in water that's a good eighty degrees warmer than what I endured when I was a boy swimming in Aberdeen – I don my favourite boxer-style cotton swim shorts. They're pink, with flamingos and palm trees dotted all over them. I could wear them to a restaurant here if I wished, with flip-flops and a cowboy hat. '*No shirt, no shoes, no problem*'. But I wouldn't dream of it. I'm a Windswept and Interesting Showbiz Personality. Times may change, but standards must remain.

ACKNOWLEDGEMENTS

This was my first attempt at personally penning a book . . . although I didn't actually 'pen' anything; I dictated my thoughts and memories into my phone. It wasn't as easy as I imagined because my phone turned out to be none too bright. I had mistakenly believed it was 'smart' enough to write down everything I said, edit it brilliantly, and send it to Nick Davies and the team at Two Roads. Unfortunately, the fucking dictation software I used couldn't understand a Glaswegian accent so my poor family had to suffer hours on end transcribing my thoughts from the audio recording. Thank you Cara, Scarlett, and Amy for all your help with that – and Pamela for the endless tea and bickies.

Aside from family, many thanks to Nick Davies for EVERYTHING – and also to Charlotte Robathan, Jacqui Lewis, Amanda Jones, Ellie Wheeldon, Alistair Oliver, Juliet Brightmore, Yassine Belkacemi, Ella Chapman, Sarah Arratoon, Laura Fletcher, Iman Khabl, Lucy Howkins, Sarah Clay, Rich Peters, Georgina Cutler and the rest of the team at Hachette.

Love and cuddles,
  Billy

PICTURE ACKNOWLEDGEMENTS

Author's personal collection: Inset I, except page 6 centre/ ©
Barry Duffy, 7 above right/ photographer unknown, 8 centre/
© Herald & Times Group Scotland; Inset 2, page 2 above, 6
above right, 8. Alamy Stock Photo: Inset 2, page 5 centre/ Movie
Collection Ltd, 6 above/TCD/Prod DB © N.Davidson. BBC Photo
Library: Inset 2, page 1 above/John Green. BBC Scotland/Martin
Shields: Inset 2, page 7 below. Nobby Clark/ArenaPAL: Inset
2, pages 3, 4 above, 5 above, 6 below left. Getty Images: Inset
2, pages 1 centre/ Julian Brown/Mirrorpix. Mirrorpix/Reach
Licensing: Inset 2, page 1 below right. PA Images/Ben Curtis:
Inset 2, page 6 below right. Shutterstock: Inset 2, pages 2 below
left/Handmade Films/Kobal, 5 below/Franchise/Brood Syndicate/
Kobal, 7 above/ Helen Osler, 7 centre/ Ken McKay.